CODE BLACK

CODE BLACK

CUT OFF AND FACING OVERWHELMING ODDS: THE SIEGE OF NAD ALI

Mark Evans

with Andrew Sharples

CORONET

First published in Great Britain in 2015 by Coronet
An imprint of Hodder & Stoughton
An Hachette UK company

1

Copyright © Mark Evans and Andrew Sharples 2015

Maps by Rodney Paull

The right of Mark Evans to be identified as the Author
of the Work has been asserted by him in accordance with the
Copyright, Designs and Patents Act 1988.

A CIP catalogue record for this title is available from the British Library

ISBN 978 1 44478 445 9
Trade Paperback ISBN 978 1 44478 444 2
Ebook ISBN 978 1 44478 442 8

Typeset by Hewer Text UK Ltd, Edinburgh
Printed and bound by Clays Ltd, St Ives Plc

Hodder & Stoughton policy is to use papers that are natural, renewable
and recyclable products and made from wood grown in sustainable forests.
The logging and manufacturing processes are expected to conform
to the environmental regulations of the country of origin.

Hodder & Stoughton Ltd
338 Euston Road
London NW1 3BH

www.hodder.co.uk

For my grandparents, parents, brother and Saethryd who are all such an important part of my life.

For Rory, Wilf and Nina who will be a wonderful part of my future.

CONTENTS

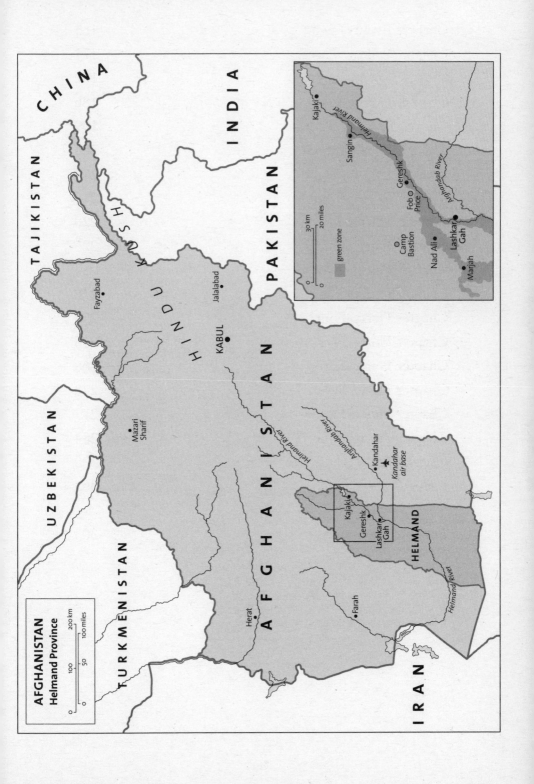

PROLOGUE

By the time I went to war in Afghanistan it felt like we'd already lost. Tired after years of fighting in Iraq, British public opinion had turned firmly against military action overseas.

The newspapers painted a bleak picture. 'Afghanistan death rate tops Vietnam' yelled one headline. 'Afghanistan falling into Taliban hands' lamented another.

Since 2006, when British troops had first gone into Helmand, casualties had mounted steadily. Defence Secretary John Reid's remark that, 'We would be perfectly happy to leave in three years' time and without firing one shot,' now seemed woefully naïve.

Then at the end of the summer of 2008, halfway through my own tour of Afghanistan, a shard of sunlight penetrated the gloom. In a daring operation, involving over 4,000 troops, the Army's 16 Air Assault Brigade fought its way deep into Taliban-held territory to transport a huge turbine to a dam that would provide electricity to nearly two million people.

The press went wild for the story, announcing that progress in Helmand was possible after all and lauding the soldiers involved as heroes. But not all the stories surrounding the operation made it into the newspapers. For instance, no one reported that British Army planners had expected to lose up to three hundred soldiers, moving the turbine straight across some of the most heavily mined ground in Afghanistan. A safer route was found only days before the operation when a private soldier casually asked a local farmer if he knew of another road leading to the dam.

Also missing from the press articles was how the operation was almost cancelled when the crane that was supposed to lift the 220-tonne turbine onto a trailer broke down. The mission was saved when the brother of a local police chief offered to lend his own crane – a service for which he charged the British Army several thousands of dollars.

These are the kind of details that make up any large-scale military operation and ensure that war is never far from descending into farce. In the end, none of these hiccups mattered and the mission was emphatically accomplished. But the lesson is clear: when it comes to Afghanistan, what you see in the press is rarely the whole picture.

The real war in Helmand that summer was fought far from the glare of the media spotlight. It's a much darker tale and it doesn't end well. There's no great victory, no triumphant homecoming. The soldiers who fought there are the only ones who know it even happened.

I was one of those soldiers.

CHAPTER ONE

I was finally on my way, the last leg of my long journey to the war. A junior infantry officer, I had been sent to Helmand to train and fight alongside the Afghan National Army.

The Chinook clattered through the air, a hundred feet above the ground, and I craned to peer through the open cargo door at the landscape as it swept beneath us. The desert spread out in an orange carpet, blank and lifeless, while our pilot banked past granite outcrops in alarming manoeuvres that produced adrenaline and nausea in roughly equal measure. They called it 'flying nap of the earth': tactical flying to avoid the enemy. I think the pilot was just enjoying himself.

Before long the desert came to an abrupt end, rocks and dust giving way to verdant colour. We had reached the Green Zone, the thin strip of cultivated land either side of the Helmand River that extended as far into the desert as the irrigation system would allow. I could see muddy brown ditches and canals criss-crossing through the crops, turning the land into a kind of green chessboard. This was the battleground for the war in Helmand. Somewhere down there, the Taliban waited.

Here and there, scattered amongst the green, were bright pink and red squares. I leant over to my neighbour, a grizzled sergeant major from the Royal Regiment of Scotland. 'What's that?' I shouted over the noise of the rotors, pointing at the colourful blocks.

'Poppies!' he yelled back.

Poppies had been a big topic during my pre-deployment training. A woman from the Foreign Office had lectured us at length on the importance of eradicating the crop in Helmand. The thinking was that opium from the poppies fuelled a drugs problem in Britain and provided funds for the Taliban. Confusingly, a colonel from the MoD later told us that poppy farmers ought to be left alone because when we got rid of their crops we destroyed their livelihoods and turned them into Taliban supporters. What we were actually supposed to do when we came across a poppy field in Afghanistan was never made clear.

Frankly, I didn't care. Not just about the poppies. I didn't care about any of the reasons we were fighting in Afghanistan. For me it was all about combat. In five years of service, I'd never fired a shot in anger. I was an officer in the Coldstream Guards, an infantry regiment, and I thought when I joined I'd be right in the thick of the fighting. But war is an elusive beast and it had dodged me at every turn. After I joined up I'd gone through eighteen months of intensive training at the end of which I assumed I'd see some action. Instead I'd spent a year marching around Buckingham Palace and the Tower of London – a role those returning from war often fought over. At first I was the proud public face of the British Army, but by the end I felt more like a tailor's dummy; a prop for tourists to use in their photos. There was no war there, a fact made clear by my company commander when he summoned me to his office one day to rebuke me for 'not playing enough tennis'.

In the summer of 2006, I'd deployed to Basra in southern Iraq. I thought I'd find the war there for sure. Well, I got close. I heard it rumbling, explosions just streets away, but by the time I arrived the war had moved on, leaving its spoor behind in the rubble, the wounded and the dead. Most of my time I spent in the desert commanding a platoon on guard at a prison. After four months I came home bored and frustrated, condemned to endure the stories of colleagues who had seen action on the ground.

4

A stream of training exercises abroad followed; in the burning sands of the Namib desert and the jungles of Brunei the Army prepared me for war. Now, two years after my first tour, I finally had my chance.

It was summer in Afghanistan – the fighting season. The severity of the Afghan winters greatly curtailed military activity but now the temperatures were climbing and the Taliban would be coming back on the offensive. As for the debates raging in the media over national security, special relationships, reconstruction – they meant nothing to me. As long as they gave me something to shoot at, as long as I could fight, I would do whatever I was told, no questions asked.

The Coldstream Guards weren't deployed in Afghanistan at the moment. I was detached from my battalion and seconded to the Royal Irish Regiment, the unit currently responsible for training and mentoring the Afghan National Army, or ANA. It was all part of the UK's exit strategy – if we could build up the Afghan security forces to the point where they were able to fight the Taliban on their own then British forces could withdraw. I'd arrived in Afghanistan expecting to take command of an OMLT (Operational Mentor and Liaison Team) – a small group of British soldiers that would train and fight alongside a platoon of up to forty Afghans from a kandak, an Afghan unit, roughly equivalent to a British battalion, comprising of around 400 troops.

We were to lead by example, showing the ANA the tactics and principles the British Army fought by. What I didn't realise at the time was how much I would learn from them in turn. In my imagination I would be posted to some remote base, where I would live alongside the native troops and lead them to victory against a tough and ruthless enemy. My fantasies owed more than a little to Lawrence of Arabia. In the weeks leading up to my deployment I'd carried around a copy of *Seven Pillars of Wisdom* in the hope that something of the great man might rub off on me. I tried to read it but gave up after one chapter of stultifying prose and settled for watching the film again.

As it turned out, when I arrived at Camp Bastion, the main British base in Helmand, they told me I was to be posted to a Combat Support OMLT in a town called Gereshk, training Afghan artillerymen. I was disappointed. I'd hoped to be on the front line. As an infantry officer, my place was in the van of battle. Gereshk had seen much fighting before the war shifted north, around Sangin and Musa Qala. However, while I anticipated my time here wouldn't be devoid of action, there was still an ever present threat from IEDs (improvised explosive devices), suicide bombers and insurgents.

We finally landed in a wide, dusty patch of ground that had been cleared and flattened out to make a helicopter landing site (HLS). The RAF loadmaster hustled us quickly out of the rear door, dragging our bergens with us. We shuffled away from the chopper, staying low to keep under the rotors as they carried on turning, and then the helicopter was gone, lifting straight up into the sky, flinging out dust which stung my face. They never liked to stay still for long in these small bases where they felt exposed and vulnerable. We were left behind, the grunts, here for the long haul.

I looked around at my new surroundings. They were desolate. There were rows of sand-coloured tents and clusters of red and blue shipping containers. A 20-foot high, double thick Hesco Bastion wall ran more than two kilometres around the perimeter. There were sentry posts every 100 metres. It was a fortress. From the inside you couldn't see anything of the country beyond. Everything was functional and drab and I felt like I'd flown into the end of the world.

'Captain Evans?' A short, dark-haired man in desert combats approached me.

'That's right,' I said.

'I'm Cpl Magoo. I'm here to pick you up.' He had a strong

Irish accent and a bouncy restlessness about him that prevented him from staying still for more than a minute.

'Magoo?' I asked.

'Well, it's MacGowan really but everyone calls me Magoo. If you've got all your stuff, sir, then we'll be off. The lads are waiting over there.' He pointed at a row of three armoured Land Rovers, known in the Army as 'Snatches', lined up by the edge of the HLS. Snatches were becoming a controversial vehicle – their armour plating was relatively thin and they were vulnerable to the increasingly sophisticated IEDs used by our enemies. Several soldiers had been killed while driving in Snatches and some of the deceased men's families had launched legal action against the Ministry of Defence, claiming negligence. I was unnerved to see that I would be driving these vehicles around Helmand. A couple of soldiers leaned against the first vehicle, smoking cigarettes.

'Off? Off where? Aren't we here already?'

'Oh no, sir. This is FOB Price – just a staging post, where the logistics monkeys hang out. The proper soldiers are in town with the Afghans. Come on. It's a short run. I'll take you over and introduce you to Major Clements. He's in charge round here, on our side anyway. The Afghan boss is Colonel Wadood – the main man – but he's away on leave at the moment.'

Magoo grabbed my bergen and slung it in the back of the lead vehicle. 'Jump up front with me. It'll only take twenty minutes. Oh, and sir?'

'Yes?'

'You're in command of the convoy. Do you know where you're going?'

Of course I didn't, but this was the job of an officer. We were expected to lead. I asked Magoo for a map and quickly scanned the route to the base in Gereshk where we were headed. It looked simple enough but I felt the pressure anyway. Magoo and the other soldiers with him were watching me and assessing my performance.

I asked Magoo if they had standard operating procedures (SOPs) in place for dealing with ambushes or IEDs should we run into trouble en route. He quickly outlined what the score was and I made sure that the men in each vehicle knew what they were doing as well.

'OK, let's go,' I said.

As we drove, I kept an eye out through the window. This was my first proper look at Afghanistan from the ground and I was anxious to drink in my new surroundings. All the scenarios from my training and all the stories I'd heard from colleagues who'd already served over here now ran through my head. I knew that the threat was very real. The road ahead might be mined and any one of the vehicles we passed could turn out to carry a suicide bomb. Magoo looked relaxed but he'd had a couple of weeks here to adjust; I was still mainlining adrenaline.

FOB Price was on the edge of the desert just a few kilometres west of Gereshk, the principal town of Nahri Saraj district. As we drove out of the main gate we passed rows of brightly coloured lorries and trucks parked up. They were all waiting to get into the FOB – Afghan civilian contractors supplying the British Army with water, fuel and other essentials. Each vehicle was searched thoroughly before it was allowed through the gate and they were made to wait for at least twenty-four hours so that a potential suicide bomber might psyche himself out of his planned attack.

We drove along a dirt track for a few hundred metres before we reached a wide metalled road, the A1, which extended all the way across the country from the border with Pakistan in the east to Iran in the west. Magoo put his foot down and the speedometer crept up.

'Steady on, Cpl Magoo,' I said. 'Got somewhere you need to be?'

'I'm on duty again in five hours. I've been up since three this morning. Once I drop you off I'll be back in my scratcher and trying to grab some kip. As they say, I'm in my own time now!'

'Well try not to get us killed,' I joked. 'So, what's it like working with the ANA?'

'They're a great bunch of lads. I really like them. They're just like us when you get down to it. They have their funny ways and they look like a bag of shite most of the time but who am I to talk?' He laughed and gestured at his own heavily wrinkled uniform. 'I'm mostly in the ops room myself so I don't see too much of them. Their CO though, the Colonel, he's a mean-looking bastard. You wouldn't want to get on the wrong side of him.'

'That's this Col Wadood, you mentioned?'

'That's right. You'll see what I mean when you meet him. Even Major Clements is a bit scared of him, I reckon.'

I could see the town, squatting on the flat, dusty plain ahead of us, an anonymous jumble of one-storey buildings that hid a labyrinth of narrow streets. We followed the road as it curved round the southern edge of the town until we came to halt by a row of Hesco that led off the highway towards a big metal gate. Painted on the gate were the words 'Joint District Co-Ordination Centre', better known as the JDCC. This would be my home for the next four months.

From a fortified sentry tower, or sangar, next to the gate, a watchful face peered at us over the sights of a PKM machine-gun, one of the weapon systems used by the ANA. Watchful eyes scanned the road below for signs of danger. I could see similar towers at the other corners of the base. The men here were clearly ready to repel an attack.

An Afghan soldier approached us, an AK-47 slung casually over his shoulder. When he saw Magoo he smiled broadly and waved, before shouting at his colleague to let us past. As the barrier swung up, Magoo waved back. 'Hello Paddy,' he said.

'Yes, hello Paddy,' the Afghan replied.

'Some eejit told him I was called Paddy,' said Magoo. 'I tried to explain but he didn't really understand and I think he thinks that all soldiers are called Paddy now. He's a friendly fellow anyhow.'

We drove into the base and parked up on the end of a neat row of vehicles identical to our own. As I jumped out I noticed a number of Toyota pick-up trucks strewn haphazardly around the camp. Some had the black, red and green tricolour flag of Afghanistan flying from their bonnets. Magoo informed me that these vehicles belonged to the ANA.

The layout was reassuringly familiar to anyone who'd spent time in a military camp. In place of temporary containers and portacabins, squat, grey concrete buildings lined three sides of a dirt parade square. Over in one corner there was an empty swimming pool, a relic from the camp's former life as a base for the Soviet Army. The Soviets had spent over a decade in Afghanistan but had never managed to complete their mission. The entire might of the Red Army, a military machine that had kept the Western world quaking in fear for half a century, had foundered and broken in this country. Our enemies' forbears had driven them out, exhausted and bleeding, precipitating the downfall of an empire. A century before, Britain, at the height of her imperial power, had been similarly crushed. This time, said the clever men running the governments in Washington and London, things would be different.

Magoo led me across the square, towards one of the buildings. A sign read, 'C Battery Headquarters, 3 RHA' in fresh paint. Once inside, the corporal rapped on the door of the ops room and swung it open.

'Hello sir, I've got Capt Evans here for you.'

I walked into a large square room. In one corner stood a couple of trestle tables with radios and maps spread across them. A corporal was hunched over the maps, scribbling in a logbook as he talked over the net to a call sign out on patrol. One wall was covered with a huge satellite image of Gereshk, overlaid with grid lines. In front of the map were rows of benches. Off to one side, sitting behind a rough wooden desk, was the Battery Commander, a major. He wore a slightly startled expression, as though Magoo had just disturbed him trying to solve a particularly complex puzzle. 'Oh, right. Thanks Magoo. Leave him with me.'

'Right you are,' said Magoo, and nodding to me: 'I'll see you around, sir.' He bounced off down the corridor towards his bed. I turned to the major who had risen to his feet and extended his hand.

'Hello,' the major said as we shook. 'I'm Richard. Mark, isn't it?' He was short with blond hair, a ready smile and a friendly, open face. His handshake was firm and his gaze was clear and level. Straight away I detected the confidence possessed by all good officers, the certainty that makes men follow them gladly.

We sat down and Richard proceeded to outline the situation. C Battery had been assigned the task of mentoring the ANA kandak stationed in Gereshk.

'The ANA is responsible for security in Gereshk,' Richard said. 'The soldiers are supposed to be artillerymen but they haven't got any guns to shoot so it's all infantry work. We go out on patrol with them and train them as we go along.'

Normally, British infantry units are divided up into platoons of around thirty soldiers but when operating in urban areas they're often divided into smaller twelve-man teams called multiples. Each multiple was commanded by junior officers like me, or by senior NCOs. On patrol with the ANA I'd been told we'd usually take just eight men, allowing the others to either carry out work within the base or rest to keep themselves fresh.

'My main job is looking after the CO,' said Richard. 'Col Wadood. He's away on leave at the moment but he'll be back soon.'

'Cpl Magoo was telling me about him,' I said. 'He seemed quite impressed.'

'I've never met anyone like him. There hasn't been much action here for a while but if the Taliban do show up I reckon the Colonel will give them hell.'

CHAPTER TWO

I'd now met my superiors and the men I would be commanding. Before I met my counterparts in the ANA, who I would be working with just as closely, I needed to pick up an interpreter. A few British soldiers had completed language courses in Pashtu or Dari, the two major languages spoken in Afghanistan, but they were mostly employed in Kabul working for generals, or at Brigade HQ in Lash. At the tactical level, we relied on the services of Afghan interpreters, hired civilians. In the JDCC, the 'terps', as they were known, had their own accommodation away from the ANA. When we needed their services we simply had to drop by and see who was free. They spent most of their time smoking and playing cards in a sort of common room, kitted out with a few tatty armchairs and a television. The air inside was dense and reminded me of those dreary booths you find in foreign airports where smokers are corralled for a last desperate cigarette before getting on a plane.

The terps were an interesting bunch. Most of them were students from Kabul. In a country convulsed by war, there weren't a lot of opportunities for the educated classes and so the risks of working on the front line had to be weighed against the prospect of unemployment. A number of them were also heavily invested in the outcome of the war and were doing their bit to stave off the return of the Taliban, who had often persecuted the intelligentsia when in power. Of course, the Taliban knew how much we relied on the interpreters and issued dire warnings to any Afghan who came to work for us. These weren't idle threats. A number of interpreters had been killed in the past, along with their families. It helped that most of our guys were deployed a long way from their homes so were less likely to be recognised by the local fighters and their spies. Even so, they all wore balaclavas or covered their faces with scarves whenever they left the base.

There was little camaraderie between the ANA soldiers and the interpreters. The two camps did not have much in common beyond a shared nationality. On the one side were the soldiers, poorly educated, overworked and underpaid, while on the other you had an intellectual elite earning a comparative fortune to hover on the fringes of the war chatting to people. I can see how the ANA guys resented this state of affairs but the reality was that we needed the interpreters' skills, and to us they were worth every penny.

There were two or three terps based at the JDCC at any one time but they moved in and out on a rota basis. Over the course of the next few months I became acquainted with all of them. Some were excellent, translating everything that was said fluently and efficiently to the point where you could almost forget that the conversation was being conducted through an interpreter at all. Others were less skilled and would mumble, mistranslate or simply stop paying attention to what was being said. A few would try to brazen it out, grabbing for any English word that they thought might sound right. When this happened, confusion reigned. I developed a good relationship with one of the best, a man called Ash. He was a young guy in his early twenties, clean-shaven and about 5'6" tall. He wore a black T-shirt and black jeans, which I was to discover were the only clothes he possessed. A student from Kabul, Ash understood idiom and nuance and was also a fount of knowledge about Afghan culture and politics. Unusually he spoke both Pashtu, the local language of Helmand, and Dari, which was spoken further north and by most of the ANA soldiers. This trilingual fluency made Ash a prized asset. Having secured his services, I decided my first visit would be to Captain Wali, the senior ANA platoon commander.

C Battery, the British soldiers, occupied a small block in the northwest corner of the JDCC, while the rest of the camp belonged to the Afghans. There was no fence, no boundary dividing our territory from theirs, but to walk a few metres from one to the other was to enter a different world. Our day-to-day lives were governed by the mores of the British sergeant major, all straight lines and shiny surfaces and clean that up and get a haircut while you're at it. Over in Afghanistan a more carefree spirit prevailed. Washing hung from tangled lines running between the soldiers' huts, like so much olive-coloured bunting, while men sat around open camp fires, chatting, cooking dinner or simply napping. I once suggested to the Battery Sergeant Major that we might share a living space with the Afghans in a spirit of closer co-operation. His reply was unprintable.

When I walked into the Afghan platoon commander's office, Captain Wali jumped up from behind his desk, smiling broadly. An unlikely looking soldier, he was in his mid-thirties, short, fat and seemingly unaccustomed to the rigours of war. He also sported an enormous black beard that, coupled with his wrin-kled uniform and lopsided beret, gave him an engagingly dishevelled appearance.

'Come in! Come in!' Wali grabbed my hand and pumped it vigorously up and down before ushering me into a chair. 'So, we are to fight together, you and I?' he said. 'This is wonderful. We shall wage a tremendous war this summer!'

I grinned back at Wali. He might look a bit odd but he seemed to share my appetite for combat. This is what I'd come for.

Mint tea was brought in and Wali poured me a glass. It was strong and overwhelmingly sweet. The English have a reputation as world-class tea drinkers but the Afghans take it to another level entirely. Tea provides the foundation of almost any social situation and refusing it provokes consternation. Over the next few months I would find myself in endless conversations with my ANA counterparts, in a hurry to get away but stuck there until my tea had cooled sufficiently to drink.

We agreed that I'd join him on patrol the following morning and he'd take the opportunity to show me around the local area. 'And maybe kill some Taliban while we're at it,' Wali added with a wink.

I asked Wali if he'd fought many battles against the Taliban. 'Of course,' he said. 'We've been in Helmand for two years. There are Taliban everywhere.'

It occurred to me that although these men were technically artillerymen, they probably had more infantry combat experience than the most battle-hardened regiment in the British Army.

Wali told me how the kandak had fired big artillery guns on only one occasion. 'We had four guns at one point,' he said. 'But we didn't have a sighting system to use with them. They were old Soviet-era weapons. Then someone in Kabul found the right kind of system — it was in a military museum there! That's how old they were.'

'So what happened then?' I asked.

Wali looked a bit shamefaced. 'There must have been something wrong with the guns. They didn't fire straight. We fired them way out in the desert but we never quite knew how off-target we were. None of the British soldiers who were training us at the time wanted to go out in front of the guns and tell us exactly where the shells landed.'

I smiled. Who could blame them?

'Anyway, the senior commanders in Kabul said that they needed our kandak to fight as infantry so that's what we do. I'd like the chance to go and shoot big guns again one day though.'

As time went on the conversation took a more personal turn.

Wali began to talk about himself, where he was from and what Afghanistan was like before the Taliban came to power. Despite his apparent enthusiasm for fighting, he was actually a reluctant warrior. Before the war he'd been a travel agent in Kandahar, spending his days organising trips for opium dealers who travelled a great deal both to Pakistan and Kabul. 'I miss my old life,' he said before regaling me with a story about how he had once booked a flight for one of Osama Bin Laden's wives. I asked him where he thought Osama was now. 'Pakistan,' he replied with certainty. 'The Pakistani government will look after him for sure. They are not to be trusted and you British should remember that.' At the time I dismissed his comments as a mixture of paranoia and xenophobia towards his southern neighbours. Of course, as it turned out, he was right on the money.

The next morning was my first patrol. Wali, along with his platoon of thirty men, arrived at precisely 0900hrs. They looked fit and the NCOs were busy making sure they were ready for the patrol. It was their weapons that drew my attention. The AK-47 is the most widely produced rifle in the world, its distinctive shape instantly recognisable. These ones, however, were something else. No two weapons looked alike. Each had been individually decorated. Some had stickers of pop stars or cartoon characters plastered on the butt and grip, while others sprouted tinsel from the trigger guard. Several soldiers had gone further and stuck flowers in their hair. I was reminded of an Eddie Izzard stand-up routine that called for the formation of a battalion of transvestites whose sheer camp improbability would lull the enemy into a false sense of security. But despite the comical decorations, these men didn't look like comedians. Their faces were hard. They'd fought through some tough battles and until I could say the same I was reluctant to tell them how they ought to dress.

The purpose of the daily patrols was to show our presence on the ground. That makes it sound far simpler than it was, and far safer. The threat in Helmand was constant and we would have to remain vigilant throughout. Keeping our eyes peeled, together we moved out of the camp's front gate, my eight soldiers arrayed among the Afghans. I was proud to see the way they immediately adapted to working with the ANA. I positioned myself close to Wali, with Ash by my side, and was able to stay in touch with my soldiers over the PRR, a small radio that each man wore clipped onto his body armour. The range was just a few hundred metres but it was enough to ensure that all the British soldiers on the patrol could talk to one another at all times.

The first thing I noticed was the heat. I'd been in Afghanistan for several days now but had spent most of that time slipping from one air-conditioned tent to another. Out on patrol, weighed down by body armour, rifle, spare ammunition, radio and seven litres of water, I began to feel how hot it really was. It was late April and the temperature was already in the high thirties. Over the next few months it would approach 50°C, a temperature at which you sweat sitting down in the shade, let alone walking countless miles with a hundred pounds of equipment on your back.

From the JDCC we moved north off the main highway and into a maze of narrow dirt streets. Mud brick walls reared up on either side, hemming us in, while foul-smelling open sewers ran along the edge of the thoroughfare, poised to snare unwary drivers should they stray too far from the central line.

Patrols with the ANA have their own unique character. Traditionally when patrolling in built-up areas, the British Army employs a system they developed in Northern Ireland that uses three twelve-man multiples simultaneously, spread between different streets. Staying in close radio contact, the multiples 'leap-frog' past one another as they move forward. This allows the soldiers in each multiple to know what is going on around them even when buildings block their view, making it harder for them to be ambushed. When patrolling with the ANA, however, it wasn't possible to use this system as the Afghans didn't have enough radios to split their men this way. In addition, I had to stick close to the ANA patrol commander so that we could talk through an interpreter. This all meant we were forced to patrol in a straight line along each road and I was acutely conscious that the enemy could surprise us at any time.

Just a couple of blocks from the JDCC we emerged into the central market-place and walked into a solid wall of sound. The yells of street-hawkers mingled with the revving of two-stroke motorbike engines while goats bleated in their pens and stereos blasted us with Afghan pop. Market stalls were crammed on either side of the road where fly-covered animal carcasses swung from hooks, attended by bloodstained butchers with their cleavers.

The market teemed with people, buying, selling, or simply loitering by the roadside, watching us through inscrutable eyes. The adults kept a wary distance from us, whether out of fear or animosity I couldn't tell. The children were a different story though. Dozens of kids, both boys and girls, swarmed around us. Over the past couple of years they'd picked up a smattering of English phrases they now gabbled at top speed. 'Hey mister! What's your name? How are you? You give me chocolate . . . five dollar . . . pens?' Their big dark eyes and barefoot poverty were an almost irresistible combination, but whenever I did succumb to one of them I always regretted it, as the rest recognised an easy touch and clamoured even louder for their share.

Being surrounded by so many people made me nervous and the market-place with its dark alleyways added to a growing feeling of claustrophobia. It would be easy for an attacker to ambush us here, to rake our patrol with a quick burst of fire, make a few quick kills and then melt away into the crowd. It was also the perfect environment for a suicide bomber. Any one of the burka-clad women could be concealing explosives beneath their billowing robes. We'd know nothing about it – one click and then oblivion.

The received wisdom was that if there were lots of people on the street then an attack was unlikely – the population supposedly knowing far more about Taliban plans than we did. A handy rule of thumb perhaps but I knew that it didn't always hold true. The enemy had no qualms about blowing up Afghans. Minimising collateral damage wasn't really on their agenda.

It might have been more straightforward to conduct our patrols in Snatches but then we would have missed out on the opportunity to talk to the locals. On foot we could present a more human face, or at last that was the idea. It was a lesson the Army had learned from fighting counter-insurgencies in Malaya and Northern Ireland – get among the population, understand them and allow them to understand you. This was difficult to achieve from inside armour-plated vehicles. Now I was going to find out just how hard it was face-to-face.

During our training we had been taught that building a rapport with the locals could help us pick up useful low-level intelligence about the area and about our enemies. Walking through the market-place with my interpreter, Ash, I decided to make a start. Just your friendly neighbourhood British officer, walking the beat, keeping the streets safe for you, the Afghan people. Who wouldn't want to help me?

A middle-aged man running a stall piled high with cabbages looked as good a candidate as anyone so I brought the patrol to a halt. 'Hello, sir,' I began. 'My name's Mark. How are you today?'

The greengrocer looked down at his wares and said nothing.

I pressed on. 'How's business? Plenty of customers?'

The man mumbled something to Ash, still avoiding eye contact.

'He asks what it is you want,' Ash explained.

'I just want to know how things are for you today and see if there are ways that we might be able to make things better,' I said.

The vendor sighed, shook his head and busied himself among his cabbages, stacking them into neat piles on his barrow.

I was starting to feel a little foolish but refused to be defeated. 'How's the security situation? Do you feel safe in Gereshk?'

'It's fine. Very good,' was the mumbled reply.

'I'm pleased to hear it. Have you seen any Taliban in the town?'

The man just shook his head and then shuffled away behind a neighbouring stall, desperate to escape from my questions.

Over the next thirty minutes I tried four more times to speak to people but all of them rebuffed me with varying degrees of politeness. Wali watched my efforts with growing amusement. 'Why do you Brits all do this?' he asked. 'Always trying to chat to people as though they're your friends.'

I explained how important it was to get intelligence from the locals and build a positive relationship with them. Wali laughed and reminded me I was a foreigner here and so fundamentally untrustworthy. 'You think you're here to help,' he said. 'But to them you're just another stranger with a gun, and people like that don't have a good history in these parts.'

'Exactly,' I said. 'Trying to break down that prejudice is the key to winning the people's hearts and minds.'

'Good luck with that,' said Wali. 'They don't even want to speak to me and I was born just a hundred miles from here. What these people really want is to be left alone.'

'Well, we did find out one thing,' I said. 'The Taliban haven't got much of a presence here and security's pretty good.'

'And you believe them? These are Pashtuns.'

The Pashtuns are by far the dominant ethnic group in south-eastern Afghanistan and almost everyone in Helmand belongs to this race. They have a proud martial history; their forbears have fought and won many battles against the British over the last few hundred years in both Afghanistan and Pakistan. As a young cavalry officer, Winston Churchill fought against Pashtuns, or Pathans as he called them, and noted that, 'Except at harvest time, when self-preservation enjoins a temporary truce, the

Pathan tribes are always engaged in private or public war. Every man is a warrior.' Wali explained that little had changed in this respect and that above all the Pashtuns did not like outsiders.

'So what's the point of us being here at all? If we can't talk to the locals how are we supposed to do anything?'

Wali grinned broadly. 'That's easy. You're here to kill Taliban.'

I was supposed to be the one mentoring Wali, tutoring him in military tactics, steeping him in British Army doctrine. A few weeks ago, sat in a cosy lecture theatre, all this had appeared straightforward but out here, among the bustling chaos of the street, I was less sure. Here and now everything Wali said made sense. And who was I to argue with him? He'd been fighting here for two years. I chose to say nothing and slowly we made our way back to the JDCC.

The heat after two hours on the ground was starting to get to me. I began to feel tired, and sucked on the rubber tube attached to my Camelbak, the portable water container strapped to my back. The water was unpalatably warm – almost as hot as tea – and it didn't refresh me at all. It was important to drink anyway though or else dehydration would swiftly leave me debilitated and put me at risk of heatstroke.

As we patrolled I stayed in constant touch with the ops room. The encrypted radio I carried made up a significant portion of the weight – some 15 pounds – but it was indispensable. I had to be able to talk to the base; if we got into a fight it would be the men in the ops room who would send reinforcements, air support or, if necessary, medics to evacuate any casualties. Without that link, we were on our own. Of course no technology is one hundred per cent reliable and sometimes the radios failed. When that happened we fell back on mobile phones. The Afghan networks surprised me with their quality but they were of course insecure and anyone with a few dollars' worth of scanning equipment could listen in on our conversations – obviously not ideal.

Today, the man on the other end of the radio was Cpl Magoo

and it turned out he liked to chat. Most conversations over the net were clipped and functional – co-ordinates, updates on the tactical situation and so forth. Magoo's style was more conversational and he saw the seriousness of our work as no barrier to enjoying himself. When he clocked my public school accent coming through the ether he spotted an opportunity to have some fun at my expense.

'I say! Hullo there. There's a friendly call sign moving three streets west of your position, yah. Pip pip. Out.'

I have to admit that it was funny, especially because he'd assumed I was exactly the kind of public-school stereotype everyone expected to find in a regiment like mine. Don't get me wrong, I had a wonderful, comfortable upbringing. And yes, I had gone to public school, but unlike some officers in my regiment my forbears hadn't been generals or peers. Apart from his years conscripted in the Army, my mum's dad worked his whole life in the village Co-op and my Grandma Evans ran the local pub. I was the first person in my family to go to university. My Mum and Dad both left school at sixteen. They worked hard and did well for themselves. They put everything they had into making sure my brother and I were given all the opportunities we needed. I probably don't tell them enough, but I'm proud of them and bloody grateful.

Not that I was going to go into all that with Magoo. I just hoped he'd knock it off if things got serious. A few minutes later I was on the net again to update the ops room on our latest position. Sure enough, there came Magoo with a cheery, 'What ho!'

Then from the other side of the ops room, I heard, 'Oi! Cut that out and do your bloody job!'

The Battery Sergeant Major clearly didn't share Magoo's sense of humour. From then on the Irishman was quite professional on the radio – except when he thought no one else was listening.

CHAPTER THREE

December 2008

I'd sold my car just before I left for Afghanistan, so my father was giving me a lift. I'd been back for a month and was now headed to Windsor where my battalion was based. I wasn't due back at work for a few more weeks but had been invited to join them for the annual commemoration of the Battle of Waterloo. Known as 'Hanging the Brick', it was a keenly anticipated event in the Coldstream Guards' calendar and an excellent excuse for an enormous piss-up. Admittedly, during the past few weeks I'd needed little excuse.

We didn't often have serious conversations, my dad and I. We'd catch up on how Southampton had been doing in the League and discuss England's chances in the upcoming Ashes but preferred to avoid any discussion of anything as messy as emotions unless it was completely unavoidable. What happened in the car, therefore, came as something of a surprise.

We'd been driving for fifteen minutes in silence. My father had the radio tuned to Radio 5 Live and the football commentary washed over me as I looked out of the window and thought about nothing in particular. At half-time, the presenter began to announce the news headlines. 'A soldier from the Royal Marines was killed in Afghanistan today.' The mere mention of that place snapped me out of my reverie and my head jerked upright.

'This brings the total number of British service personnel killed to . . .' Dad reached over and turned down the radio. My eyes were fixed

straight ahead on the motorway but for a moment I thought I saw rocks and sand.

'Mark?'

I swung round and glimpsed a soldier in the seat beside me, twisted in an awkward, broken pose, agony etched across his features. Then I blinked and focused on my father's confused face. The spell was broken. 'Are you all right, son?' he asked.

I coughed and ran my fingers through my hair, feeling my forehead damp with sweat. 'Huh? Yeah, I'm fine. Why do you ask?'

'You don't look fine,' he said.

I shrugged. 'Probably hungover. Late one in the pub last night.'

I kept my gaze forward, preferring not to catch my father's eye.

'Oh,' he said. 'Right.'

Another minute passed in silence; then, 'It's just you haven't seemed quite right since you came back.'

More silence.

'I don't want to pry but did something happen over there?'

Screwing my eyes shut, I thought hard. In the few weeks since the end of my tour in Afghanistan, I'd not discussed it with anyone. I hadn't known what to say or to whom. My parents seemed to sense this but up until now hadn't asked. I searched my mind but couldn't find any words. You can't just sweep up the shattered bodies and blood-soaked memories of war and dump them on your father's lap halfway down the M4. The two worlds were so far apart and I had no business spoiling my family's peaceful reality with the carnage I'd found in the desert. I could feel tears springing up behind my eyes and I blinked fast to push them back.

'There was some stuff,' I said. 'It got hairy sometimes. We got shot at a bit. But here I am. It turned out OK in the end.'

My father pursed his lips and nodded. 'OK. If you want to talk about it, though . . .' His voice trailed away, the offer of help unspoken. I was grateful that we could leave it there and we lapsed into quietness once more.

Before long we'd arrived at Victoria Barracks in Windsor and I jumped from the car with a cheery, 'Thanks. See you in a few days.'

I took my rucksack from the boot and walked through the gate and back into the Army for the first time since I'd landed in the UK.

I made my way to the Officers' Mess, a three-storey redbrick building overlooking the parade square. As I walked, I passed neat rows of Land Rovers parked up on the square. It felt comforting to be back in this military environment. I hadn't realised how conditioned I'd become to the distinctive feel of Army life. Previously I'd always found the discipline and uniformity oppressive but now I craved these things.

Along the way I came across groups of soldiers ambling about the place. On the day of 'the Brick' there wasn't much work being done and there was an unusual holiday feel about the place, like you'd get among a group of lads at Luton airport waiting for their flight to Magaluf. The atmosphere was charged with a potent mix of booze and testosterone.

There must have been thirty or forty officers already milling around the anteroom when I arrived. It's a big room that oozes tradition even though the Mess was re-built just a few years ago. At one end there's a Georgian fireplace they salvaged from the old Mess, and pulled up around it are a number of leather wingback chairs. In the corner stands an ornate writing desk where you can find the Mess gambling book containing records of officers' debts from the late 1800s up until 1980, when some puritanical commanding officer banned the practice. As I walked in, it seemed that all eyes turned to watch me. I felt suddenly self-conscious.

Looking around, there were a few unfamiliar faces, men who had commissioned since I'd been away from battalion, but most I knew. All officers of the Coldstream Guards, we were supposed to be comrades and friends, brothers even. They'd not been with me in Afghanistan, having mostly deployed on an earlier tour while I'd been off training recruits in Yorkshire. In my absence they'd forged new bonds with one another during the long months overseas and now, even as they welcomed me back into the bosom of the Coldstream family, they seemed like strangers.

Jamie Russell, the adjutant, approached me first, grabbing my hand and pumping it enthusiastically. He'd known me since my first day in the Regiment but we'd not seen one another for almost a year. This greeting was at least genuine. As others came up to say hello, I felt myself become awkward and formal. I'd trained with some of these men for years, shared water-filled shell scrapes dug into windswept hillsides and afterwards we'd got roaring drunk together. We had, I thought, been as close as it was possible for men to be, but now I feared a veil had fallen between us. Although most of them had been to Afghanistan, they hadn't seen what I'd seen, done what I'd done.

It was the questions about my tour that I found the hardest to endure. These were military men. It should have been easy. They, more than anyone, were equipped to comprehend what I'd been through. But as I began to talk I was aware of attentions wandering and eyes glazing over. They didn't want to know. Of course. Telling war stories is a competitive sport in the Army. These officers had been in Afghanistan during the winter and while they had endured their share of fighting I suspected it had lacked the intensity of my encounters with the enemy. But who wants to hear that? The last thing I was interested in was a game of one-upmanship, especially one in which what counted as winning or losing was becoming increasingly unclear to me. Under fire in the desert, I'd longed for days like this when I could share my experience with fellow-warriors who could appreciate all the hardship and the tough decisions. But now I had my chance, I found that neither I nor my audience wanted to play. The longed for glory had evaporated like morning mist in the desert.

Thankfully all conversation was soon quelled by the start of the proceedings that comprised 'Hanging the Brick'. We filed out of the Mess, clutching G&Ts or Bloody Marys, and ranged ourselves about the lawn that looked over the parade square.

The eponymous brick refers to a lump of masonry that was taken from the farmhouse of Hougoumont, a building the Coldstream Guards had successfully defended at the Battle of Waterloo. History records that the French were attempting to breach the gate of the farm when two men, Lt Col Macdonell and Sgt Graham, averted disaster by fighting through the enemy lines and forcing the gate shut. Wellington later described holding the farmhouse as the key to the battle. The brick has consequently assumed talismanic status in the regiment, a symbol of the bravery and selflessness to which all Coldstreamers should aspire.

As we watched from our vantage point on the steps, the parade began. Two of the burliest members of the Sergeants' Mess escorted the brick from the guardroom, carrying it in a custom-made cradle along a route that took it around the perimeter of the square. Another forty men, the remainder of the Sergeants' Mess, marched behind to the beat hammered out on the drums. Every man was wearing fancy dress. Axe-wielding Vikings walked beside witches with their brooms while street-sweepers and police officers followed behind. The one commonality was that all the costumes required the wearer to carry an object that might function as a weapon. You see the escort was not merely ceremonial – tradition stated that should the junior soldiers successfully capture the brick then they could legitimately hold it hostage until the sergeants paid an appropriate ransom in booze. The threat therefore was very real and the sergeants were ready to do battle.

The brick got as far as the first corner of the square without incident when from around the side of the Quartermaster's stores a column of screaming dervishes fell upon the parade and surged towards the brick. Play acting this was not. Each man on the square was an infantryman, trained in violence. A few pre-match beers had lowered inhibitions and as fists began to fly, the scene quickly descended into a bad day at Millwall. We officers looked on from our perch like patricians in the Colosseum, radiating jovial approval as the men we commanded knocked seven bells out of one another.

The running battle continued as the brick made its slow progress around the square. When one wave of attackers had been repulsed, fresh men would take their place. The spectacle grew steadily closer and I could hear the crunch of fists on flesh, the laboured breathing of the combatants. This was not just fun. Adrenaline was pumping. One man caught my attention, dressed in the robes of a Bedouin Arab. Below the band of his headdress, I could see his eyes burning with the thrill of battle, as I'd seen in the eyes of my comrades in Helmand. Yes! This is what the Army was for. It liberated all our base instincts, made savages of civilised men, allowed us to act as nature intended.

I felt my blood pumping hard and around me I could hear the cries of the other officers, shouting at the sergeants, exhorting them to a still greater pitch of savagery. And then I wasn't cheering the men on the square but was back in Helmand, yelling at the Afghans beside me to move forward and engage the enemy. The wall of sound around me became rifle fire and the explosions of rockets as they launched.

'Steady on there, Mark.'

I looked around wildly to see James, another captain, smiling at me. 'There's a whole day of drinking ahead of us. You look a bit glazed already.'

I nodded vacantly. 'Feeling rather odd,' I said. 'Late night last night.'

James had already turned his attention back to the melee below us and I backed unsteadily away up the steps and into the Mess. Once inside I blundered towards the gents. I pushed open a stall door and locked it behind me before collapsing on top of the toilet seat. My body shook as I sat there and for the first time I asked myself the question, 'What the fuck is wrong with me?'

I drank away the rest of the day in the Sergeants' Mess where, in the name of tradition, anyone who touched the brick was obliged to buy a round. If volunteers were not forthcoming then the NCOs would forcibly grab an officer and propel him headfirst through the air towards the brick, which was suspended from a rope above the bar. It was considered good form to resist but only up to a point. Struggling too much would cause the NCOs to push your head into the brick with considerably more force than was necessary. So it was that I woke the following morning with a crashing headache, but that was not what was bothering me most. I got up and went to see the regiment's medical officer.

'I can't stop thinking about Afghanistan,' I said.

'How long have you been back?'

'About three weeks.'

'Yes, that's standard. Here, have some sleeping pills. You'll feel better soon.'

Everything was fine. This was all quite normal. I felt relieved. Better have a drink to celebrate.

CHAPTER FOUR

After the initial hurricane of work that comes with starting any new job, life began to settle into a recognisable pattern: twice-daily patrols, writing reports and, my most important task, the planning of operations. So called patches of time emerged of (what might laughingly be referred to as) recreation. There wasn't a great deal of choice when it came to leisure activities. Sleeping, reading and watching DVDs were the chief pursuits, interspersed with odd bouts of masturbation. Given the close confines of our living quarters, it was best for one's peace of mind not to dwell too heavily on the frequency of this last activity.

Of all our pastimes, the most productive was exercise. In the Army it's instilled into us that fitness is next to godliness and competitive 'phys' was actively encouraged. However, it was difficult to run due to the layout of the base, and obviously jogging through Gereshk itself was a non-starter, so instead it was all about the gym. We had no proper equipment but enterprising sappers from the Royal Engineers had improvised an extensive fitness studio out of assorted junk, fashioning dumbbells out of discarded oil cans they'd filled with rocks.

Soldiers can never resist the urge to give something an absurd nickname and hence weightlifting was known as Op Massive, so named for the overdeveloped physique to which participants aspired. In Gereshk I made an effort – keeping fit is an important part of being an officer as we need to be able to keep up with our men when in the field and remain alert enough to make crucial decisions. With this in mind, I diligently presented myself at the gym, ready to pump some iron.

'Fuck me, sir, my grandmother's got bigger arms than you.'

'I've never seen a man lose a fight with a punch bag before.'

Banter, smack talk, taking the piss is the way men bond the world over. My rank didn't protect me from this, but I gave back as good as I got.

So the days passed. Patrol followed patrol without incident, and boredom began to set in. I yearned for action. I'm sure many people might see this hunger for battle as the craving of a madman. At this point in history, with two world wars behind us, surely no reasonable person could view armed conflict as anything other than a catastrophe.

But going to war is all I ever wanted. It was my obsession since before I can remember. From those earliest playground games, using sticks for guns and arguing over who was dead, I wanted to be a soldier. For a while my childhood companions all shared the same dream and together we watched the films, read the books and debated the merits of different types of gun. As we became teenagers, however, new fascinations emerged and the platoons of our imagination were overrun by girls. Girls didn't think war was cool, so we pushed down our darker impulses, banishing fantasies of combat in favour of other more readily obtainable pleasures.

For my friends, this was as far as it went. They grew up, dreamed new dreams and forgot their childhood obsessions. They joined civilisation. I was different. War never relinquished its foothold in my mind and by the time I finished university it was rampant once more.

In 2003, a million Britons took to the streets to protest against the invasion of Iraq. A girl I liked was going so I went along. We ended up on the Embankment, being crushed by the weight of the gridlocked crowd. All around me people with placards were chanting slogans like 'No War' and 'Not in my Name'. The anger was tangible. It felt like the entire nation was rising up and declaring a universal commitment to peace. I looked at the faces of the protestors and saw such certainty in their eyes. War was evil.

Maybe they were right. I've certainly had times since when I've questioned the morality of the whole enterprise. But not back then. Then all I saw was opportunity. We were living in extraordinary times. It had been years since we in Britain had had the chance to go to war. Stories of real combat were the preserve of our grandparents. Now, here was our chance, our moment to prove ourselves in the ultimate test. The drums were beating, urging us to war in a far-off land and here I was, the only person who could hear the call. I turned around and forced my way out through the crowd. A month later I presented myself at an Army recruiting office.

The selection process through which one must pass to gain entry to the Royal Military Academy Sandhurst was seemingly straightforward, but many candidates failed to make the grade. The main hurdle was a four-day assessment that took place in the grounds of a grand country house somewhere in Wiltshire. They tested our fitness with an assault course and bleep test, our mental agility with timed essays and general knowledge quizzes, and our communications skills with debates and public-speaking exercises. Finally there were the so-called command tasks, where we took it in turns to take charge of a team transporting heavy barrels over imaginary crocodile-infested rivers with various planks and lengths of rope to aid us. When it was all over, through some esoteric process they made a call as to whether we had what it took to be an officer.

Arriving at Sandhurst I found myself in the company of like-minded men, most of whom shared my own hunger for war. I wasn't a freak and this really was an adventure. We were captivated by the romance that we believed existed in combat. That our views flew in the face of popular opinion only drew us closer together and cemented our faith. We were an elite, set apart from the civilian masses by our selfless willingness to risk our lives for the United Kingdom. In the chapel on Sundays, we would sing 'I Vow to Thee, My Country' and feel our hearts swell in patriotic fervour. Except, of course, it was more about the fighting than the country.

The early weeks of the course consisted mostly of intensive lessons in how to walk in a straight line, otherwise known as drill; how to iron knife-edge creases into our shirts and trousers, something I never got the hang of; and how to buff our shoes until they shone like the sun. None of this seemed to have a great deal to do with the business of soldiering or leadership but was rather an exercise in humility. The most useful part of it for me was learning how to function on less than four hours sleep a night.

Gradually, under the patient yet acerbic tuition of Colour Sergeants 'Proxy' Smith and Graham Hales, we began to learn some more useful skills – how to shoot, how to write a set of orders and, crucially, how to look after ourselves in the field. Over a series of freezing, rain-soaked exercises we were schooled in the dark arts of sleeping in a water-filled hole in the ground, trying to stay awake while staring into the darkness for signs of a non-existent enemy, and walking a long way while carrying large amounts of weight.

Eventually we came to the end of our first term and the syllabus took on a more cerebral nature. At least it purported to do so. We slumbered our way through lectures on international affairs, military strategy and ethics, exhausted from our more physical outdoor exertions. No one seemed to mind if we paid attention or not in these classes; it was only our performance out on exercise that counted. This was an attitude that prevailed throughout the Army. Independent thought was generally discouraged. The Army had a procedure for everything – why would you need to question it when you've already been told the correct approach for handling any situation? In fairness, this system was effective – it meant that under pressure the training conditioned you to act a certain way, and allowed you to predict how others around you would respond too.

As the weeks became months, the platoon grew ever closer and almost without noticing we sloughed off our civilian identities and became soldiers. Our sense of humour darkened and gradually we came to accept the brutal realities that military service involved. Our moral code subtly shifted over the course of our training. We became fiercely committed to values of integrity and honour while at the same time ready to accept orders without question and prepared to kill for our country. I suppose it was a form of brainwashing, but one that we all embraced.

The course was hard work and not everyone made it through. We lost four guys to injuries, while another three were deemed not to have made the grade and asked to leave.

The last term of Sandhurst passed by in a blur. My place in the Coldstream Guards was confirmed a few weeks in and after that it was head down and sprint for the finish line. In the final months we moved away from conventional military training and began to learn how to conduct more complex counter-insurgency operations, more akin to the situations we would one day find in Afghanistan or Iraq. It was more interesting, but by that point I had had enough of training, just wanted to commission, take my place in the real Army and maybe, if my luck held, go to war.

Finishing Sandhurst was not the end of training, however. As an infantry officer I was required to complete another three-month course, conducted largely in the inhospitable Brecon Beacons. Known as the Platoon Commanders' Battle Course, this was a fearsome and intense training package that taught us in more detail about the job of infanteering. The infantry's official job description is to 'close with and destroy the enemy'. Not for us the more impersonal means of delivering death used by the Artillery with their long-range guns or the Air Corps with their helicopters. Over the three months in Brecon we practised the tactics and methods that would enable us to kill people up close. It's a brutal and dangerous business but by the end of the course I felt ready to go out and do it for real.

CHAPTER FIVE

My first real test came about three weeks into my time in Gereshk. I was called to the ops room one morning where Richard, the Battery Commander, informed me an IED had been discovered in the market-place. Dealing with IEDs was the preserve of the Ammunition Technical Officers or ATOs, the British Army's name for bomb disposal experts. When a bomb is discovered, it's the ATO's job to crawl up to it and poke around inside until it's safely defused. Of course, the IEDs are often highly unstable and they frequently blow up, taking the poor ATO with them. The brave men and women who do this difficult and dangerous job have all undergone about eighteen months of training to qualify and only a handful of the strongest candidates complete the course successfully. As a result, ATOs are always in short supply and their deployment within theatre is strictly controlled by the Brigade Headquarters. Calling out an ATO is a big deal and we were always wary of wasting their time on false alarms. So when Richard received the report of an IED he first had to confirm whether or not it was accurate.

'Mark, I want you to go with an ANA platoon and check out this bomb,' he said. 'If it looks genuine then we'll get an ATO flown in from Lashkar Gah. We've already alerted them.'

I picked up my blokes and together with Wali and his platoon we headed out. I walked with the Afghans while the other British soldiers followed in the Snatches. As I walked, it occurred to me that I didn't know what an IED looked like. They could be disguised as almost anything, from an obvious shell casing, to a drinks can, or even a simple box.

When we arrived at the edge of the market-place, an Afghan in police uniform waved us down. The Afghan National Police (ANP) has a poor reputation among the British military. They aren't thought to be of the same calibre as their ANA cousins, but more significantly they aren't considered trustworthy. The ANA has a policy of deploying troops in parts of the country away from their homes. This is intended to reduce corruption and prevent local warlords and gangsters from wielding influence. The ANP, however, tend to be recruited locally and their allegiance is often called into question.

I approached the police officer warily, fearful that I might be being led into a trap. Wali looked glum, as relations between the ANP and ANA were famously strained. His discomfort did nothing to calm my nerves. The market-place also made me uneasy – too many buildings overlooking us, too many alleyways from which an ambush could be sprung. Patrolling through it was one thing, but we were going to be stuck here for a while. Any one of the people crowding around the stalls could turn out to be a suicide bomber.

Wali ordered his platoon to form a cordon around the market-place to keep the crowds back, outside of the danger zone. A big enough bomb could take out half a street and throw shrapnel even further.

Controlling the public was a difficult task in itself as the locals, far from being panicked, followed our antics with curiosity. The sight of a British soldier prodding away at a bomb that might go off in his face was apparently fine sport. They jostled against the ANA men manning the cordon, trying to get the best possible view. I found their nonchalance in the face of danger quite unsettling but I supposed that years of warfare and the daily threat of violent death had made the Afghans hard. Steeling myself, I allowed the police officer to lead me on foot further into the labyrinth, towards the bomb.

The police officer came to a halt opposite a heap of rubbish piled up by the side of a narrow alley. 'It's in there,' he said.

I saw it at once, sticking up out of the mound of discarded metal and wire, a rusting artillery shell. It was big, at least 100 pounds by the looks of it – about the size of a scuba diver's air tank. The real deal; enough to make a mess of anyone standing in this street. The police officer just stood there, hands on hips, looking utterly relaxed. I began to sweat. For a moment I considered getting a bit nearer to see if there were any visible wires leading away from the IED that could be used to trigger it, but swiftly dismissed the idea. The ATOs might enjoy getting intimate with high explosives but this was quite as close as I wanted to get.

'Yep, that's a bomb,' I stammered.

The police officer just shrugged.

'Let's get back behind the cover of the vehicles,' I said.

We beat a retreat to the corner of the alleyway. My companion sauntered while I tried my best not to break into a run until I was safely crouched behind my Snatch. I got on the radio and asked the ops room to call in the ATO.

'Expect them within forty minutes,' I was told. 'In the meantime, wait there and maintain the cordon.'

Now that I'd seen the bomb, I wasn't sure that the crowd had been pushed back far enough to guarantee their safety. Luckily, the British Army offers its commanders a handy solution for dilemmas of this nature. It's called the TAM, or Tactical Aide Memoire. This remarkable document is an A6-sized ring binder that fits in your pocket and contains procedures to deal with almost any conceivable military problem one might encounter. Being shot at and not sure what to do? Get out your TAM and it will take you step by step through an assessment of the tactical situation and help you make a plan. Puzzling over the correct drill for setting an ambush? It's in the TAM! Obviously there's not always time to read through a set of instructions but right now it was just what I needed. I pulled the green covered binder out of a webbing pouch and flicked through it until I found the section on IEDs. It was all there. For a bomb of 100 pounds – there was a helpful illustration of how big that might look – the cordon should be 200 metres in radius. I looked around at the troops holding back the crowd. The distance seemed about right. I decided to leave things as they were.

At that moment, there was a loud commotion over by the cordon and I heard a British voice shouting, 'Halt! Get back!' I ran over to find one of my soldiers holding back a middle-aged Afghan man who was pressing against the thin strip of tape that we'd stretched across the road to mark the perimeter of our operation. He had the long, pointed face of a rodent, a likeness exaggerated by two overgrown front teeth that protruded slightly beneath a manicured moustache. Rivulets of sweat ran down his face as he argued with the soldier in Pashtu. He was clearly furious and the more incomprehensible we found him, the more animated he became. His gesticulations grew increasingly expansive until a particularly theatrical flourish caused the front of his leather jerkin to gape open. Underneath, slung over his right shoulder, I could see the stubby shape of a cut-down machine-gun.

This was it. I brought my rifle up to point at the man's face. To my surprise our would-be assailant shrank away, covering his face with his hands. I stopped and stared at him. This wasn't the kind of behaviour I associated with a Taliban insurgent.

'Ash,' I said to my interpreter. 'Who the hell is this guy and what's he doing parading a weapon around in front of us?'

Ash shot a series of questions from over my shoulder, sensibly keeping an armed man between him and his interviewee. Before the man could answer, Captain Wali arrived on the scene. He took one look at the man on the other side of the tape and grimaced. 'It's all right,' he said. 'Put your weapons down. This is Major Haider. He's with the National Directorate of Security.'

'The what?'

'Secret Police,' said Wali. He turned to Major Haider and politely invited him to cross the cordon.

Major Haider had quickly recovered from the shock of two British soldiers threatening to shoot him and was working back up to his previous pitch of angry indignation. Ash had stopped translating but it was clear that the Major was tearing a strip off Wali about something. Whenever there was a gap in the torrent of abuse, Wali would patiently try to interject, only to be shouted down again.

Eventually Major Haider ran out of steam, allowing Wali to get in a few words. The secret policeman stiffened. He glanced over in the direction of the IED, and without further ado ducked back under the cordon and vanished into the crowd. Wali burst out laughing. 'He's always playing the big man. Thinks he runs this town with his secret operations and his "I answer directly to the President's office." Put him next to a bomb and he pees himself and runs back to his mother. Ha! He always gets uppity when Col Wadood's out of town. The CO will squash him like a slug when he gets back.'

The National Directorate for Security, or NDS, were rather a law unto themselves. They didn't fall under the British forces' training remit and we had very little direct contact with them. I believe that the Americans did some top-level liaison in Kabul but, like secret services the world over, no one on the outside really knew what they got up to. And also like any other secret service, their colleagues in the regular military and police were pretty wary of them. Rumours of kidnapping, torture and murder surrounded the NDS and I even heard they had links with Iranian intelligence. Whatever the truth, I was happy to keep my distance.

Reaching into my trouser pocket, I pulled out a pack of

Marlboro Lights. The police officer who had directed me to the bomb gratefully accepted my offer of a cigarette. I lit one for each of us. My fear began to recede as we smoked. I felt guilty about my initial suspicion of my companion. I'd judged him based on the received wisdom about the Afghan security forces and I'd been proved wrong. I resolved from now on to treat our allies with greater respect.

In due course the ATO arrived. Although he was around my age, his haggard face aged him considerably. 'This is my third IED since this morning,' he said.

'Busy day?' I asked.

'About average,' he sighed. 'So what have we got?'

I briefed him on the situation and he nodded. 'Yeah, sounds typical. We've had a lot of artillery shells being used recently to make IEDs.'

The ATO clambered into his protective gear, a thick padded outfit with a helmet and visor that resembled an old-fashioned diving suit. The temperature inside must have been unbearable. I speculated that the equipment's main purpose must have been psychological; if that bomb went off I couldn't see it offering much protection. He made his way towards the alleyway at a slow waddle.

After twenty restless minutes the ATO returned. He took off his helmet and grinned. 'Not a bomb after all, mate,' he said. 'Probably just a metal mould from a factory. Looks quite like a shell, mind you. From a distance, anyway.'

I felt myself flush red. 'God, I'm sorry. I was so sure.'

'Don't worry about it. Do you know how much I long for false alarms when I get called out? I've seen quite enough of the real thing. There's only a month left till I go home and if every time between now and then I only see duds, I'll be a happy man.'

I thanked him and set about the business of collapsing the cordon and getting back to base. On the drive I reflected on my performance. Confronting the bomb was the first time I'd felt real fear since arriving in Afghanistan. I'd held it together though and for that I was pleased.

I found myself wondering how my own grandfather would have performed in such circumstances. He was the only surviving member of my family to have fought in a war, the Second World War in his case. I didn't know much about what he'd done. The old man had never spoken about it, supplying only the barest details when I'd pressed him and those were given up only after I had myself embarked on a military career. He had been an infantry soldier in the 14th Army in India and Burma – the so-called Forgotten Army. I knew that he'd spent a period as a sniper and I often tried to imagine him squinting down the sights of his rifle at a Japanese soldier, slowly squeezing on the trigger.

He'd suffered afterwards, apparently. Again, I didn't know the ins and outs of it but whenever a war film came on the television he'd quickly change the channel and he refused to have anything to do with Remembrance Sunday. The smell of curry used to set him off too. Just walking past an Indian restaurant was enough to transport him back to the war and you could see his eyes grow hollow and vacant. Growing up, I found my grandad's war record a subject of intense fascination and wondered incessantly about the adventures he must have had. In place of any concrete information I pictured all kinds of heroism under fire. Now I had gone to war myself, I felt his imagined valour weigh heavily on my shoulders.

My grandfather had been ill for some time before I'd left for Afghanistan. It was emphysema. No one knew how much longer he had but my parents had agreed with me that should he die before I got home, they'd keep it from me. There was no sense breaking bad news while I was stuck here, unable to attend a funeral. 'You need to stay focused,' they'd said, and they were right.

The night after the false alarm with the IED I slept fitfully and woke the following day unrested. After breakfast I went for the morning briefing with Richard. After a well done to me and the lads for the way we'd handled the IED operation, he rattled through the usual intelligence summaries and orders for the day. Nothing much seemed to be on the cards and the whole thing was done in twenty minutes. As we filed out of the briefing room, Richard called me over. 'Mark, have you got two minutes?' he said. 'Walk with me back to my office.'

We strolled together across the parade square.

'You haven't met Col Wadood yet, have you?' said Richard.

I shook my head. 'No, he's been up in Kabul ever since I arrived.'

'Of course. He's due back later today and you ought to go and introduce yourself.'

'Oh right. Well, no problem. I'll go and see him before dinner when I get back in from patrol.'

'Good. Um, there's one other thing.' Richard looked shifty and fumbled with the keys to his office as he spoke.

'Yes?'

'I've had the Brigade Chief of Staff on the telephone this morning and he wants to know why the kandak hasn't been patrolling on Fridays. I tried to bring this up with the Colonel before he went on leave but it didn't go too well. I was wondering if you might mention it at your meeting this evening.'

'The ANA don't patrol on Fridays? What? Not at all?' I hadn't been on a patrol on a Friday in the three weeks since I'd been in Gereshk but I hadn't realised that it was an ANA policy.

'It's not a rule, but generally they prefer to take Fridays off,' said Richard. 'It's religious, I suppose. A bit like Sundays for Christians or Saturdays for Jews. They go out if they have to, for arrest ops and so forth, but they don't conduct routine patrols. Brigade's in a bit of a wax about it.'

'OK. I'll let you know how it goes.'

Richard turned his attention to the papers on his desk and I took this as my cue to leave. Although I hadn't yet encountered the Colonel, I'd sensed his shadow. From hundreds of miles away he still managed to dominate the lives of everyone in the camp. None of the ANA officers and soldiers did anything without first considering what the CO would have to say about it. He'd been in command through the past two years of brutal fighting in Helmand and now, at my first ever meeting with him, I had to tell him he was doing it wrong.

CHAPTER SIX

That evening I made my way over to the concrete building that housed the Colonel's office, walked upstairs and paused by the door. I straightened my beret and glanced at Ash before gulping down my anxiety and knocking. A growl from within granted me leave to enter and I swung open the door.

The room was about ten metres by four and sparsely appointed. On the far side was a rickety wooden desk covered in maps and neat stacks of paper. Behind the desk was a long window which was open, allowing the noise and fumes of the traffic on the road to drift inside. In the centre of the room a square table was covered with a giant map showing the whole of Gereshk district. A bare electric bulb cast a dim glow and in one corner a battered old television sat on an upturned packing crate. On the wall was a huge framed print of an Afghan man, painted so that his head emerged from a cloud, like some kind of god.

The Colonel was sitting behind his desk when I came in, head down, poring over his papers. He glanced briefly in my direction and held up a hand to acknowledge my own rather shabby salute while continuing to scribble notes in the margins of a document. His face was thin and pointed with a sharp nose that gave him a hawk-like appearance. A narrow, carefully trimmed moustache adorned his upper lip, hinting at a fastidious character.

As the Colonel finished his writing he stood up to greet me, unfolding his long frame from behind the desk. He was in good shape, lean and wiry, as befitted a soldier who'd been fighting for over twenty years. His appearance was really quite unremarkable but there was something about the way he held himself, a certain imperiousness in his bearing that radiated power.

'Captain Evans,' he said. 'Come on in. Please sit down.'

The Colonel spoke with a heavy accent, but although we henceforth used an interpreter, I suspected his English was better than he let on. He often reacted to what I said before he'd heard the translation, using the time it took for the interpreter to speak to formulate his own reply. Translating back into English, the interpreters, even Ash, lacked the fluency to make a precise rendition of the Colonel's words. Instead I heard a simplified approximation and so relied a great deal on visual cues from the Colonel's body language and expression. I think we understood one another well enough, and over the time we worked together this became easier.

Now I steeled myself for the conversation that lay ahead, but before I could find a suitable opening remark Col Wadood interrupted me.

'I was just about to have supper. Why don't you join me?'

I thought of all the work that awaited me after I finished my business with the Colonel that evening. There were today's reports, planning for tomorrow's patrols, a training plan that needed writing. Afghan dinners could drag on for hours. But it would seem rude of me to refuse, and besides, a meal would allow me to put off the dreaded conversation just a little longer.

'Thank you, Colonel. I'd be delighted.'

At that moment, there was a knock at the door and one more ANA officer entered. He was the S2, the captain in charge of intelligence. I never found out his real name; he always went by his title of S2. He was a behemoth of a man with a big, black beard and a belly protruding several inches over the top of his waistband. He was strongly allergic to most forms of exercise but made special exception for the traditional Afghan sport of buzkashi. Similar to polo, it's played on horseback but in place of a ball the two teams compete for possession of a headless goat's carcass. As we got to know one another, the S2 would often regale me with tales of his nail-biting victories on the buzkashi field. When he told me his dreams for a future after the war, being reunited with his favourite horse received equal billing with his wife and children.

The Colonel's desk was too small for a dining table but the four of us made do and squeezed in. I was particularly excited after spending the past week eating nothing but boil-in-the-bag rations. I had long ago lost any fondness for preserved corned beef hash and chicken stew, the greasy taste of which lingered on the palate hours after the last mouthful. Tonight we dined on runny, salty yoghurt, with spring onions stirred in. The sloppy mixture was served in a blue washing up bowl and we passed around a ladle from which we took it in turns to scoop out some yoghurt and slurp it down. Watching the S2 lick the ladle clean before handing it to me did little for my appetite but nevertheless the yoghurt was tart and refreshing, and slaked my thirst as well as my hunger after a long day in the sun. Once we'd finished the yoghurt, we were presented with our main course – an altogether less appetising prospect. On top of a generous heap of rice and vegetables sat lumps of glistening animal flesh, which defied more accurate classification. I'd heard that eating meat in Afghanistan was to play Russian roulette with one's digestive system, but the dish's spicy aroma was enough to suppress my natural caution and I tucked in.

Before we began to eat, the Colonel had switched on the television, explaining that he always liked to listen to music while he ate. Women in saris swirled across the screen in bursts of colour that contrasted with our drab surroundings. Bollywood musicals were the movies of choice throughout the ANA and from the rapt attention of the S2 I could imagine why. The dancers skipped down the staircase of a sumptuous palace in outfits designed to best show off their toned stomachs and thighs. 'Whores,' muttered the S2 and shot me a glance, looking for my reaction. I smiled politely and he grinned back, his mouth still full, and winked. He clearly thought the British are all obsessed with sex. Thinking about all the naked flesh spilling from the magazines in our ops room, maybe he had a point.

I found my eye drawn again to the picture of the man on the wall and Wadood caught the direction of my gaze. 'Do you know who that is?' he asked.

'No, I don't.'

'That is Ahmad Shah Massoud. The greatest Afghan of our time.'

I'd heard of Massoud, of course. He'd been a legendary mujahideen commander during the war against the Soviets and after they'd left had become one of the top men in the Northern Alliance, fighting the Taliban. In 2001, just two days before 9/11, two Tunisians posing as journalists had killed Massoud in a suicide attack on the orders of Osama Bin Laden.

'Did you know him?' I asked Wadood.

'Know him? I was his aide. I was there when those dogs killed him. If he still lived, this war might now be over. The Lion of Panjshir would have chased the Taliban all the way back to Pakistan and we'd have a very different kind of government in Kabul.'

I probed Wadood further for his views on the Afghan government but he just smiled ruefully and brushed aside my questions. 'I'm just a soldier,' he said. 'I'm not political.' Ash shot me a warning glance and I decided to dig no deeper.

After we finished our meal the orderly came in to clear the plates away. The S2 passed around a blue packet of Mild Seven cigarettes. Mild was a serious misnomer here, but to avoid giving offence I took one and was soon enjoying the rasping sandpapery feeling at the back of my throat. Col Wadood looked forlornly at the packet and looked hopefully in my direction. 'Mark, do you have any fancy Marlboros?' he asked.

I patted my pockets helplessly. 'Sorry, I've run out.'

Wadood sighed and glumly accepted a Mild Seven. 'When there is no more decent tobacco, you know the war is going badly,' he said.

Richard had told me that the Colonel seldom smoked and I took this rare indulgence as a sign he was feeling relaxed. The moment had come to broach a delicate issue.

'Colonel,' I began, 'I'm sorry to talk shop straight after dinner, but there's something I need to speak to you about.'

Wadood leant back in his chair, half raising an eyebrow. He was an inscrutable fellow, but just for a second I fancied I saw a glint of fire in his eyes. He might have been a foreigner but he was still a colonel and irritating senior officers seldom produced good results.

'You see the thing is, sir, that last Friday your men didn't go out on patrol. And, well, they didn't go out on the Friday before that either.'

The Colonel's stare was quite expressionless and I shuffled my feet under the table before continuing.

'It's Thursday today and they were wondering at Brigade whether you might be planning on doing any patrolling tomorrow?'

I pulled on my cigarette and tried to arrange my features into an expression that was stern yet also deeply respectful. My question hung in the air with the smoke and the seconds dragged past. The S2's eyes flicked over to the television where the dancers had left their palace and were now capering along a riverbank. I tried desperately to retain eye contact with the Colonel and prevent my gaze slipping to the floor in embarrassment.

Before the pause extended into the realms of farce, the Colonel replied. 'Captain Evans, why do you think we haven't been patrolling on Fridays?'

'I know that Fridays are an important day in your religion,' I replied. 'And I appreciate that you want to observe that. The

British Army wouldn't try to interfere with your customs unless it was important.'

Col Wadood's eyebrow arched a few millimetres higher and he said, 'It's good to know that. Of course, the Taliban would say that interfering with Afghan customs is exactly why you are here. Luckily, we in the ANA know better.'

This was worse than I'd expected. Anger I'd been prepared for, but the Colonel's gentle mockery stripped away my credibility far more surely. I tried not to rise to it.

'Yes, sir,' I said. 'So you see, it's only strategic imperatives that would force us to intervene.'

Col Wadood finally lowered his eyebrow and offered me a perfunctory smile.

'Patrolling on a Friday is a strategic imperative?' he said.

'We feel it is. You see sir, when we're fighting a high-tempo counter-insurgency, we can't afford to slacken off or we risk giving an advantage to the enemy.'

'The enemy, yes. That's the Taliban. A group of ultra-conservative Muslims, who are so devoted to the teachings of Islam that they won't even let people listen to music because they think it goes against their religion. What do you think they are doing tomorrow?'

Seeing where the Colonel was going with this, I hesitated, but thinking about how the conversation would sound when I reported back to Richard, I ploughed on regardless.

'That's just it, sir, we don't know,' I said. 'If we're not out on patrol ourselves, they could be digging in IEDs, setting ambushes, intimidating the locals. We need to deny them the ground.'

The Colonel was now grinning widely and had produced a toothpick, which he was now using to excavate the remnants of his dinner. 'But they do all those things anyway. Every other day of the week we find their IEDs, walk into their ambushes and hear the locals moan about their interference. What can you possibly think is going to happen if we stay in camp tomorrow? Will the Taliban take over the country in a day?'

'That's not really the point, sir,' I muttered. 'It's the principle that matters.'

'Listen, Mark, you can talk to me about principles for the rest of the evening. I'll tell you what the Taliban are doing tomorrow. They are praying. They are sleeping. They are defiling goats. It's a Friday. They are not a problem for us tomorrow.

'Look at this another way.' Col Wadood was suddenly serious. 'How long are you in Helmand for? Six months. How long will your replacement be here for? Six months? And his replacement? Now, how long has the S2 been here?'

The S2 looked round from the television. 'Nearly three years,' he said.

'I've been here for two,' said the Colonel. 'We don't know when we'll leave. Back in the UK, do you work seven days a week?'

I shook my head.

'No, you don't. But you come here for a few months, run round in circles, work every hour in the day and look at us like we are lazy for taking a day off each week.'

The anger I'd feared had finally arrived. It felt worse because I knew that he was right.

The Colonel continued, 'Every six months I have this same conversation. It never gets through. Do you understand?'

I nodded dumbly.

'Agh. What's the use? You know you'll be back here again, asking the same dumb questions, after your bosses have shouted at you for not sorting out those crazy Afghans.'

'Colonel, I really am very sorry.'

Wadood shook his head and sighed. 'Don't worry about it, Mark. Like I say, it's nothing new. Now, it's getting late. You'd better get back. It's been a most enjoyable evening. You're always welcome here.'

I spluttered my thanks for his hospitality and apologised again as I stood up and left. When I reached the door, Wadood called to me. 'Mark, you should cheer up. I guarantee you a hundred per cent that the Taliban won't try anything tomorrow. Tell Richard not to worry.'

'How can you be so sure, sir?' I asked.

'Because their commander rang up just before you came over to tell me. He just wanted to check we weren't going to do anything crazy ourselves and start patrolling on a Friday like the British! Goodnight.'

I stood there gaping at him in the doorway before turning and stumbling out into the night. The Colonel's laughter drifted after me as I went.

CHAPTER SEVEN

Two days after my dinner with Wadood we received a tip-off that a Taliban unit was hiding out in a village called Saidan, 15 kilometres to the east of Gereshk, on the other side of the Helmand River. The place had an ugly reputation after some fierce fighting there the previous summer. There was a great deal of excitement on the British side – it was going to be the first strike operation of our tour. The kandak was going to raid the village and arrest or kill any enemies they found inside. We would accompany them to make sure it all ran smoothly. I couldn't wait.

We drove out of Gereshk in WMIKs – a kind of cut-down Land Rover with no roof and a .50cal machine-gun mounted on the back. These are fearsome weapons that fire over 500 rounds per minute with a range of up to 2,000 metres. Unlike the Snatch, WMIKs have no armour to speak of, leaving driver and passengers dangerously exposed to attack. On the flipside, they are more manoeuvrable than Snatches and their crews have a much greater field of vision. They bear a certain resemblance to the kind of vehicles the Long Range Desert Group used to drive during the Second World War and most soldiers love them, the perceived 'cool factor' far outweighing the increased vulnerability.

First we moved to a deserted compound a few kilometres outside of Gereshk where we met the other units that Brigade had sent to support us in the operation. A hundred men from the D company, 5th Battalion, the Royal Regiment of Scotland (5 Scots) had turned up to provide a cordon that would catch any enemy fighters who tried to escape when we went in. We also had three dogs to take with us on the raid. Two were search dogs – an amiable-looking Labrador and a Retriever – and we all fell in love with them at once. We weren't allowed to get too close though. 'Don't be affectionate,' their handlers told us. 'It over-excites them and messes up their training.' The third dog none of us wanted to get close to. It was a massive and ferocious Alsatian, trained to attack the enemy, or indeed anyone who wasn't its handler. Every time I walked near the animal it snarled through its muzzle and strained on the leash. The ANA, not well disposed towards dogs at the best of times, were visibly terrified.

We remained in the compound all day and prepared for the operation. Richard and Wadood were in charge overall, but Wali and I were responsible for the troops on the ground that would make the break-in and carry out the real work. We were to move to Saidan that night, under the cover of darkness, and then hit them at dawn. We would have gone in earlier but the ANA didn't have night-vision goggles and so we were compelled to wait for the sun to come up. Wali's thirty-man platoon, along with my multiple, was to be the first unit into the village.

Together Wali and I prepared a model of the target buildings and the surrounding area. Model making is a real art in the military, and most officers carry with them their own kit which they have built up over the years, containing all the materials that will help bring their miniature world to life. Coloured ribbons can represent anything from rivers to roads or boundary lines. Talcum powder is also useful for marking the positions of units or various obstacles. Anything not in the pack can usually be improvised on the spot – leaves to represent wooded areas, pebbles to show buildings, and so forth. The relief of an area is best shown by piling up the dust and sand into the required shape. This may all sound a little ridiculous but making sure › everyone has a good visual picture of the ground before an operation begins is essential to prevent confusion once things start to move.

When the model was ready, Wali and I gave orders to our respective soldiers and then started on a series of rehearsals. We acted out what was going to happen the following morning so that everyone understood the particular part they would have to play. Using the compound we were currently occupying as a stand-in for a building in Saidan, we lined up in the correct order and practised forcing our way inside and securing the area. We did this without body armour and radios. It took us five attempts before I was content we had it right. We were shattered after three. Christ knows how it was going to feel with all the equipment on.

While all these preparations were going on, I began to feel the after-effects of Wadood's hospitality the night before. The mystery Afghan meat dish was working its black magic on my intestines and there were ominous stirrings inside my gut. I briefly considered reporting to the medic but feared he might try and ground me. There was no way some half-digested Afghan food was going to get between me and the war. I knocked back four Imodium tablets and hoped for the best.

We finished our preparations at about ten in the evening and tried to snatch a few hours of sleep before we hit the road again at 0300hrs. When I woke I felt worse than ever but with the help of some more drugs forced myself upright and headed out. We stopped in the desert around three kilometres from the edge of Saidan where we set up a leaguer, a sort of improvised temporary camp. After posting sentries we settled down to wait.

Saidan itself was about two hundred metres square and really just a loose collection of buildings rather than a proper village in the Western sense of the word. Under normal circumstances I imagine the place would have been home to perhaps a hundred people but if the Taliban had moved in then hopefully the civilians would have had the good sense to leave. Our intelligence was sketchy but we believed there were up to thirty insurgents in the village – certainly enough to make this a real fight. Just the thought of it made my palms begin to sweat as adrenaline flooded my system.

It was a clear night and the full moon cast a faint glow, illuminating the outline of the distant village. This was a nuisance, for as much as the light helped us to see our way to the target it was just as likely to betray us to the enemy. After all the preparations, these last few moments before the attack dragged. I checked my equipment again and again. I felt excited. Excited and sick. I couldn't tell if this was adrenaline or if my drugs were wearing off. I nervously checked and rechecked my pouches to make sure my spare ammunition was easy to get to. I forced myself to concentrate. After all the years of training, this was it. The real deal. I was going into battle.

The sun was beginning to gather on the horizon when we started our engines and moved off on the final stretch towards Saidan. I was supposed to be in the lead but one kilometre from our target the Afghans could contain themselves no longer and surged past me in their Toyotas. They piled into Saidan with accelerators pressed firmly to the floor while we desperately tried to keep up. What the fuck were they doing?

We screamed straight through to the far side of the village where we jumped out of the vehicles and the ANA began to kick in the doors to the compounds. There had been a detailed plan for how we were going to clear through the village but as soon as we arrived pandemonium broke loose. The ANA charged through the village like men possessed. I had no idea where Wali was or how to get the situation under control. I followed a group of Afghan soldiers into one compound, hoping that Wali might be inside.

The compound was in uproar, women and children were crying as the ANA soldiers herded them from their homes and pushed them towards a holding area beside our vehicles. Old men muttered defiantly but no one tried to resist. There were no young men there at all. I ducked through one of the low doors into a room off the compound's central courtyard. It was dark inside but I could make out a sleeping area in one corner that was piled with blankets and cushions. The rest of the room was a combined living area and kitchen with a big earthenware cooking pot next to a clay oven. A wooden bench stood against the wall and spread across it was a tangle of wires and electronic components. My heart skipped a beat – it must be bomb-making equipment. I was joined by one of the search dogs, which darted quickly around the room searching for a scent. I pointed at the equipment on the bench but the dog's handler dismissed it with a quick shake of his head. 'Bits of radio,' he said.

Back out on the road, the radio crackled in my ear. It was Richard, speaking from a vantage point 200 metres away on the cordon. 'Send a situation report,' he ordered. This was easier said than done. We'd assigned codenames for different areas of the village so that we could report when they had been cleared but looking around me now, Wali's men were running in different directions all over the place. I had no idea what sectors were clear. 'There's no sign of the enemy,' I told Richard. 'It's a bit chaotic though.'

Eventually I caught up with Wali in the prisoner holding area where he was jabbering enthusiastically into his mobile phone. He finished his call as I approached. 'No Taliban here today,' he said to me. 'The Colonel's coming over now to have a look.'

By the time Wadood and Richard appeared, Wali's men had searched over half the village, turning up nothing of interest and I was beginning to feel ill once more. The Colonel chatted to a few of the locals and asked them where all the young men were. They told him that they were all out working on the poppy harvest. Of course no one had seen any Taliban. Overhead circled an Unmanned Aerial Vehicle, better known as a UAV or drone, relaying thermal images of the scene back to the ops room in Gereshk. It too had seen no sign of the enemy.

Richard, always keen to do things by the book, wanted to continue until the whole village had been cleared but Wadood was bored and eager to head back to Gereshk – he didn't think we'd find any enemies here now. Just as the Colonel's view was beginning to prevail, we heard an urgent message come over the radio. The UAV had picked up a heat signature moving towards us from outside the cordon. The Taliban were counter-attacking.

We quickly assumed defensive positions while the soldiers on the cordon moved to intercept the attackers.

After a couple of tense minutes, a Scottish voice came over the net.

'We've got eyes on the target.'

There was a pause.

'It's a goat.'

That was the big Taliban counter-attack – a bloody goat. How that could have confused the people back in the ops room ana-lysing the UAV feed I have no idea. It seemed there was little more to do but pack up and go home. I felt a hand on my shoulder and turned to see one of Wali's corporals proffering a cigarette.

'Thanks.' I reached out and took the fag. As I did so, another wave of nausea hit me. I doubled over, retching. Hot vomit gushed out of my mouth and spattered on the Afghan's boots. Backing away, wiping my mouth, I stammered an apology. 'I'm so sorry. Really, awfully sorry.'

The corporal gave me a long, level stare. Then he shrugged, put his cigarette to his lips and lit up. I guess even being vomited on couldn't make this morning any more disappointing.

CHAPTER EIGHT

Before I knew it, three months had passed since I'd arrived in Gereshk and still the enemy had failed to show themselves. I had almost completely lost hope that they ever would. So the explosion that shook the building, ripping me from sleep, was a massive shock. My first thought was that we were under a mortar attack but there was only one bang and it sounded much bigger than any mortar I'd heard before.

Dressing quickly, I ran to the ops room, passing two ANA Toyotas speeding towards the gate. The watchkeeper on duty was occupied on the net, scrabbling for information. As I stood there two US Marines rushed into the room. 'We've been hit,' panted one. 'It was a suicide bomber. We've got several dead men. Our platoon sergeant's been killed. We're just outside the gate.'

I'd heard that the Americans were sending a brigade into Gereshk. These guys must have been an advance party. Such was the level of communication between our forces, we'd had no idea that a US patrol would be passing so close to the base.

At that moment Richard arrived and took control. He spoke briefly with the two Marines and ascertained that they'd been patrolling with their platoon when a man had walked up to them and detonated a bomb. They didn't know how many were dead but the explosion was huge.

Richard turned to me. 'Mark, take your multiple and secure the area. Talk to the ANA guys out there and make an assessment. You've got your vehicles. Get the American troops safely out of the area.'

I hurried outside to get my blokes together; they had responded immediately to the noise of the explosion and were kitted up, ready to go. As I approached the front gate I saw the ANA Toyotas coming back into camp. A man, a woman and two children were stretched out in the back of the first vehicle. They were badly wounded. The truck's floor was slick with blood. I paused, wondering if I should help, but the medics soon ran over and I gratefully left them to get on with their grisly business.

Outside the gate we came upon a scene of brutal devastation. The bomb had destroyed half the street and the three shops nearest to the blast had been reduced to ruins. Spread among the shattered glass and rubble were fragments of human tissue, charred and bloody. Closest to the blast it was all just red mush but a few metres further away, recognisable limbs were dotted about. A severed arm lay in the centre of the road, the fingers of its hand splayed outward clutching at the dust.

Marines knelt here and there on either side of the road in a rough defensive perimeter while their platoon commander sagged against the wall, his face drained of colour. I tried to speak to him but he just stared at me with big, vacant eyes. Shock had hit him hard and he was quite unable to command. Meanwhile, one of the Marine corporals was issuing orders. His shirtsleeve was torn and a crimson-soaked bandage was wrapped around his upper arm but he was focused and getting a grip on the situation.

'We've got two dead,' he said. 'No, three. Our interpreter's dead too. Five wounded but they'll be all right.'

The bodies were lined up side by side in the middle of the road. They lay awkwardly, twisted and broken by the explosion. Two of them stared sightlessly at the sky. The third was missing its head.

Dozens of ANA troops were milling around and I grabbed

one of them and asked who was in charge. He yelled down the street and Capt Wali turned and walked towards me. I was pleased to see someone I knew and after a short conversation we had divided up the tasks between our two units. My multiple would deal with the Marines while Wali and his men secured the scene and awaited the arrival of the British forensics team who would try and glean some useful information from the carnage.

'I know who did it,' piped up one of Wali's soldiers. 'It was a Pakistani. The suicide bomber was definitely from Pakistan.'

'How do you know that?' I asked. 'Don't you believe an Afghan could do something like this?'

'Oh no,' the soldier replied. 'It's his hair. The bomber's hair was very dark and curly. Pakistani hair.'

'How do you know what his hair was like?'

The soldier grinned and held his hand out towards me. In it he held a greasy, tangled mess of black fibre and skin. It was a human scalp. 'This bit normally comes off when they blow themselves up,' he said.

I managed to usher the Marines towards a couple of American vehicles that had turned up, and bundled them into the back. We zipped the dead into black bags and loaded them aboard our vehicles before driving to the safety of FOB Price. Once the corpses were inside the bags they stopped being people and became anonymous, mere objects to be transported.

When we got to Price I sent my soldiers away to sort out their equipment and prepare for the day's patrolling. Our vehicle, I noticed, was awash with blood. Taking a hose, I splashed water in through the rear door and watched the red liquid wash onto the dirt. I tried to mentally block out the horror of what I'd seen. In a few hours I'd be out on patrol myself and if I allowed myself to dwell on the terrifying possibility that the same thing could happen to me, I'd never be able to walk out of the gates again.

CHAPTER NINE

December 2008

After I joined the Army I'd tried hard to keep my two lives separate: the off-duty civilian versus the professional soldier. The thought of becoming a chino-clad, polo-playing stereotype filled me with dread. And despite the months of indoctrination and the insidious pressure to conform, I felt like I was succeeding. Being at work often felt like playing a part in a play. Dashing Captain Evans on parade at Buckingham Palace; stern Captain Evans reading the riot act to an unruly guardsman; tough Captain Evans marching across a frigid Welsh hillside at dawn. But come the weekend, it was as simple as changing clothes. Swapping combats and desert boots for jeans and trainers was when I said goodbye to Captain Evans and became Mark again, and he was someone else entirely. My military disguise, put on and discarded as required, seemed to me most efficacious. But Steph never quite bought it. She saw the parts of Captain Evans that I couldn't leave behind.

Steph had been my friend since our first term at university. She was funny and clever and entirely immune to my clumsy undergraduate attempts at charm. We shared an anthropology class focusing on the tribal rituals of Papua New Guinea and got to know one another through long discussions about the relative merits of cannibalism versus human sacrifice.

An ardent pacifist, Steph had never understood my decision to join the Army, but over time I wore her down with the glamour of dinners at St James' Palace and drill ceremonies at the Tower. Gradually she fell in love with the pomp and pageantry but I could never quite complete her military seduction. She could never forget, or let me forget, the true purpose of my job. Arguments of patriotism, national security or moral obligation did nothing to sway her. Killing was just wrong.

Today was the first time I'd seen Steph since I'd got back. I had been looking forward to it. My other civilian friends were full of questions about Afghanistan and would badger me for war stories I didn't want to tell. But Steph didn't want to hear about the war and so we spent a morning walking in the cold winter sunshine, talking about music, her boyfriend, a recent holiday. It should have been pleasant but I still couldn't shake feelings of unease. As we walked down Oxford Street I kept staring at the floor, searching the pavement for IEDs. I tried to snap out of it but the habit was too deeply engrained and whenever I looked up, I found myself scanning the horizon for potential enemy positions, mentally noting what cover was available should we be attacked.

Spending time with a civilian prompted me to consider my own future. I wasn't sure I wanted to be in the Army anymore. When I'd left Afghanistan, I was simply happy to be shot of the place. My thoughts about the future hadn't extended beyond getting home alive – something that had for a while seemed in doubt. However, after my brief return to battalion for 'the Brick', I'd felt much less committed to a military career. It had been fun while I'd been chasing war but now I couldn't quite see the point. Of course, if I wasn't going to be a soldier it raised the question of what was I going to do. While I'd been away the economy had gone into free fall and with my CV – strong on guns and killing but weaker on anything else – I doubted my chances of landing a job.

It was Steph's idea to go to the National Gallery. Normally I was interested in art but today I was just content to spend time with my friend. We drifted from one room to another, my gaze sliding over the canvasses. When it happened I was standing in front of an image of Mary, dandling an overweight and miserable-looking Christ-child on her knee.

Some small sound made me turn away from the painting and I saw a woman wearing a hijab standing next to me. She had her head turned away, talking to a child holding her hand. I couldn't see her face. Who was this woman? Why was she hiding herself?

And then I knew. She was going to kill us. All of us. It was someone like her who'd come for the US Marines in Gereshk. Any moment now. I recoiled from the explosion that was about to come.

I looked around. No one had noticed. They didn't know. I had to warn them. We all had to get out of there.

Even as this terror gripped me, I picked apart my logic. We were in London, not in Afghanistan. The war was thousands of miles away.

But they did it here too, didn't they? They had done it. On tubes, on buses. The war had come to London before.

It was them. They did it. They didn't look like us. They weren't like us. They hated us. I knew them. They wanted us dead. This woman, she wanted to kill me.

A scream bubbled up inside me. I swallowed it and grabbed Steph by the arm, marching her from the room without explanation.

We sat on the steps outside and smoked. Vague arrangements were made for dinner the following week and we hugged our goodbyes. I thought I'd hidden my fear and panic, but years later I found out that, walking away, she'd held back tears only as far as the first corner.

CHAPTER TEN

One night, two weeks after the Americans died, I was once again woken from a deep sleep, this time by someone shaking my shoulder. Through the gloom I saw Magoo looking down on me – not the first thing I'd choose to see on any morning. 'What time is it?' I muttered.

'Just gone midnight,' he said. 'They need you in the ops room.'

I dressed quickly and made my way outside where dozens of ANA soldiers were running about with weapons and packs. In the ops room I found Richard talking to Col Wadood.

'Are you sure?' Richard was saying. 'We've received no reports about this.'

'They are moving now,' said Wadood. 'A large Taliban force is coming up from the south and it's going to attack Marjah. Our sources are certain.'

'Give me some time. I want to corroborate this. I need permission from Brigade before we start charging into someone else's Area of Operations.'

Wadood looked irritated. 'We haven't got long. If we delay they will have already begun their assault. I can't wait. We're leaving now. You always say that we should be ready to move quickly and that's what we're doing. I've heard a lot of words about your Taliban-killing capabilities. Now is the time to prove it.'

The Colonel turned and walked out of the room. Richard sighed and ordered me to round up my multiple. He told me that the company from 5 Scots responsible for the Marjah Area of Operations, or AO, knew nothing about it but we would rendezvous with them at Brigade HQ in Lashkar Gah before moving to Marjah to investigate. 'Personally I think the whole thing is going to be a wild goose chase,' he said. 'But we can't let the Afghans go and do this on their own. If the intelligence turns out to be accurate, they'll need our support.'

Marjah is a rural district about 35 kilometres southwest of Gereshk, centred around a small town, barely larger than the average English village. It was a major centre for poppy cultivation and up until a year ago the Taliban had controlled the area, before being forced out by local government-backed militia and the ANA. British troops rarely entered the district and so our knowledge of the place was limited. This air of mystery, coupled with rumours of the drug cartels that operated there, made Marjah sound exciting, lawless and potentially very dangerous.

Barely an hour after I'd left the comfort of my bed, I was bumping along in a Snatch, following a fleet of ANA Toyotas heading out of town. We travelled in strength – two multiples from the battery and one ANA company; around a hundred men. Our convoy stretched almost half a kilometre down the road. Unlike other operations, when I'd had the chance to plan, select routes and brief everyone properly, now we were just trying to keep up with the Afghans.

We took a route east out of Gereshk, crossing over the Helmand River on the A1. It was one of the few tarmacked roads in the province and it was a fast, comfortable way to travel compared to the jolting cross-country journeys we sometimes made across the desert. It was impossible to relax though; the road was a favourite target of the Taliban for IEDs and ambushes. The standard operating procedure was to stop at every vulnerable point, such as the drainage ditches that ran under the road at regular intervals, and physically search for bombs, but today there was no time so we just ordered the drivers to put their feet to the floor and trust that speed and the element of surprise would protect us. It was a relief when we swung right off the highway and onto the road towards Lashkar Gah.

We were still on tarmac but the road was pitted with craters and we were forced to zigzag across the carriageway as best we could. We drove without lights so as not to broadcast our position. The soldiers in the back of the open-topped Toyota in front lurched from side to side, bouncing high in the air as their driver failed to spot yet another pot-hole. Their discomfort was hidden behind tightly wrapped shemaghs that shielded them from the clouds of dust kicked up by our convoy.

Around an hour into the journey the Toyota suddenly disappeared in an enormous cloud and our vehicle was buffeted sideways by the force of an explosion. We skidded to a halt and through the dust-stained windscreen of the Snatch I saw the ANA vehicle lying on its side by the edge of the road. Flames sprang into the air and soldiers scattered for cover. The fire in the back of the vehicle had ignited the crates of ammunition piled up against the cab. When subjected to very high temperatures a cartridge will heat up until the explosive powder inside ignites. The pressure inside pushes out in all directions simultaneously and because it isn't confined inside the chamber of a rifle, the round will explode. The ammunition crate began to fizzle and crack like a kind of deadly popcorn, each bullet a mini hand grenade. Tiny shards of metal pinged off the sides of the Land Rover and I realised that if there were any bigger explosions, we would be right in their path. I ordered the driver to back up twenty metres, jumped out of the vehicle and hurled myself into the roadside ditch.

I assumed the Toyota had been hit by an IED and that somewhere nearby the enemy was now poised to spring an ambush. My heart raced and I offered up a silent prayer that I might be right this time. We were here in force and I was ready to give the enemy hell.

Just then I heard a faint sound carrying over the shouting and the exploding ammunition. It was screaming coming from the stricken vehicle. Someone was still alive inside and, judging by the noise they were making, in a great deal of pain. A figure slowly emerged through the shattered windscreen of the cab, inching his way clear of the wreckage. As he rolled onto the road, we could see flames flickering around his legs. The man was on fire.

Three ANA soldiers who had been riding in one of the lead vehicles rushed forward to help him but still ten metres from the man they were forced to the ground by the exploding ammunition pinging around them. The burning man struggled to his feet and stumbled towards us. For a second I glimpsed his face; his features were contorted in agony. Then he checked and swung round, back in the direction of the Toyota. It was as though he was blind, or perhaps the pain had stripped him of his faculties. We called out to him, urging him towards the sound of our voices but he was powerless to heed us and make his way to safety.

Suddenly the man dropped to the ground, as if realising for the first time that his legs were burning. Either that, or a piece of shrapnel found him. He rolled desperately on the floor and after maybe thirty seconds the flames went out. Thereafter he lay still and screamed. I wanted to go to him and drag him to safety but the exploding rounds pushed me back. All we could do was lie there and listen to the man's agony.

Another minute went by, and the man's screams began to tail off. As they did, the explosions also became less frequent and three ANA men were able to crawl out to reach him. They grabbed him by his shoulders and dragged him to the ditch.

I'd been following this gruesome drama intensely, mesmerised by the horror. With a wrench, I forced my thoughts once more to the subject of the enemy. Where the hell were they? And why hadn't we been hit? But there was no time to dwell on the whys and wherefores of the Taliban's continued absence; we had to get the wounded man to a hospital as fast as possible. Richard had been on the radio to Brigade at Lashkar Gah and called in a medevac chopper, known as a MERT or Medical Emergency Response Team, but apparently there were concerns over the security of the landing site. Without a secure cordon in place, and the area swept for mines, the helicopter wouldn't even take off. This was standard procedure but I couldn't help wondering if the response would have been quite so sluggish if the wounded man had been a Brit. Wadood decided that enough time had been wasted already and ordered his men to put the casualty in the back of one of the remaining Toyotas. We drove the last few kilometres into Lash at breakneck speed.

When we got to the base the medics came and took the casualty off our hands. I heard a few days later that the soldier had died that night in the hospital. We figured afterwards that the explosion hadn't been an IED strike but instead been caused when one of the soldiers in the Toyota had accidentally discharged his weapon as they went over a pot-hole, detonating the explosives. Even without the enemy, there were plenty of ways to die in Helmand.

In Lash we were due to team up with B Company from 5 Scots, which used to be known as the Argyll and Sutherland Highlanders. I didn't know much about them beyond the reputation of their soldiers for tough professionalism and impenetrable Glaswegian accents. The officers were different. They all came through the same Sandhurst route I had and it was rare for a commissioned man in these regiments to actually be Scottish himself – although many claimed Celtic heritage. In a Scottish Officers' Mess you were most likely to encounter the same modulated public school tones endemic throughout the officer corps.

The first person I saw when I walked into the Company HQ was a friend. Captain Colin Wood and I had trained together at Sandhurst and the Platoon Commanders' Battle Course, then we'd served at Catterick in North Yorkshire where we'd spent a year training new recruits and getting drunk. I'd known that he was coming out to Afghanistan on this tour but hadn't counted on bumping into him. Woody, as I knew him, was a short, sandy-haired fellow with a desert-dry sense of humour that often left people unsure as to whether he was joking or not. Aside from this he was enormously enthusiastic about the business of soldiering. By this I mean that he didn't merely hanker after the thrill of combat as I did, but that he really enjoyed the physical challenges that came with the job. While I suffered the early starts, arduous marches with heavy kit and poring over maps in the freezing dark, he relished every backbreaking minute.

I shook Woody's hand and we spent the first couple of minutes catching each other up on our experiences. It turned out he'd fared rather better than I had at finding the war. He'd been in a number of firefights but I was surprised to find that he was reluctant to discuss them with me. The company had lost a few soldiers in these contacts and I wondered if for Woody some of the shine had been taken off the war.

While I was talking to him another officer walked in and introduced himself as Simon de Boulay. 'Call me DB,' he said. He was tall and rangy with a shock of dark hair. His face had the fresh and unlined appearance of youth, a look that made sense when he explained how he had arrived in theatre just two days previously, fresh off the Platoon Commanders' Battle Course. His wide eyes betrayed the shock he must have been feeling, suddenly dropped from the familiar certainties of training into the alien environment of Helmand. He was desperately eager to please, to make his mark with the older, more experienced hands such as Woody and me.

'No space for newbies on this trip to Marjah,' said Woody. 'You can mind the shop until we get back. Make sure Lash doesn't fall apart while we're away.'

DB looked crestfallen.

'Don't worry,' Woody went on. 'There's plenty of time left before we go home. You'll get your pop at the Taliban yet. Of course, you've got more chance of getting killed than you have of winning a medal.'

The intelligence picture in Lash was no less sketchy than ours in Gereshk and Woody had nothing to add about the supposed enemy attack. 'You'd better go in and see Harry,' he said. 'That's our company commander. He takes things a bit seriously but he's a good bloke really.'

I knocked on the door and walked straight into the company commander's office. A stocky, balding man with a soft face and small, earnest eyes was standing beside the desk, brow furrowed as he studied a map pinned to the wall. He was my senior by rank, and by at least ten years.

'Hello,' I said, throwing up an untidy salute. 'I'm Mark Evans, just come over with Col Wadood's kandak from Gereshk. It's Harry, isn't it?'

The man turned towards me and looked me up and down. The curl of his lip indicated that he didn't much like what he saw.

'Don't you normally address a major as "sir"?' he asked.

My heart sank. Usually being on operations meant an escape from this kind of nonsense but every now and then you ran into a real stickler for military discipline. I probably should have just apologised, but I couldn't help myself.

'Well actually, no. In the Coldstream Guards we only call officers who have commanded a Guards' Battalion "sir".'

The major's face coloured as he searched for a suitable response. 'The Army's bigger than your regiment so try being more respectful. Now, I need to have a word with this Afghan colonel you've brought and find out what he wants.'

Together we walked towards the main briefing room to attend an Orders Group that would hopefully shed a little light on the situation now developing in Marjah. We hoped in vain. No one at

Brigade HQ seemed to understand what was going on any better than we did. All anyone had heard was rumours of an impending Taliban attack; we hadn't the faintest notion of what that might entail. What we did know was that if Marjah did fall, it would be a major propaganda victory for the Taliban and provide them a base uncomfortably close to Lashkar Gah, the provincial capital.

It was decided that Wadood's company, Richard's multiples and a platoon from B Company – in all nearly 150 men – would proceed to Marjah and then 'see what happened'. Harry was particularly unhappy with this vague and open-ended mission but orders were orders and there was nothing any of us could do about it.

After snatching a few hours' sleep, we left Lash at 0300hrs and covered the remaining 20 kilometres to Marjah. The journey seemed to go on forever. The roads were terrible and we had to stop every hundred metres or so to check for IEDS. When the sun came up we found ourselves driving past dazzling emerald fields, but there was no time to take in the scenery. We expected to be ambushed at any moment and my finger hovered over the safety catch on my weapon. By the time we made it to our destination it was past midday and there was much we had to do before darkness fell.

With no new intelligence available, Col Wadood arranged for a meeting with the local police chief, a man called Haji Tor Jan. In addition to his position at the head of the area's ANP unit, Tor Jan doubled up as the regional drugs kingpin. I'd heard that the British Foreign Office had pushed the government in Kabul to have him arrested but for the moment his political clout was too strong and so he stayed put, playing off both sides of the law, and doubtless the Taliban too, against one another as suited his personal needs.

Wadood, Richard and Harry made up the delegation for the meeting, while to my displeasure I was left to organise the cordon. The rendezvous took place at a compound on the edge of the district centre. It looked like every other residential building I'd seen in Helmand but apparently this was the local ANP HQ. It was really Haji Tor Jan's home, but since he conducted the majority of his business from here it had become the de facto centre for police activity.

A couple of men leant against the wall beside the gate. One was dressed in a blue police officer's shirt while the other wore a shalwar kameez, the traditional outfit of loose-fitting trousers and long shirt worn by most men in this part of Afghanistan. Both carried rifles and had the same sullen, uncooperative expression shared by bent coppers and assorted lowlifes the world over. I recalled meeting two similar characters at the border crossing between Thailand and Malaysia, an encounter that had left my wallet $80 lighter. Today, however, I too carried a gun.

With the meeting safely under way, I took the opportunity to conduct a low-level investigation of my own. I wasn't sure if I'd get anything out of the two goons, but it beat standing around, counting the seconds till the meeting was finished. I approached them, Ash by my side, a reluctant companion. He too had had his experiences with this kind of policeman.

'*As-salamu alaykum*,' I said.

They stared back at me and said nothing. One of them spat in the dust.

'Do you ever get the feeling you're not welcome somewhere?' I asked Ash.

'These are not good people,' he said. 'You should leave them alone. The Colonel will be finished soon and we can get out of here.'

I wanted to give this one last go. Supposedly these people were on our side but there was something about their attitude, not to say what I knew of their boss, that made trust impossible. Maybe they weren't Taliban but in the shifting fog of allegiance and betrayal that was Helmand, they could be the closest I'd ever get to the enemy.

'Have you heard anything about this Taliban attack?' I asked. Ash nervously translated the question, which provoked laughter from the two guards.

'Don't bother with these bastards,' said Capt Wali as he approached, scowling at the guards. 'The police round here are nothing more than gangsters.'

The guard in plain clothes began to shout at Wali. Ash didn't translate but I got the gist. Wali shook his head and spat back a sharp retort that did nothing to calm the situation. I heard the sound of a rifle being cocked and the uniformed policeman took a step forward. For a moment it seemed as though we were one insult away from a murder. Then Wali's sergeant stepped out of one of the Toyotas parked nearby. He was a huge Pashtun and towered over the rest of us. The two guards still didn't back down but then half a dozen more ANA soldiers jumped out of the vehicles. The two guards turned on their heels and pushed their way through the gates into Tor Jan's compound.

Wali watched them go and then turned to me. 'Never forget that the police are just one pay cheque away from joining the Taliban. We are the only ones you can trust to keep this country in line.'

Some time later the meeting concluded and Wadood and the two British officers emerged from the compound. The Colonel looked pleased while Richard and Harry looked bemused.

We headed back to the desert outside of the town to re-group. On the way Richard briefed me on what had happened. It seemed that Tor Jan had corroborated the threat of an imminent Taliban push but was sketchy on the details. He'd been adamant that we should stick around to reinforce his garrison but had been reluctant to go into any detailed planning for the defence of the district centre.

'I'm not sure our translator was getting everything,' said Richard. 'The Colonel clearly has no time for Haji Tor Jan and the feeling seemed to be mutual. It doesn't look like we'll be working closely with the ANP here.'

Wadood had gone on to explain to Richard how Tor Jan was currently embroiled in a feud with some of the other gangs in the area. The politics of Helmand were entirely opaque to us. Knowing where the legitimate government stopped and criminal warlord power structures began was nigh on impossible. The Taliban fitted in with all this somewhere too. Identifying our true allies and enemies in this shifting landscape was a complex task that we never seemed to be on top of. We relied on Col Wadood's word simply because we knew him the best, and we were never given reason to doubt him. But who knows where his allegiances truly lay? British policy was to support the ANA and to destroy the Taliban – beyond that we really didn't know what we were doing. I'm sure that when Richard wrote his report he found some rather more strategic rationale for the operation but right now we were here because Wadood had told us we had to be.

We spent the next few hours before darkness establishing a leaguer in the desert where we intended to spend the night. With British units everything was done by the book. All the vehicles parked in their assigned spots, regulation distance between each one. There was a designated place to sleep and eat and each sentry was placed where they could command the widest arcs of fire out over the desert. Harry imposed stringent rules regarding the use of light after dark and ordered everyone to limit noise so as to make the leaguer as inconspicuous as possible. This was all very sensible, the hallmark of good soldiering, but of course the Afghans approached the leaguer in their own style. The ANA Toyotas were scattered in an approximation of a defensive position. Their sentries were just as informally situated and I saw at least one of them casually making a cup of tea, looking up every so often to confirm that the enemy hadn't arrived while the water boiled. The rest of the soldiers spread themselves out, seeking out the flattest, most comfortable pieces of ground on which to sit and later sleep.

Harry watched the Afghans with jaundiced eyes, desperate to grip them and knock them into shape. That Wadood outranked him made it difficult for him to intervene. Also, mentoring the ANA was my boss Richard's remit and Harry was reluctant to tread on his toes. Instead he contented himself by taking me to task.

'What have you been teaching them, these past three months?' he asked. 'They look like a fucking rabble. You can barely tell them apart from the guys we're supposed to be fighting.'

As daylight began to fade, the Afghans began lighting fires to cook their dinner. One man clicked on a small transistor radio and the tinny warbling sound of Afghan music drifted across the leaguer.

'That's it,' snapped Harry. 'We're not sharing a space with these lunatics. I'm ordering my soldiers to move out and set up a separate site. I'm not risking good men's lives at some Afghan cook-out and karaoke contest.'

'Whatever makes you think they're at risk?' The sudden rumbling intonation made us both jump and I turned to see Wadood standing behind us.

Harry quickly recovered his poise. 'Well, Colonel, it's just that your men are making a lot of noise and you can see those fires from miles away.'

'Who is around to hear this noise?' Wadood replied. 'Who will see these fires? We are in the middle of the desert. We can see all the way to the horizon. Where do you think the Taliban are? Hiding under rocks?'

I had to admit, much as I'd been conditioned by my training to see Harry's point, the Colonel made a convincing case.

'It is good for the men to get into the right habits,' said Harry. 'It teaches good discipline.'

'Major Clark, you must realise that we are not newcomers to

war. I would not have lived to be as old as I am if I didn't know when to hide and when to be comfortable. The Taliban know where we are. You cannot move this many soldiers about the place without people seeing and those people will talk. Like I said, if the enemy want to visit, we can see for miles. We'll be ready.'

I looked over at the Afghan troops as they lounged by their fires, chatting, smoking, laughing. Even though they had weapons, the scene reminded me a little of a small summer music festival and I'm sure I caught the sickly scent of hash in the air. The Jocks under Harry's command went about their business with the serious intensity that you might expect of soldiers about to go into battle. I liked the Colonel but you couldn't argue over whose men looked the more professional. Should I have done more in Gereshk to impose British military standards? I realised that even after four months together, I didn't know the true mettle of these warriors. We hadn't been tried in combat and that I knew was the only test that mattered. I had been working alongside them, training them, and when the time came it wouldn't just be my own skill and nerve by which I'd be judged but theirs too.

We spent the night out in the desert, sleeping in shifts, on edge, waiting for something to happen. Finally, around 0500hrs, something did. The dull thud of an explosion came from the north, somewhere near the district centre, about two kilometres away. That was it. One bang and then silence. Wadood had informers patrolling the streets and got straight on his mobile phone demanding information.

A bomb – that was all we knew. Apparently no follow-up though. Perhaps it was a ploy to lure our main force into the confines of the built-up area where an ambush might be sprung.

As dawn broke we drove back towards the district centre. The streets were empty when we arrived and the place had an eerie desolate quality about it. This was often an indicator that the local population expected a fight and were keeping their heads down so as not to be caught in the crossfire. We proceeded with caution.

Over at Haji Tor Jan's compound there were signs of life. We stopped outside the gate. In place of yesterday's pair of thugs was half an ANP platoon and two Toyotas with PKMs – the Soviet version of our GPMG – mounted on the back. It was a significant increase in security levels and could only mean trouble.

Wali approached the men and asked what had happened. It turned out that the explosion we'd heard had been a huge IED. It had been planted by the side of the main road overnight and discovered by a passing police patrol. They'd supposedly defused it and called Haji Tor Jan over to examine the bomb once it was safe. It seemed however that the men on this patrol were double agents and had lured Tor Jan into a trap. When the police chief walked up to the bomb it had been detonated remotely, killing him instantly. Suddenly leaderless, the ANP were trying to work out what happened next. Within Marjah's arcane power structure, the killing of the police chief didn't leave an automatic replacement and the scene was now set for a power struggle.

Wadood did not appear much concerned by the death of Haji Tor Jan. I suppose for him it meant that there was one less powerful man in the region who could stand up to him. The implications for the British were less clear. Woody was convinced that it would bring no good. 'Tor Jan was a bastard and a drug runner,' he said. 'But at least he wasn't fighting against us. God knows who'll take over now but I reckon today was a good day for the Taliban.'

A few weeks later, I would learn just how right Woody was.

CHAPTER ELEVEN

January 2009

I'd only been back at work for a week and I was already on Guard. On top of our role as a light infantry battalion, the Coldstream Guards are obliged to carry out public duties, which involve providing soldiers to protect the Royal Palaces. This has been the job of the Foot Guard Regiments, of which the Coldstream is one, since the days of Charles II when they formed the King's personal bodyguard. You'll have seen us standing guard outside Buckingham Palace, the Tower of London and, as I now found myself, at Windsor Castle. As an officer, I didn't have to shiver for hours in the cold outside but I did have to be there. Being Captain of the Guard was thought by outsiders to be a glamorous job, and when we marched into the castle in our red tunics and bearskins, past the hordes of slack-jawed tourists and perky American backpackers, it almost felt like it was. What would the men in Afghanistan have made of it? In my mind I heard Magoo's commentary, 'I say, sir, you look really spiffing in that bright red outfit. It'll really hide the blood-stains when you get yourself shot.' I couldn't even imagine what Wadood would say. This pageantry was my reward for surviving Afghanistan.

Once we'd taken over the Guard we settled in for a 48-hour stay in the castle, me and my gang of sixteen soldiers. The men were over in the guardroom, a sparse dormitory full of metal bunk beds and one incongruous 52" plasma TV. I, on the other hand, was entitled to my own flat in which to hunker down for the duration. It's a cosy little bolthole, entirely private, and once in I was quite self-sufficient. There's a small kitchen with a microwave where I could whip up a basic meal and a large bedroom that is rather how I imagine Sherlock Holmes' study might have looked. The walls are lined with heavy oak panelling and a wingbacked armchair takes up one corner. It's the carpet that lets the place down – grey, threadbare and stained, it doubtlessly prevents the beautiful oak floorboards from being ruined by our ceremonial boots. An enormous double bed is tucked into an alcove and the headboard is lavishly decorated with hand-carved stylised grenades – the badge of the Grenadier Guards. To one side of the bed there is a wooden carving of a mermaid, which if you look closely is cracked all around the edge. Reaching up, you can prise the carving from the wall, revealing behind it a secret compartment containing a packet of condoms. This stash is available should the Captain of the Guard wish to invite one of the aforementioned American backpackers to join him in the flat. Should an officer make use of the supplies he is expected to replenish them the following day. Today, though, I just wanted to be on my own.

Two days before, despite my misgivings about a future military career, I had extended my commission, committing to at least one more year in the Army. My battalion had one too many captains on its books and so there had been some debate over what job I might be given. The problem had eventually been resolved by my commanding officer, who had devised a plan to mount expeditions taking wounded soldiers around the world to undertake such adventurous pursuits as diving, sailing and mountain climbing. It now fell to me to make this vague but ambitious vision a reality. The job was a fairly cushy number, as my friends never ceased to remind me, keeping me in London and away from the bureaucratic drudgery attached to service with a regular battalion in the UK. I guess I was lucky, but really I wanted to run as far and fast from the Army as I possibly could. It was only fear that stopped me – fear of the unknown civilian world that now seemed every bit as terrifying as the IEDs in Helmand.

Dotted around the flat were mementoes donated by Guards officers of yesteryear. There were souvenirs from British conflicts dating all the way back to the Crimea. I found myself pondering the sacrifices that my forbears had made and wondered how my own exploits measured up. Had my encounters with the Taliban alongside Wadood and Wali really made any difference to the future of Afghanistan? And did the future of Afghanistan make any difference to my own country? The newspapers didn't seem to think so, echoing public demands for 'our boys' to be brought home. At least the men who'd fought in the two world wars were involved in a more urgent battle for national survival, which must have given them some sense of purpose. Or perhaps not. The painting that was framed over the small portable television set depicted the carnage from the first day of the Somme. Arguably the thousands of lives lost there hadn't made much difference to the progress of the war.

Across the walls were etched the names and initials of dozens, if not hundreds, of bored Captains of the Guard who had lain here over the years. The graffiti had not been universally appreciated and a typewritten note, yellowed with age, was tacked to the wall, proclaiming that, 'By order of the Warden of Windsor Castle, officers are to desist from defacing the walls.' When I'd stayed in this flat before I'd deployed to Afghanistan, I'd stared at the scratched markings and imagined my roguish predecessors, wondering if they'd managed to have more fun here and bag more women than me. Now, however, I couldn't help but ask how many of them had gone on to reach old age and how many had been cut down in a hail of bullets on some distant battlefield. All roads led me back to a miserable contemplation of my time in Afghanistan and nothing about the Army, not even the boozing and shagging, seemed like a game any longer.

There was a small casement window near the door of the room, which looked out over one of the castle courtyards. Peering through it I could see one of the guardsmen standing stock-still in his sentry box. In front of him the crowd jostled one another as they fought to pose for their quintessential British holiday photo next to the red-coated toy soldier. I felt a flash of irritation. The man on duty down there, now reduced to the status of a tourist attraction, was an infantryman. Away from this place he would risk his life for this country but the snap-happy throng saw only a quaint slice of tradition.

Taking a knife from the kitchen, I carefully carved the initials M.E. into the wall above the bed. It was as though I was taking my own small place in the history of this hidden shrine to the military way of life and I imagined the ghosts watching me. They knew. They understood. I smiled and for a moment felt a little less alone.

CHAPTER TWELVE

The sun inched towards the horizon, its dying rays setting the desert floor aflame. We sped over the blood-red rocks in a race against the coming darkness. Navigating the wilderness was harder after nightfall and my levels of concentration were already depleted by a long day on the move. It was a few days since we'd returned from Marjah. We'd started out early, driving 40 kilometres east from Gereshk to the imaginatively named Patrol Base Four to carry out a training package with the ANA garrison there. I'd taken with me eight British soldiers, split between two Snatches, and a dozen Afghan troops in three Toyota pick-ups. Job done, we were now driving back in convoy. In the back of my vehicle was an Afghan interpreter, and a bombardier called Grey on top cover, scanning the desert for potential threats. My driver for the journey was a lance bombardier known as Stocky, so called because of his rail thin frame. In his mid-twenties, he was a cheerful sort who kept smiling despite having what I thought to be one of the worst jobs in Afghanistan. On top of the stress of driving a four-ton vehicle across appalling terrain, while the rest of us were able to jump out when we reached our destination, poor Stocky was condemned to wait in a stifling, airless cab until we finished whatever task we were about.

Our outward journey had been uneventful, a straight two-hour slog through the dust. The A1 main road would have been faster but it was infested with IEDs. We avoided it whenever possible and stuck mainly to the desert.

The rule of travel in Helmand dictated that one never took the same route on the homeward leg of a journey in order to avoid potential ambushes. So it was that we found ourselves that evening driving in a long loop, several kilometres north of Gereshk, through a patch of desert none of us had previously visited. On my map I could see two minefields in the area, left behind by the Soviets. They were clearly marked on the page but quite invisible on the ground. Running between them was a narrow sliver of desert that was our route home. My map-reading skills were usually OK but there was little margin for error. The only alternative route was a narrow, single-track road that British patrols had used several times over the past week and I feared that the Taliban would have recognised this and dug in IEDs. With this in mind, the route between the minefields seemed the lesser of two evils.

Frequently in Helmand the ANA travelled at the head of a convoy and Brits followed on behind. The unspoken rationale was that if a bomb went off, it would more likely be the Afghans who'd die. This ugly brand of self-interest might work for those who only liaised occasionally with the ANA but for us, patrolling alongside them every day, it wasn't going to fly. Which is why I was leading the convoy. Besides, being at the front made it easier for me to see the way ahead. Facing the task of threading our way between two minefields, I wanted every advantage I could get.

There were no markers on the ground to indicate that we'd entered the danger zone but, checking my GPS, I was sure we had. My watch read 1745hrs. I radioed the rest of the patrol and reminded them to follow the tracks of my vehicle closely. The minefields were supposed to stretch 400 metres – just a few of minutes' drive over this terrain. I squinted through the wind-screen, trying desperately to make out some indication that we were clear. The seconds ticked past. I looked at the GPS again and saw we were safe. I blew my cheeks out in relief and grinned over at Stocky.

I didn't hear the explosion. There was just a lurch as the ground moved away and then we were done. An acrid smell filled the vehicle, like tarmac melting on a hot day. My head was pushed back against the radio block behind my seat. I couldn't see anything as thick black smoke palled in front of my eyes. No noise at all. Sound had been sucked out of the world.

'I'm dead.' The thought bubbled to the front of my brain. 'This is what death feels like.'

I found myself in an almost transcendental state. Everything else drained away. All responsibility, all fear, gone. It was like being at the top of an enormous rollercoaster, that brief moment where you teeter on the edge anticipating the plunge. I was completely out of control, my whole life flapping out behind me as I balanced here on the edge between this world and the next.

Then I breathed, a huge gulp of air and smoke rushing into my lungs, shattering the illusion and sending me into paroxysms of coughing. I'd been holding my breath, I don't know for how long but the suddenly overpowering urge to breathe at least proved I was still alive.

My first instinct was to run my tongue over my teeth. I wanted to know they were all there. I don't know why. I tapped them individually. All intact, no gaps. I felt strangely elated.

Only then did I think of my legs. I didn't want to check, scared of what I might find. I steeled myself and reached down to grope into the footwell. Yes. Both there. I was all right.

My senses came flooding back to me. The smell of burning sand and cordite stung my nostrils, and I could hear Stocky screaming, crushed against the steering-wheel. Suddenly it wasn't about me anymore. I had to get out of there, get help.

The Snatch had been flipped sideways by 45 degrees and my

passenger-side window was now pointing up towards the sky. I was held in place by my kit, which was jammed hard against the driver's seat. The weight of my body armour was pulling me down and I struggled against it as I tried to reach the door handle. I pushed hard but the handle wouldn't budge. The whole door had buckled in the explosion and was stuck solid. I would have to try to reach the door on the driver's side, which now looked out over the desert floor.

Stocky was deaf to my shouts, lost in his own world of pain. Shutting my ears to his cries, I pushed past him and managed to reach the door handle. It moved easily enough but with my arm fully extended I couldn't push hard enough to open the heavy armour-plated door. I apologised pointlessly to Stocky as my body armour scraped across his exposed face. I braced my feet against the driver's seat and strained against the door, which finally swung outwards. I crawled out and flopped onto the ground.

Of the other two men in the vehicle, the interpreter had managed to get out through the rear door while Bdr Grey had been thrown straight out of the top cover hatch and deposited on the ground five metres away, where he still lay. The crew of the Snatch that had been following us were crawling around the back of their vehicle, metal detectors in hand, probing the ground with their bayonets, testing every inch for mines. Even though we'd already driven over that ground, there might be mines that hadn't been set off by a vehicle but could still be det- onated beneath a soldier's boot.

Meanwhile, the ANA had driven their five Toyotas into a defensive perimeter around our position. They crouched behind their machine-guns, scanning the horizon for enemies swarming toward us out of the dusk. The threat of the mines didn't seem to scare them, or if it did they pushed straight through their fear.

The radio in my vehicle had been broken in the explosion and so I was forced to conduct a shouted conversation with the corporal in the next wagon, who relayed my words back to the ops room in Gereshk. As far as I knew, Stocky's life was ebbing away. Bdr Grey had by now managed to crawl the five metres back to the vehicle from where he'd been thrown, disregarding the danger of setting off a mine, and was giving first aid to Stocky.

I'd made sure that all the soldiers under my command knew how to send a casualty report over the radio but now the chips were down, I quite unfairly lost faith in their ability. Maybe I was suffering from shock, which had addled my thought processes, but I felt I had to be the one to get control of the situation and I was never going to be able to do this from my own stricken vehicle. There was no time to wait for the route to be cleared back to the second Snatch. It went against all my training, which dictated that one should avoid making oneself a casualty, but I screwed up my courage and stepped out into the danger zone.

If I kept to the tracks my vehicle had made in the sand, I reasoned, I should probably be safe, but in my mind's eye I saw myself being engulfed in a firestorm with every step I took. I had only 20 metres to cover. It can't have taken longer than a few seconds. It seemed an eternity.

When I reached the safety of the second Snatch it turned out that one of the soldiers had already sent the casualty report, exactly as they had been trained to do. I got straight on the radio and spoke to the ops room in Gereshk. The news was not good. We were once again told that a helicopter required a secure landing site before it would fly in. No pilot would risk landing on top of a mine so we would have to clear the whole area. With a multimillion-pound flying machine at stake I understood their caution but for us grunts stuck out in the middle of the desert it seemed like the same old story. For a moment I considered lying – yep, sure we've sorted that HLS out for you. Now why don't you haul your lazy, overpaid arses down here and get our wounded man to the hospital? Instead I began to make plans to clear the HLS.

After being injected with morphine, which all of us carried, Stocky wasn't shouting anymore and was sitting silently in the driver's seat with his eyes closed. 'He's ok,' Bdr Grey shouted over to me. 'Two broken legs and both his feet are fractured but he'll make it.'

With his injuries confirmed as non-life-threatening, I stood the helicopter down. This was a relief because we lacked sufficient troops to properly secure the area. Co-ordinating the ANA troops was extremely difficult due to the language barrier and we didn't have enough Brits to form a secure perimeter. This was a perennial problem in the OMLT role and now I realised just how dangerous it was to operate in such small teams.

Instead of the helicopter a medical team would travel to us overland. They would also bring a recovery vehicle to come and drag my stranded Land Rover away. The other option would have been for us to blow it up, thus preventing the enemy from helping itself during the night, but the MoD lacks the bottom-less pockets of our American cousins and the loss of important equipment was much frowned upon by senior officers.

I knew it would be a long wait. Even with help on its way I felt exposed and vulnerable. The ops room in Gereshk was telling us that they were monitoring Taliban radio communications that suggested they knew we were stranded in the desert and were now planning an attack. There was little we could do about this. The ANA were already in defensive positions and although we kept a look out towards the horizon we were really just waiting to get hit.

I lit a cigarette and took a moment to assess the situation, trying to figure out what else I could do. I hadn't taken more than two drags when I was interrupted by a shout of 'Medic!' Assuming that Stocky had suddenly taken a turn for the worse, I looked over to the lead Snatch but in fact it was Bdr Grey that I saw slumped unconscious on the sand.

One of the other soldiers was also qualified as a patrol medic and he ran to Bdr Grey along the path that had now been cleared between the two vehicles. After a cursory assessment of the casualty the medic said, 'I think he's broken his back.' I was astonished; just a few minutes before he'd been moving around quite freely, administering first aid to Stocky. How was that possible for a man whose spine had been snapped? The medic was adamant about his diagnosis. 'It's quite common,' he said. 'You can walk around for weeks with a broken back sometimes and Grey would have been buzzing with adrenaline which just kept him going.'

'Will he live?' I asked.

'We need to keep him still. Every time he moves, he could make the injury worse.'

We rolled Grey carefully onto a stretcher and strapped him in. He'd regained consciousness and started to feel pain so we stuck him with a shot of morphine.

The ops room informed me that the relief would be with us in two hours. They also told me that they'd heard the Taliban were moving fighters towards our position. I was terrified that we would end up fighting our way out of the minefield – there was no chance we'd keep Bdr Grey immobile in that case.

I began to chain my way through an entire packet of cigarettes, while the ops room continued to feed me reports of increased Taliban radio chatter in our vicinity. The men began to clear a new path from our position towards the A1, 300 metres away. This would allow our relief to reach us more quickly when they finally arrived on the scene.

All our nerves were shredded by the time we heard a convoy of vehicles approaching. We peered through the sights of our rifles, fingers tight on the triggers, ready to fire. I exhaled with relief as I saw a column of armoured vehicles hove into view. Help had arrived.

Our rescuers were from a Danish battalion based at FOB

Price. They brought with them an ATO to make a quick assessment of the ordnance that had caused our predicament. He agreed that it was most likely an old Soviet mine and commented that the softness of the sand had probably allowed the mine to drift over the years as the sands shifted, moving it beyond the confines of the minefield marked on my map. Having said that, the same soft sand had absorbed most of the blast and this had likely saved our lives.

'You're lucky,' he said. I stared blankly at him. I didn't feel lucky, just acutely conscious that I had no control over my destiny.

Four hours later we made it back to Gereshk. I walked into the ops room to make my report. Richard was waiting for me. He listened to my story and then curtly told me to write a full account of the patrol immediately and that an investigation would be launched. An investigation? Into what? Was I being held responsible for what had happened? No one told me. Suddenly I felt like I was on trial and I had no idea what the consequences might be if I was found guilty.

I sat on my bed, tapping away at my laptop, transforming the evening's events into bloodless, bullet-pointed prose. As I typed I began to think that perhaps it actually was my fault. It had been my decision to take the patrol on that route, to thread the needle between two minefields. There were other routes I could have picked but I'd chosen this one. Maybe my map-reading skills weren't as good as I thought they were. God knows we'd all made navigational errors going through training. Why should I have so much more confidence in my abilities now?

The following day, Richard ordered me to take another patrol out to Patrol Base Three. It was the same ground I'd covered the day before. Everyone on the patrol knew what had happened and as I climbed into the Snatch, taking the lead once again, I imagined the whispered conversations behind me.

'Fucking officer. He can't even read a map.'

'Oh shit, it's Captain Evans. We're all dead.'

'Bloke drove straight into the middle of a minefield and came out OK the other side. I'll follow him.'

'He broke my mate's legs and now he's coming after mine.'

Up until this point, every day I had gone out the gate in a state of excited anticipation, hoping to meet the Taliban. Now all I wanted was to get through this next patrol and then the next and the next, until it was time to go home. At the end of all this I wanted to be able to say, 'No one died.' The weight of responsibility for the lives of the men under my command pressed down heavily, more now than it ever had before.

Darkness fell before we set out on our way back to Gereshk. It was always hard driving without lights. We had night-vision goggles (NVGs), which obviously helped, but looking through them one loses all perception of depth and after a while the green tinted images start to play tricks on one's mind. We hurtled forward into the mine-infested void and I felt the beginnings of panic, cold electricity that ran up from the pit of my stomach through my chest and burst inside my head. I wanted to open my mouth and shout. I wanted to shut my eyes and for the shuddering, dark, terrifying world to dissolve away. Fear prickled at my skin. I bit down hard on my tongue to keep the screams inside. Next to me the driver stared straight ahead, oblivious to my silent meltdown.

It was no good. I was staring so hard into the darkness that my vision was beginning to blur and the view through the NVGs was beginning to play tricks on me. I fancied I saw explosions leap from the ground in front of me. I suddenly told the driver to stop. He shot a worried glance at me but complied with my instructions. I flung open the door and jumped down onto the desert floor. I leant against the side of the vehicle and breathed in the cool night air, trying to steady my nerves. 'Turn on the headlamps,' I said.

This was in direct contravention of our procedures. In the dark our lights could be seen hundreds of metres away. Fuck it. I had to see what was ahead, even if only for a moment. The twin beams cut through the darkness and revealed ... nothing. The desert stretched out in front of me, seemingly endless. My fear was still there but I pushed it down once more and climbed back into the vehicle. Ordering the driver to kill the lights, we continued on our way.

I have no idea how long the journey took. Two hours, perhaps. Maybe longer. It ended anyway and no one said anything about my unscheduled stop. In reality it was more straightforward than many of the other patrols I'd made over the previous four months but it was by far the most harrowing. My nerves were fraying fast. I still hadn't been shot at but I'd lost a lot of my old confidence. And there were still over two months left until the end of my tour.

The following day was a Friday and the ANA had no plans to patrol. I was in no mood to push them. After doing a little work in the morning, I sloped back to my room where I spent the rest of the day. I read a few chapters of my book and started writing a letter home to my parents.

The words wouldn't come. '*Dear Mum and Dad.*' My pen hovered over the paper as I contemplated the next line:

Sorry I haven't written in a while but I wanted to wait until there was something exciting I could tell you about. We were blown up two days ago. Stocky might lose his legs. Grey broke his back.
Apart from that, things have been pretty quiet.
Your loving son, Mark.

I screwed the paper into a ball and chucked it at the wall. Writing wasn't going to help anyway. The gym – that was the thing I needed now. I didn't usually box but an hour pummelling the punch-bag suddenly seemed appealing.

As I was walking across the square Richard shouted over to me.

'Just to let you know,' he said, 'all the reports are in on your mine strike. No one to blame. It was a stray mine, outside any of the known danger areas. Nothing you could have done about it.'

I was stunned into silence. 'Anyway,' Richard went on, 'it's all as I expected. See you later.'

He sauntered off towards the ops room. Nothing I could have done about it. All as expected. So casual. I'd been tormenting myself that I'd been responsible for smashing Stocky and Bdr Grey's bones and putting everyone's lives at risk. Here in this place it was apparently all part of the routine.

Two days later Richard saw me off on leave in the UK. Every soldier was entitled to a fortnight's leave at some point during their tour but I couldn't help questioning the timing. I asked Richard if it had anything to do with the explosion, an excuse to get me away from patrolling. He said it wasn't. I didn't believe him.

The following day I was on a plane, heading home. I resolved to forget Afghanistan and for two weeks embrace my old life once more. It wasn't that easy.

CHAPTER THIRTEEN

I spent my two weeks of leave in London. It was a pleasant enough fortnight, the days merging in a haze of alcohol as I hurried between a series of parties. There were so many people to see and everyone wanted to know, 'What's it like, over there?' I found I had no words to describe my experiences. I fobbed people off with glib remarks like, 'It's a bit hot,' or 'The food's not up to much.' I said nothing of the mine that had so nearly finished me, yet the acrid odour of the explosion was still strong in my nostrils and I kept reliving the shock and the terror I'd felt. My brush with death had woken my sense of mortality, but as the days passed I was surprised to find the same old urge to fight reasserting itself. My mind was drawn constantly back to Helmand, fearful that the war might erupt in my absence. I devoured the news, desperately checking for word of renewed fighting in Gereshk. It was with relief that I arrived at RAF Brize Norton and embarked on the journey back to Afghanistan.

Darkness had fallen by the time I arrived in Lash, my final stop before Gereshk, and I almost walked straight past the lonely figure lurking in the shadows by a row of Hesco.

'Hey, Mark!' the figure called out. It was John Toomey, a Royal Irish captain I knew from Sandhurst.

'Hello mate,' I said. 'I'm just passing through on my way back to Gereshk. What's going on?'

'You're not heading to Gereshk anymore. It's all changed since you've been away. Everything's gone to shit. The Taliban have gone nuts. Marjah's fallen. We're getting our asses kicked. Everywhere, all the way up to Lash.' This certainly hadn't been in the papers back home. His news was grave and you'd have thought his demeanour would have matched his words but Toomey's face shone with a feverish excitement.

'Now we're in a real war,' he finished with a broad grin.

When I'd left two weeks ago, we'd had a tight grip on Helmand province. The locals were talking to us, the Taliban were keeping a low profile and the war seemed to have gone away. All before I'd fired a shot. It had seemed I was to end my campaign untested, destined to return to London to endure the bragging of other more heroic officers. But that script had been ripped up. I grinned back at Toomey.

'So what now?' I said.

'There's an O-Group about to start. They told me to take you straight there.'

Ducking through the door of the briefing room, I saw Nick Bridle, the 5 Scots Operations Officer, standing in front of a map marked with all the British and Taliban positions. A cluster of red pins, representing enemy forces, extended from Lashkar Gah westwards, right the way to the border. All the territory our predecessors had sweated and bled for was under serious threat. Fifteen kilometres to the northwest of Lash and ten kilometres from Marjah was a town with a solitary blue marker depicting British troops and a single green marker for an ANA unit, both isolated in a sea of red. I peered at the name of the town written on the map – Nad Ali.

As the briefing wound on, the picture grew bleaker. An operation by US forces in the far south of Helmand had forced enemy fighters north towards Lash and the assassination of Haji Tor Jan, the Marjah police chief, had kicked off a wave of Taliban attacks. Once Marjah had fallen, the Taliban had moved on to Nad Ali. Col Wadood's kandak had deployed there to stop the

Taliban advance. They'd established a new patrol base but had been encountering heavy resistance and requested major British reinforcements to back them up. Brigade, used to Afghan hyperbole, had sent just over forty men, about half of B Company, to find out what was going on. They were under the command of Harry Clark, the same major who'd come with me to Marjah a few weeks before.

'They got smashed,' said Nick. 'Seems the ANA had it right for once. We had to send the rest of the company in straight away. They were about to get completely overrun.'

Another fifteen men from B Company was all Brigade could spare. The biggest operation of the summer was about to begin. All available troops were committed to moving a turbine from Kandahar to a dam at a remote village called Kajaki, 100 kilometres northeast of Lash. The dam housed a massive hydroelectric plant that provided electricity to half of Helmand province. It was built in the 1950s with American aid money but only two out of three turbines had ever been installed and so wasn't producing enough power. The US had decided now was the time to rectify this, and in doing so, hopefully win some public support in Helmand. Brigade had been planning the operation for months but had struggled to find a safe route along which to move the turbine. One where it wouldn't be destroyed by the Taliban. Now time had run out. Rumour had it that Condoleezza Rice herself had called the Brigade Commander, Brigadier Mark Carleton-Smith, and ordered him to put things in motion. 'Just get it done,' she'd allegedly said. There was major concern at Brigade HQ, staff officers running from one meeting to another, wearing identical worried expressions. If this thing went wrong and the Taliban pulled off a spectacular attack on the turbine it could precipitate the end of British involvement in the war. Anyone not directly involved in the operation was suddenly relegated to a lower priority and that included Harry and his beleaguered company. So far they had managed to hold out, but if the Taliban continued to pour more men into the battle they were going to be fighting for their lives.

Nick explained how the enemy had systematically dug up most of the road network between Lash and Nad Ali. There was just one road remaining, which would allow one last convoy to get through.

'They're surrounded,' Nick went on. 'They've taken over an old schoolhouse and have built a strong defensive position but they're really up against it. They've already had eight men wounded and evacuated out on helicopters. The ANA have taken about ten casualties, including one man killed. On top of that, Harry's told us that the ANA are now refusing to patrol.'

Nick turned towards me.

'So this is where you come in, Mark. We need you to get over there and persuade the Afghans to re-engage. There's an eight-man OMLT flying in now from Bastion with a colour sergeant in charge. But we need an officer there. Someone the Afghan Colonel will listen to. You've been with the ANA long enough and seem to know what makes them tick. I don't care how you do it – just get them back in the fight.'

Before I left the ops room, there was time for one more question. 'Who is the Afghan commander in Nad Ali?' I asked.

Nick consulted his notes. 'It's a guy called Col Wadood.'

I felt a thrill of anticipation. Working with Wadood in Gereshk and Marjah had been an education, even though the Taliban had failed to materialise. If there was going to be a scrap then there was no Afghan I'd rather have alongside me.

There was no time to prepare. There was a re-supply convoy due to leave for Nad Ali in just a few hours' time and I would be going with them. I was confronted with the perennial conundrum: did I spend my time preparing or take what would probably be my last opportunity to sleep for the next 48 hours? I managed neither. Establishing a hideaway in a nearby tent, I crammed myself onto a short couch opposite the television.

Between the broken air-conditioning and my racing brain, I sweated three restless hours away on cushions already stained by the countless sleep-deprived soldiers that had gone before me. I was much too excited to sleep. The thrilling prospect of finally seeing some action quite eclipsed any fear I might have felt about setting out on another dangerous journey across the desert.

We left camp at 0300hrs in a convoy of one drops vehicle, (a kind of big flatbed lorry with a crane mechanism attached to hoist large shipping containers on board), two four-tonners and six WMIKs, mounted with .50cals as an escort. In addition, there were two further WMIKs, which were being delivered to Nad Ali for use by the OMLT that I would be taking command of. I was riding shotgun in the cab of the second four-tonner, sick from fatigue, my rifle jammed awkwardly between my knees.

Our route was only 15 kilometres long and in ideal circumstances we might have expected to cover the ground in three to four hours. Today, however, progress was even slower because of the state of the road and the constant stops we had to make to check the road for IEDs. We found that sections of the road had been freshly dug up by the enemy and had to slowly manoeuvre our way past. Every time this happened, the convoy was brought to a standstill and then, one by one, each vehicle would ponderously reverse and turn to find a new route in. I came here expecting explosions and gunfire but now the blaring of reversing sirens was the soundtrack to my war.

In the driver's seat next to me sat a heavily tattooed private soldier from Birmingham. His was an unglamorous job, six months rumbling back and forward across the desert in an HGV for a little over half the salary of his civilian counterpart doing the same up and down the M5. Except over here there was always the chance that the road might explode at any moment.

By six in the morning the sun was up, bringing with it oppressive heat, and we were still in the desert, trying to find a safe route in. I lay prone in the dust by the roadside, squinting through my sights as my ride waited for its turn to back up. I was still keyed up. The Taliban wouldn't want us to reach our comrades in Nad Ali. I expected an ambush at any moment.

The desert around us stretched out to the horizon. It was the same flat, featureless landscape I'd driven across near Gereshk. The occasional settlements we passed through consisted of scattered mud-walled compounds set back from the main road. There was no indication of what went on behind the walls or who lived inside. This was an anonymous world.

To reach the schoolhouse where Harry and B Company were based, we had to drive through the middle of Nad Ali District Centre (DC). There wasn't much to it, covering maybe 300 by 600 metres. Within this area was a small market-place strung out along the main road, a police station, mayor's office and a few other scattered buildings. Along the entire eastern edge of the DC, ran the ruins of an ancient mud brick wall that had once marked the perimeter of a great fort. The ANA had set up four positions in the town. There was the school in the northeast corner. Around this, the kandak had established three smaller bases, one a hundred metres or so to the north, one to the east and one to the west. Each of these positions was manned by two dozen Afghan soldiers, leaving just over a hundred ANA in the school, along with Harry's force. The police station was in the southeast corner of the DC and I'd been told in my briefing that there were around thirty ANP officers who were nominally on our side. After my experience with the police in Marjah, I wasn't sure they counted for much.

The most striking thing about the DC was the absence of people. In Gereshk the streets had teemed with men, women and children. Here there was just eerie silence. The abandoned buildings appeared as relics of a lost civilisation. What had driven the people from this place? It would be too easy to point the finger at the Taliban but they'd been in town for some time while the locals had continued about their daily business. Really, it was us who had pushed the population out. It was when the kandak arrived that the fighting began and then later the presence of British troops made things worse, attracting Taliban fighters like a jar of honey brings wasps at a picnic. I was sure we were the good guys but I don't think the locals gave a damn. Brits, ANA, Taliban – they wanted no part of our war and just wanted to be left alone.

Perhaps the enemy weren't ready for us or perhaps they were waiting for us to reach Nad Ali before they sprung their trap. Whatever the reason, we made it to our destination without incident. As we approached the school, I could make out the tops of the sentries' helmets peeking over the wall and the barrels of heavy machine-guns pointing out at the surrounding area. We drove through the main gate and rolled to a stop. I jumped down from the cab and took my first look at my new home.

The school had been built by American aid agencies in the 1970s. A seven-foot high concrete wall marked the square perimeter of a dusty area, around the size of a large football pitch. In the northeast quarter stood the old schoolhouse, a squat one-storey building constructed out of the same grey concrete that, along with mud, seemed to be the only building material available in Helmand. On the other side of the compound were two newer looking classroom blocks that now served as dormitories for the troops. At each corner of the makeshift base was a hastily constructed sentry post, consisting of two WMIKs parked flush against the wall. From these platforms, the soldiers could look out over the top of the wall and command wide arcs out over the surrounding area. The soldiers had rigged up ponchos on either side of their vehicles to produce a kind of lean-to, which they now called home.

'Evans, you massive prick. Welcome to Nad Ali.' I turned around to see a familiar diminutive figure standing there, one hand in his pocket, the other dangling a lit cigarette. He looked exhausted.

'Woody,' I said. 'I didn't know you were here.'

'I thought we were being sent a proper officer but now here you are.'

I looked at Woody's deadpan face. I was never quite sure if he was joking or not.

'Come and say hi to Harry,' he continued. 'He'll be delighted to see you.'

It was only a few weeks since our tempestuous encounter in Marjah. I only hoped that the recent fighting had softened the major's demeanour and made him more approachable.

It hadn't. 'Oh, it's you,' he said. 'I hope your drills have got slicker since the last time I saw you. There is a war on, you know.'

We sat outside the ops room and smoked while Harry briefed me on the situation. In the schoolhouse there was Colonel Wadood and his men; Harry and his Jocks; myself and my OMLT, whose job was to patrol with the ANA; in the ops room with Harry were the rest of his command team, including the company sergeant major and Woody.

As Harry related the events of the last few days, I realised the severity of the situation. Col Wadood had moved to Nad Ali with 200 men from his kandak about a week ago, after intelligence reports had suggested a major build-up of Taliban fighters in the area. The exact numbers were unknown but the upper estimates suggested around three to four hundred, more than the ANA kandak could deal with alone. Brigade had sent Harry and his men to assess the situation before they committed any more troops. After Marjah, where the Taliban had managed only one solitary bomb – albeit one that had killed the local police chief – Harry had believed that this 'crisis' in Nad Ali would fizzle out in the same way. A quick in-and-out patrol, he thought. Chat to the Afghan commander, establish the threat wasn't serious and head back to Lash. It didn't quite work out that way.

When Harry arrived he'd rendezvoused with Wadood at the police station in the south of the DC. All was quiet and it had seemed like his cynicism was justified. Twenty minutes later, however, the enemy attacked the police station with a heavy barrage of RPGs and small arms fire. The Jocks, ANA and ANP, manning positions on the roof, were able to repel the assault but several police officers and Afghan soldiers were seriously wounded. Harry was ordered to stay and hold the DC at all costs.

The following day, Harry and his men relocated to the school-house where Col Wadood had set up his headquarters. That night the Taliban attacked again – this time with a force of some two hundred fighters intent on storming the schoolhouse. As he briefed us on the details, Harry's face turned ashen. They'd managed to hold on, but only just. 'We had fighters running at the walls from every direction,' Harry said. 'I thought we were going to be overrun.'

Only the firepower of the .50 cals Harry had placed on the roof of the schoolhouse prevented the enemy from swarming over the perimeter wall. From this elevated position the men manning the guns had commanded a 360-degree field of fire and had swung the barrels with deadly effect. Harry estimated that the gunners had killed twenty enemy fighters between them. The rest of Harry's soldiers had accounted for around that many again. With nearly a quarter of them killed and more wounded, the Taliban had retreated. Miraculously only one of Harry's men had been wounded, and that had been the result of a misguided rocket launched by one of the ANA soldiers. It had exploded against the base's western wall, embedding shrapnel all down the left side of the man's body. This incident did nothing to improve relations between the Jocks and the ANA, who had lost one of their own in the fight.

After the attack, Harry had needed no further evidence that, this time, Wadood's information was accurate. He radioed back to Lash and requested for all the remaining available troops from his company to join him. Only twelve more men, but Harry was desperate for the extra firepower and supplies that they would bring. He realised that the battle for Nad Ali would not be over quickly.

The reinforcements drove to Nad Ali that night under the cover of darkness. The move did not go smoothly. As they approached the outskirts of the DC from the east, a Snatch vehicle lost its bearings in the dark and rolled into a deep water-filled ditch. The four men inside nearly drowned and barely escaped with their lives. All four of them were injured. They were forced to throw grenades through the back door of the vehicle, blowing it up to prevent the enemy salvaging valuable equipment from the wreckage.

The next day Harry sent out a platoon in four vehicles to investigate enemy positions to the north of the DC. The enemy were waiting for them in strength. They ambushed the patrol as they drove along the road. Rocket-propelled grenades exploded beside the vehicles, wounding another four of the Jocks. The rear vehicle in the patrol was disabled and the men ran to a nearby compound, where they hid for three hours, hoping that their comrades would be able to reach them before the Taliban worked out where they were. It took four attempts for the other members of their patrol to get to the compound as the Taliban kept up their attacks. The platoon commander was shot in the arm and his sergeant was wounded by shrapnel from an RPG. They all finally made it back to the schoolhouse, having taken six casualties in total. The wounded were all airlifted back to Lash within a few hours, where they were operated on prior to being shipped home. A second night of attacks followed. For a second night they held them off. Harry's force was now down to just forty-six men. It was astonishing what they had been through in the past 72 hours. No wonder they were so relieved to see us.

'It was like something out of *Zulu*.'

I heard a voice behind me and looked round to see another man standing there. It took me a moment but then I recognised him as DB, the brand new officer that I'd met in Lashkar Gah before I'd headed to Marjah. The change in him couldn't have been more startling. Gone was the fresh-faced look of wonder, replaced now by the grimly fatalistic expression of a man who'd seen too much. The fighting over the past few days had transformed DB from inexperienced rookie to tough combat veteran. I tried to keep up a serious and professional front but on the inside I was delighted.

'So there are still Taliban out there?'

'No shit,' DB replied. 'We're surrounded by the fuckers. There are at least a couple of hundred out there, in compounds less than 100 metres away.'

I thought back to all the seemingly empty buildings I'd seen on my way in. The invisible enemy. This was what I wanted. Finally it looked like I had found my war.

My first job, Harry told me, was to get the ANA back in the fight. They were happy to defend the patrol base but moving out of the DC and taking the fight to the enemy was apparently out of the question. I asked Harry what he thought the problem was. 'It's the ANA!' he replied, suddenly shouting. 'Who knows why they do anything?' It was that same old British refrain. If I knew anything about Wadood, he would have a bloody good reason for not patrolling – the Colonel wouldn't shirk from a fight unless he had to. For the first time since I'd been in Afghanistan I felt like my skills and experience just might make a real difference.

· 'You've got to talk sense into the Colonel,' Harry went on. 'There's now fifty-five British soldiers here, including your eight-man OMLT, who flew in last night. Then there's thirty ANP men on the southern edge of the DC. That's not enough to take on hundreds of Taliban. Wadood's got two hundred soldiers. We need them to start pulling their weight or we're in serious trouble.'

The dull thud of an explosion cut Harry off mid-flow. In the distance we heard the sound of gunfire and the unmistakable noise of multiple RPGs. It was about a kilometre away but sounded heavy. It had to be the convoy I'd arrived on just an hour previously. Having delivered their cargo, they were heading back on the road towards Lash. There were no other call signs out on the ground. The Taliban must have been lying in wait, allowing the convoy to reach Nad Ali and then ambushing them on its way out. Through the open door of the ops room, the radio hissed. 'Contact. Wait out.' Harry and Colin glanced at one another, their faces tense. No one spoke.

From so far away, the battle didn't seem real. We couldn't see the vehicles anymore but tracer fire flickered on the horizon as the WMIKs opened fire with their .50cals.

We followed the firefight over the radio net, its drama reduced to a staccato series of questions and answers, confirmations followed by clipped orders. Only briefly did a sense of crisis intrude as the convoy commander declared his intention to abandon a vehicle and extract from the contact. The response from HQ was immediate and uncompromising. Leave nothing behind.

The battle was brought to a swift conclusion by the arrival of an Apache attack helicopter, which roared low over the schoolhouse on its way to the battle. It blasted the enemy with four Hellfire missiles, and battered them with rounds from its 30mm cannon. The Taliban melted away, leaving the convoy to drive on unmolested. Over the radio we heard that the men in the convoy had killed ten enemy fighters while miraculously sustaining no casualties themselves. We didn't know it then, but those trucks disappearing over the horizon were to be our last glimpse of friendly ground forces for two months.

Half an hour later, the net crackled into life again. The road to Lash had been completely destroyed and with it our last land-based supply line. From now on, only helicopters would be able to reach us and with so many enemy fighters in the area they were dangerously vulnerable to attack. I looked out over the walls of the base and pictured the Taliban hidden just a few hundred metres away. We were now a force under siege.

CHAPTER FOURTEEN

Before I went to see the Afghans I wanted to meet the men of the OMLT who would be under my command here. My deployment to Nad Ali was a hasty affair, no time to plan, just hop on a truck and get down there. My team had been given no more notice themselves and had been dragged in just last night. There were eight men, six of them infantrymen from 1 Royal Irish with one medic from the Royal Army Medical Corps and a Kiwi from the Territorial Army who had been on a course to learn Pashtu.

For the past twenty-four hours the man in charge had been Colour Sergeant Mason, a grizzled soldier of the old school. I say 'grizzled' but really he can't have been more than a few years older than me. His face was heavily lined and his eyes were locked in the perpetual squint common to those who have spent most of their life outdoors. He was of average height, 5'9" or 5'10", but he stooped, making him appear shorter. He had a bit of a belly and pale skin, even after months of exposure to the Afghan sun. Perched at the corner of his mouth was a half-smoked cigarette – an accessory, I was to learn, he was rarely without. Above all, CSgt Mason exuded an air of toughness and competence. Over the coming weeks he would prove himself time and again as a tremendous soldier and leader of men. For now, however, he just looked pissed off.

'Sir,' he said, acknowledging me with a curt nod.

'Capt Evans,' I said, stretching out a hand.

'Yes, sir. I'm Colour Mason. They said that they were sending an officer.'

'So what's the score with the Afghans then?' I asked. 'Why won't they fight?'

Colour Mason admitted that he didn't know the answer. 'The Afghan colonel wouldn't go into much detail when I spoke to him. He just said that he didn't take his orders from Major Clark. To be honest,' he was suddenly conspiratorial, 'those two don't really get on.'

It figured. Harry's disdain for the Afghan way of soldiering had been apparent in Marjah and I doubted that he'd changed his opinions since then. Before I left, I asked Mason for his assessment of our situation.

'It's shit,' was his succinct reply.

Soldiers use the adjective 'shit' to describe a great many things ranging from the merely annoying to the prospect of imminent death. I looked into Mason's eyes and for the first time since I'd arrived, I felt a twinge of fear. What had I got myself into? Some of this emotion must have found its way to my face for Mason suddenly laughed. 'Don't look so worried, sir. It'll turn out OK. Anyway, if the ANA lads aren't going to fight then we can stay tucked up safe in here. Come and find me after you've seen the Colonel and we'll figure out how we can make this thing work.'

'Thanks, Colour,' I said and went in search of the Colonel.

Before I could talk to the Afghans I had to pick up an interpreter. The Argylls had brought a couple of their own with them but I was delighted to discover that Ash had made it down from Gereshk with the kandak. I greeted him enthusiastically but his reciprocation was somewhat muted.

'What's up, Ash?' I asked. 'Why so cheerful?'

'This place is a deathtrap,' he replied. 'I'd never been shot at before I came here and now there are hundreds of men with guns who want to kill me.'

'Fun, isn't it?' I said. 'Now come on, let's go and see the Colonel.'

'Sorry,' said Ash. 'I can't help you right now. Major Clark has asked me to go and see him.' He called across to one of his fellow interpreters, a gloomy looking older fellow who I didn't recognise. 'Wasim will go with you.' I shook hands with the new interpreter and together we walked over to the Colonel's office.

Wadood had set himself up in what had once been the head-master's office in the main schoolhouse. It had the same sparse expeditionary feel as his office in Gereshk, except this one had a couple of fold-up beds crammed in beside the desk. One was the Colonel's while the other belonged to the S2, Wadood's buzkashi-loving right-hand man. We must be in a tight spot, I thought, if Wadood was willing to share a quarter with the S2's rumbling digestive system and powerful personal aroma.

The Colonel looked about as cheerful as Wasim when I walked in, but he said hello warmly enough and I tried to convince myself that he was pleased to see me.

'So you are here to be my teacher?' he asked.

I smiled nervously.

'I used to get majors to show me what to do,' said Wadood. 'Now, it's Captain Mark. What next? Yesterday that Colour Sergeant came to talk to me. I sent him packing. Tell me, where is our friend from Gereshk, Major Richard?'

I'd heard in Lash that his promotion to lieutenant colonel had come through while I'd been on leave. 'He's been promoted,' I said. 'Flown back to England to start his new job.'

Wadood drummed his fingers on the table. 'Good,' he said. 'Richard is a talented officer. His promotion is certainly deserved. So for me, you must be the new Richard. I hope you are ready to fill his shoes. Now, what can I do for you?'

The Colonel was being polite but I could tell that my rela-tively low rank was an issue. It wasn't so much to do with Wadood's pride – he was utterly self-assured and confident enough in his own position not to worry about any insult that might have been implied by sending a junior officer. He was

107

more concerned about the limits of my influence with Brigade HQ in Lash. He knew well enough that when a major picks up the telephone or gets on the net people pay attention but when a captain puts in a request he is likely to be fobbed off or dismissed out of hand. Without a heavy hitter pushing his case for him, Wadood could find himself left out in the cold when it came to the allocation of equipment or vital air assets.

I took a deep breath. 'Well, sir, perhaps you remember the first time we met in Gereshk.'

Wadood began to smile and clapped his hands together. 'Aha! So you want to know why we're not patrolling. That man Harry has sent you over here to chastise me.'

'Not at all, sir,' I said. 'It's just . . . Er . . . Well, what is the situation?'

Wasim, the interpreter, paused for a moment before translating. He then proceeded to talk for a full thirty seconds. I'm not sure what he said but it provoked an instant reaction from the Colonel, who picked up a helmet lying on the floor behind his desk and swung it hard at Wasim's head. He dropped to the ground while Wadood stood over his prone body and subjected him to a tirade of invective. I stood there stunned, unable to make out what had just happened. Wadood jabbed his finger towards the unfortunate man and continued to yell before launching the helmet at the wall in a fit of rage. As the Colonel ran out of steam, Wasim climbed unsteadily to his feet and shuffled towards the door. Wadood now looked at me. 'Get another interpreter,' he said, in English. I tried to ask him what had just happened but he just waved towards the door. I made my way back to the interpreters' room.

Ash had finished with Harry. I told him what had occurred. He nodded. 'Wadood doesn't like Wasim,' he said, as though this explained everything. 'It's been a difficult few days. I'll come with you. Best to keep Wasim away from the Colonel now.' Together we went back to Wadood's office.

'I'm sorry about that,' the Colonel said. 'Now where were we?'

I never did find out what Wasim had said to deserve such rough treatment, and a few days later he left for good on a helicopter. Tensions were clearly running high.

The Colonel proceeded to lay out the situation for me. His orders from General Mahayadin, the Afghan officer in command of all ANA forces in Helmand, were to hold the Nad Ali DC. As far as he was concerned, that's exactly what he was going to do. His men occupied strong defensive positions and Wadood saw little value in moving his men about the battlefield just because a British major thought it was a good idea.

British Army doctrine demanded that we take offensive action whenever possible, so I asked, 'But don't you want to take the fight to the enemy? I'd have thought you'd have loved the chance to kill a few more Taliban.'

Wadood sighed. 'Of course you're right. But it's not just about killing Taliban. There are other considerations. I have to think about the safety of my own men.'

'What do you mean? I know it's dangerous but the men take risks all the time. They're soldiers.'

Wadood slapped his hand down on the table. 'And any single one of my men is willing to die if that's what duty requires him to do. Never call into question the bravery of my men. All I'm asking is that we share the risks equally. You say that British soldiers put themselves in as much danger as Afghans . . .'

He glared at me, daring me to contradict him.

I nodded dumbly.

'. . . But what do you have every single time you go out on patrol?'

My mind was blank. I had no idea what he was talking about. 'Er, better boots? More ammunition? Radios that work?' I suggested.

'Ha! Right on all counts – especially about the boots.' Wadood looked briefly at the cracked leather of his own footwear. 'But that's not what I mean. Helicopters! That's what you have. Planes too. Every time you go outside, you can call in firepower from above. When my men go out, their best chance of seeing something in the sky is taking a kite with them.'

He was quite right. Air power was the crucial difference between us and the Taliban. Yes, we were better trained, had superior weapons and more of them, but on any given day all that could be negated by the terrain, by a shortage of troops or by the cunning of our enemies. When things weren't going our way, when we found ourselves on the losing side in a battle, we'd bring in the helicopters. An Apache hovering overhead was always a cheering sight to beleaguered British troops. Its effect on the enemy was even more spectacular. With its 30mm cannon it could destroy an infantry platoon four kilometres away. It can fire Hellfire missiles even further. Those are designed to blow up tanks. You can imagine the impact on the Taliban's foot soldiers. In an environment as dangerous as Nad Ali it was British policy not to patrol without air support either up above or waiting on call.

'We want them,' said Wadood. 'Treat us the same as you treat your own men and we'll patrol to the edge of the world if you want.'

I couldn't argue with him. He was right. If we wanted to call the Afghans our allies we had to show that we stood shoulder to shoulder with them. Why should we ask them to take bigger risks than we would? It was clear in my own mind what we had to do, but would the officers at Brigade see it the same way?

As it turned out, Brigade was happy to supply us with the choppers. I think the Brigade Commander, the senior officer directing all British operations in Helmand, was spooked by Harry's reports of how hot things were getting in Nad Ali. His attention may have been focused on the big turbine operation but he also realised that successfully fixing Helmand's electricity problem would seem much less of an achievement if the Taliban took over half the province in the meantime.

Now we'd negotiated this first obstacle, Harry and I set about planning a patrol for the very next day. Wadood was as good as his word and entered into the preparations with gusto. As I'd seen before, given any opportunity to kill the Taliban he was game, provided it didn't conflict with any of his other objectives. Most of the kandak was to take part in the operation, leaving behind a few essential sentries and the Jocks to take care of the patrol base. The only Brits heading out would be me and my OMLT. It was time to catch up with Colour Mason.

I found Mason sitting on the veranda outside the ops room. Together we pored over a map and smoked while we figured out how eight men could best support a force of two hundred.

The two of us had to work out how the OMLT would function on a day-to-day basis. The initial plan, to which I reluctantly agreed, was that I would spend most of my time in the ops room, liaising with Brigade, Col Wadood and Harry while Mason commanded the team out on the ground. I had two problems with this approach. Firstly, I worried about how I'd manage to exert any influence over the team this way, and secondly, I wanted to be in the thick of the action.

Woody wandered over, clutching a sheet of paper in his hand. He handed the sheet to me. 'Patrol schedule,' he said. 'This is what Harry wants the ANA to stick to from tomorrow.'

Mason peered over my shoulder as I read the details. Harry had decreed that the kandak should put out at least two patrols every day. The problem was this meant the OMLT would have to follow suit.

'Two patrols a day?' Mason was incredulous. 'The lads'll be knackered.'

He was right; with only eight men at our disposal, each soldier would end up deploying on the ground twice in one day. The Afghans could vary which sub-units they used and so give their men time to rest but we would quickly become exhausted under this punishing regime. Two patrols a day may not sound like a great deal but when you consider that each one could last up to five hours, longer if the enemy chose to intervene, and that each soldier carries over 100 pounds of kit in temperatures above 40°C, you start to understand the scale of the undertaking. Harry's Jocks weren't going out more than once a day so it seemed a bit much that he should ask us in the OMLT to shoulder a greater burden.

The more we talked about it, the more difficult it became to justify keeping me confined to base, while Mason led the men on the ground. I realised that even if I were to stay behind during the patrols, there was no obvious place for me to work. There were currently two separate ops rooms within the base, one for the ANA and one for the Brits. Harry insisted that no Afghan could be admitted to his ops room in case they gained access to 'secret material'. As far as I was aware, Harry didn't have anything more secret in his ops room than Richard had had in Gereshk, and there Wadood had popped in an out as he pleased. Anyway, what Harry said went, and without having Afghan commanders in the ops room, there was little point in me basing myself there. I suppose I could have sat in the Afghan ops room, but without being able to speak the language it would have been difficult to follow the action and make a meaningful contribution. I was beginning to realise how difficult my job in Nad Ali might be, caught on this active fault line between Wadood and Harry.

We decided that the second patrol each day would merely be a short sweep around the perimeter of the base to ensure the Taliban weren't getting too close and to keep Harry and Brigade happy. We also agreed that I would deploy on the ground. There was no other way to make this work with the limited resources at our disposal. I'd get my chance at combat yet.

As darkness drew in, I went to meet my team. I'd seen them

knocking around the yard earlier but in the hurry to unload the convoy, and the toing and froing between Harry, Wadood and Mason, there'd been no time for proper introductions, or even to find out where we were sleeping. Mason ushered me into the accommodation. While the Jocks were dotted around camp in various improvised shelters by their vehicles and sangars, we were lucky enough to have a proper room in one of the old classrooms. Mason had secured his own private quarter at one end of the block and was clearly not about to give it up. 'You can bunk in with Magoo,' he said. Magoo! Another familiar face from Gereshk and a welcome one.

'All right, sir,' said Magoo, raising a hand in lazy salute from where he lay on his camp cot. 'Heard you were on your way.'

'Hello Cpl Magoo,' I said.

'Actually it's Sergeant now. I picked up last week.'

'Congratulations. Maybe your new-found responsibilities will leave you less time for taking the piss out of me.'

'Not a chance, sir,' he said with a grin.

'So they finally let you out of the ops room,' I said. 'They must have thought you were getting too fat, sat on your arse all day next to a radio.'

'It's about bloody time. I'm a soldier, not a radio ham.'

It was true. Magoo's talents had been wasted stuck behind a desk in Gereshk. He was a graduate of the Platoon Sergeants' Course, a notoriously punishing three-month thrashing up and down the Brecon Beacons. You have to be pretty tough to make it through, and those that do are some of the best infanteers in the world. I was pleased I'd have Magoo alongside me when we went looking for the Taliban. I knew his cheerful piss-taking would be a welcome relief when things threatened to get serious.

There were six other members of the motley crew – strangers for now, but I'd get to know them well over the coming days.

Sat cleaning their rifles were Cpl Beattie, Charlie and LCpl Ramsay. Cpl Beattie was an Ulsterman like Magoo, but a completely different character. Where Magoo kept up a non-stop stream of cheeky banter, Beattie was a much quieter fellow, who liked to carefully observe and listen. Every now and then he would cut through everyone's raucous bullshit with a wryly delivered joke that sent us all into stitches. Out of all of us, he was the most experienced in terms of Afghan combat. He'd fought a series of bloody battles around Musa Qala on his last deployment. This was to become a source of much amusement and not a day went past without someone asking the question, 'Hey Beattie, is this as bad as Musa Qala then?' For the first few days he'd reply with a flicker of a smile and a quick shake of the head. After that it was a different story.

Charlie was a broad-shouldered, baby-faced New Zealander and a corporal in the Territorial Army. He was a quiet man who had spent a year in the UK learning to speak Pashtu. Most of the ANA soldiers we were with spoke Dari and Charlie, with his flair for languages, had picked up a fair bit of that language too. He frequently eschewed the rowdy company of the OMLT to spend his downtime with the Afghans, with whom he developed a closeness most British soldiers never achieved.

LCpl Ramsay, or Ram for short, had been in the Army for some ten years but never looked like he enjoyed it much. He'd signed off, the military term for giving notice, and was only a few months away from going back to civilian life. I think this made it harder for him every time we went on patrol as, so close to leaving, he saw the odds of making it back in one piece shortening fast. He was the consummate professional and never had to be told the same thing twice.

Helping Mason arrange the stores were Griff and Stan.

Griff was the youngest member of the team. A ranger and only nineteen years old, he was quick-tempered and seemed hugely unenthusiastic about the business of soldiering. He was very much in love with a girl back home and he took every opportunity he could to use the one satellite phone in the base to call her. They were due to be married although, perhaps uncharitably, no one thought it had much of a chance of working out. He just seemed too young for that kind of commitment. We spent a great deal of energy trying to get him to focus on the job in hand rather than the girl at home.

Stan was a soldier of the old school. He'd been dug out of the QM's store in Lash to make up the numbers for our little band in Nad Ali. He seemed quite unfazed by the sudden shift from accounting for equipment in the safety of headquarters to fighting alongside the ANA. He kept up the same unflappable jollity and talked mostly about the pub he planned to open with his wife when he finally left the Army.

Lastly, we also had our own medic, LCpl Gurung, whom everyone called Gee and who, other than Charlie, was the only non-Irish member of the team. He was the son of a Gurkha but had been raised in the UK. I think his foreign heritage helped him to identify with the ANA guys as they strived to understand our British way of doing things. Like Charlie, he built up a strong relationship with the kandak and he and Charlie could often be found in their lines, chilling out and finding ways to bridge the cultural divide.

All the men acknowledged my presence with a certain wariness. I was an unknown quantity to them and they realised that over the coming days I might hold their lives in the balance.

CHAPTER FIFTEEN

March–April 2009

In the months after Afghanistan, the women came and went. You can get a lot of mileage with some girls when you tell them that you're fresh back from war, and I helped myself to more than my share. Not that I remember much about them. I was drinking properly by now. The booze helped to slow down my thoughts, which if left unchecked would instantly pluck me from the present and deposit me right back in Helmand. The Army made it easy; everybody boozed and you could hit it hard without anybody raising an eyebrow. Since I'd come back from Afghanistan I'd start as early as I could, as often as I could, whether I had anyone to drink with or not. I would often take a bottle of wine to bed with me and the next morning I'd kid myself that I ought to finish it to stop it going off. This way I started many days with a buzz that I liked to top up with a pint or two over lunch. I used to worry that a senior officer might notice my lack of sobriety but soon discovered that a packet of chewing gum and five fags could mask most sins. If not then there was always the excuse of a late night in the bar the previous evening – provided one was punctual, this was never unacceptable, even in today's modern Army.

All my liaisons were fuelled by drink. I'd pick up a girl in some exclusive, horrendously overpriced cocktail bar. Many of them seemed to believe that Army officers had a certain social cachet, even drunken, shambling ones with wine stains down the front of their shirt.

None of them lasted. They all wanted to talk afterwards and I never

116

did. When I started my seductions, I genuinely wanted to reach out to another human and hopefully find some measure of understanding, but there was always a gap that I couldn't quite bridge. After the second or third drink, I always gave up and henceforth floated on autopilot through endless conversations about I don't know what. By the time we reached the bedroom, I was zoning out, never listening to the murmured words from the pillow next to me. My behaviour was bad – I knew this but didn't care. I'd had enough of taking responsibility for others and now it was all about number one. If these girls were misguided enough to fall into my bed then that was their lookout. I felt guilty afterwards but it never stopped me going out and doing it all again. Of course there were even more nights when I passed out alone in a puddle of my own vomit and, frankly, that was fine with me too.

Then there was Sophie. She was different. We'd known one another for years; since school, in fact. She'd attended an all-girls college not far from my own school. Back then we were acquainted in that vague sort of mutual friends, go to the same parties kind of way. I'd always fancied her but she was utterly unobtainable. Attractive, interesting and self-possessed, she was always dating someone older, richer, or more interesting than me. When I finished school and went off to university, I lost touch with Sophie and slowly her memory faded. I hadn't seen her or really thought about her for almost ten years when we met at a party thrown by my friend Dan at his house in Brighton. Our eyes didn't meet across a crowded room. In fact I don't remember much about that night, as it passed in the usual blur, but the following morning we ended up catching the same train back to London. We sat opposite one another and for the whole hour-long journey I stared at her across the table top, utterly captivated. Sophie was about 5'7" and slim, with chestnut hair that reached down just below her shoulders. She was pretty with delicate cheekbones and deeply tanned skin. A long, slightly crooked nose just held her back from achieving classical beauty but to me it was one of her best features. To top it off, she had the most extraordinary eyes – not icy like blue eyes can be. Hers radiated warmth, and when I stared into them I felt curiously comforted.

After we arrived back at King's Cross we'd already started on our separate ways when I shouted after her, brought her back and asked her on a date. She hesitated for a moment, seemingly reluctant, but then agreed.

I went in hard, taking her out as often as I could. Dinner, lunch, the theatre, clubbing, Sophie lapped it all up. It cost me a small fortune. Her father had been a cavalry officer while she'd been growing up and that counted in my favour. She was, to some degree, already familiar with my world and was neither repelled nor cloyingly fascinated by my military stories. A journalist, Sophie worked for a fashion and design magazine, which had her flitting back and forth across Europe between a succession of glamorous parties and shows. This meant that she was often away but when she was back her time was mostly her own and much of it she would spend in my company. In my new job organising the expeditions there were very few people who knew what I was supposed to be doing, so I could sneak away for extended periods of time without anyone really noticing. Sophie and I were able to spend all night partying and enjoying long, lazy lunches the following day.

As I've said, I drank a lot, but Sophie didn't mind. She was a work-hard, play-hard kind of girl and no stranger to hedonistic excess. She went away a lot and I think she forgot that my own behaviour didn't calm down while she was out of town.

One morning she casually asked me if I'd like to go with her to the BAFTA Television Awards Ceremony. I'll admit that I came over a little star-struck. The military world and the celebrity one rarely intersect, not counting the odd visit of a topless model or C-list comedian to Camp Bastion in the name of troop morale.

Arriving at the Royal Festival Hall, I felt rather let down. The red carpet was everything I'd hoped it to be. We'd swanned our way past the cheering crowd behind the ropes, pretending that the adulation was for us. But inside I'd expected real showbiz glamour, waiters ploughing through the crowd with champagne, some witty repartee with Stephen Fry before settling down to a four-course feast, that kind of thing. I spotted Alexa Chung deep in conversation with Sir Alan Sugar and I made a beeline for them. Unfortunately, a BAFTA flunky intervened before I could reach them, and I found myself herded to the rear of a crowded auditorium, crammed next to a fat journalist, sweating through his bulging tuxedo. Luckily I'd squirrelled away a small hip flask into my jacket pocket, which helped me get through the first hour of the interminable series of sycophantic speeches and backslapping that comprised the ceremony.

If I'm honest, I wasn't really disposed to have a good time that night and my thoughts had already turned bleak before the evening began. Earlier that day I'd seen the Operational Honours and Awards List, all the names of those soldiers who had been selected to receive a medal during my tour of Afghanistan. I'd not expected anything for myself but I'd hoped Magoo would pick something up. Harry and I had written a citation for him and sent it over to his superiors in the Royal Irish. 'In the face of the enemy, Sgt MacGowan, at great personal risk to himself, exposed himself to sustained fire in order to provide his commander with vital information on the course of the battle that prevented a British position from being overrun.'

He'd got nothing. The Jocks had got nothing. Harry had got nothing. We may have had our differences, but he'd commanded a company under the most incredible circumstances. It seemed so unfair. They even gave pilots medals. I'm not saying the flyers aren't brave guys, but they at least got to fly back to a comfortable, secure base after their shift, while we were left in the shit, getting shot at. The whole system made no sense. We'd done it gladly, expecting no reward, but when I saw others being recognised for less, it seemed wrong. Fuck it. I was mixing with the stars now. What did I care about the war?

The ceremony had been under way for two long hours when they announced the award for Best Factual Series. First up was some documentary about a bloke who'd been on a trip down the Amazon. I watched the big screen as he paddled his way along the river, chatted to tribesmen and freaked out on their mind-bending drugs. Who cared? Certainly not the journalist next to me who was now lolling in his seat, mouth agape and beginning to snore.

The second nominee was announced, Ross Kemp, the EastEnders actor, who'd made a series about being embedded with the British forces in Helmand. In fact he'd been out there at the same time as me. I remembered some of the Jocks talking about him, having bumped into him before they'd come to Nad Ali. I hadn't resented him then and had actually heard good things about his films. But now he was up for an award. He was sitting down there by the stage, while we all sat around and applauded his achievements. His achievements? He'd been in the country for three weeks and thought he could tell us how it was out there. Fuck him. And fuck the Army.

The lights went down and the clip began to play. Familiar images flickered across the screen. The desert at dawn, men lying flat in the dust as bullets wing past. And then the whump-whump-whump of a helicopter overhead.

The screen went blank and the audience whooped and clapped their appreciation for the daring film-maker. And the images carried on. I closed my eyes but the film kept playing in the darkness. Not Kemp's pictures now but my own memories.

I was straining to see, my eyes fixed on the horizon. Somewhere out there were the enemy. The floor beneath me was slick with blood and my boots skidded as I ran to the empty window. I could feel the walls shaking as the world outside exploded. Inside, the screams of the wounded man filled my brain. The eyes of the men, Afghans and Brits alike, turned to me. 'What now?' they implored.

'Don't look at me. Look out there. Find them. Find them now, or we're all fucking dead.'

In my mind I struck upwards, kicking for the surface and tried to break out of this deep well of memory. Faintly, through the blood and the dust, I could make out Sophie's face turned towards me, shock and concern etched in her expression. I gasped and tried to speak but no words came out. I flailed in my seat, pushing myself upright and forced my way out past the journalist's sleeping carcass to my left. Staggering down the aisle, I found the door and exited to the sounds of applause and gunfire.

Sophie found me some time later outside the theatre, smoking and staring out across the river.

'Hi,' I said. 'Sorry. Needed some air.'

'What happened?' she asked.

'It's nothing. Just got a bit claustrophobic. Goes on a bit, this show, doesn't it?'

'You looked like you were having a stroke,' she said.

I shrugged and looked away. The truth was that I didn't know what had happened. The playback in my head was on a continuous loop. Whenever my mind wandered, it was filled with the sights and sounds of war. This time had been more visceral and taken me somewhere new but really it was situation normal. Another day in Afghanistan, in London. I didn't want to talk to Sophie, to pick at this thread of memory. It was private, my own. Not her business. Not anyone's business.

I turned back to Sophie. 'Has it finished in there?'

'More or less,' she said. 'Why don't we take off anyway?'

'Excellent,' I said. 'I know a bar nearby.'

I took her hand and we walked together down the steps. As I relaxed, I heard the faint sounds of screaming tugging at the corners of my consciousness. I squeezed Sophie's hand harder.

CHAPTER SIXTEEN

My first morning in Nad Ali dawned clear. I made breakfast alone on the veranda. As I watched my sausage and beans boil in my mess tin I felt a sense of calm descend upon me. Just being here, so close at last to real combat, made me contented for the first time in months.

Today was the first of September, which was also the first day of Ramadan and the ANA took their obligations seriously. During the hours of daylight they would neither eat nor drink. This would be a tough undertaking for anyone, but these men would be forced to patrol for hours in the hot sun. I was worried that they would collapse under the strain. Before we headed out on our first patrol I asked Wadood what he thought. He looked surprised, as though the idea of not fasting simply hadn't occurred to him. 'We're Muslims,' he said. 'It's Ramadan.'

'But what if they collapse on patrol?' I pressed him.

'Then we'll give them water. We're not barbarians, Mark.'

At 0700hrs we set out to patrol the local area in a display of military might designed to show the Taliban what force was now ranged against them. There were over a hundred soldiers with us, spread out across the landscape. Up above us an Apache circled, clearly showing Wadood that Brigade had listened to his concerns. Overseeing the spectacle was Col Wadood himself, sauntering among his men, bare headed and without body armour, as though he held the enemy's bullets in utter contempt.

We headed west, away from the DC. It was mostly fields with

a few lonely compounds dotted here and there. The crops had reached almost their full height and the harvest was only weeks away. Who was here to gather the crops though? Only the bravest or most suicidal of farmers would dare to linger when his field could become a battleground at a moment's notice. Then again, maybe they would take the risk. Losing an entire crop would bankrupt a farmer here.

Running between the fields was the usual network of irrigation ditches. They paralleled all the dirt tracks on both sides, which made it almost impossible to manoeuvre a vehicle. All our patrols here would have to be on foot.

Wadood pointed at one prominent compound that lay about 400 metres due east of the schoolhouse. 'We call that Compound Green,' he said. 'Taliban often snipe at us from there.'

I regarded the building warily, conscious that we were exposed directly in front of it. Wadood read my mind. 'Not today,' he said. I asked him how he could be so sure. He dismissed my concerns with the ghost of a smile. 'The Taliban are staying in today.' Such certainty; once more I got the impression that the Colonel wasn't telling me everything. Had he done some kind of deal with the enemy? Was he privy to special intelligence? I felt uneasy but also had to acknowledge an increasing respect for this man. Here with Wadood was my best chance of understanding Afghanistan and the war we were fighting.

We looped northwards and moved back into the DC. It was still deserted, the market-place devoid of both goods and traders. We passed quickly through the streets and pressed on in a south-easterly direction along the main road. We walked past yet more fields and headed towards a large village called Luy Bagh, which lay a kilometre from the DC.

Before we reached the village we encountered our first signs of life – a few solitary individuals standing in the fields dressed in shalwar kameez and turbans. They all stopped what they were doing and stared as we came into view. It was a disconcerting feeling to be the object of such scrutiny. Their eyes tracked our movement ceaselessly. I suppose it was only natural to respond this way, seeing over a hundred soldiers walking down the road armed to the teeth, but in my racing imagination I saw each of them as a potential enemy. Maybe they were. The Taliban were a local force; they had no uniform. These same men who leaned on their hoes could tomorrow be kitted out with AK-47s.

Every now and then Wadood would pick out one of these onlookers and subject him to a rudimentary interrogation. His exchanges were much more direct than my own attempts at local engagement in Gereshk. No effort at pleasantries, just, 'Are you Taliban?'

'No.'

'Any Taliban around here?'

'Yes.'

'Where?'

The farmer would gesticulate in a vaguely westerly direction.

'If you see any of the Taliban, tell them to leave this district. If they don't, we'll kill them.'

I asked Wadood if he thought these men were telling him the truth.

'Of course,' he replied. 'They know that if they lie, that if they try to protect the Taliban, I'll kill them.'

I believed him, and the brutal frankness shocked me. As far as he was concerned, he was fighting an entirely different kind of war to us. For us, the stakes were no higher than getting out of Afghanistan with our lives, but Wadood was fighting for the future of his country. For him, there was no middle ground. When the chips were down, you either rejected the Taliban or you paid the price. He was a surgeon cutting out a cancer and if the cells around it became infected then they had to go too.

Luy Bagh turned out to be a bigger place than the DC, about four times the size. It was centred on a large mosque at the cross-roads. The remainder comprised of large compounds, high-walled enclosures that housed entire Afghan families in a number of separate buildings. We couldn't see behind the high walls but the gaily painted gates were more ornate than the basic corrugated iron sheets I'd so far encountered. There was clearly money here, generous pickings for brigands or for the Taliban.

Patrolling through a village is a tougher proposition than the open countryside. Narrow alleyways and high rooftops offer all manner of cover where a sniper or ambush party might conceal themselves. Still Col Wadood ambled along, quite unperturbed by the threat.

We walked west from Luy Bagh, following the track until we came upon a long wall that extended some two hundred metres along the southern side of the thoroughfare. Green trees peeked over the top of the wall, branches drooping down towards the ground, heavy with red apples. Wadood reached up and plucked a piece of fruit which he passed to me. 'Orchard,' he said and then indicated rows of bullet holes that pockmarked the wall. 'Taliban are often here.' He paused. 'Not today though.'

Over the coming weeks, this copse would attain an almost mythical status among us, as we came here again and again to find our foe. Today all was quiet. I chafed yet again at the absence of an enemy to fight.

That night, my second in Nad Ali, a helicopter visited us. Now that the road to Lash was destroyed this was the only way that Brigade could get supplies to us. In order to transform our rough and ready camp into a proper fighting patrol base, we needed tents, generators, radio equipment and a constant stream of water, food, fuel and ammunition.

What we didn't need was a Code Black: a point-blank refusal by the RAF to fly in. It hadn't happened since the early days of the war, but in the most dangerous situations they could be compelled to make that call. The night before I arrived, the Chinook carrying Mason and the others had almost been shot out of the sky. We responded by going to extreme lengths to provide the safest cordon possible. Without the RAF we really would be completely on our own, cut off by enemy forces.

Every day I would submit a report detailing the supplies that the OMLT needed. Woody would do the same for the Jocks and one of Wadood's officers for the kandak. Then all we could do was hope a helicopter would turn up every two or three nights, bringing us what we'd requested. Even if they did, each chopper could only carry a small amount of stores. Just enough to keep us in food, water and ammo for seventy-two hours.

Putting in place the protection helicopter pilots required before they would land was a complex and time-consuming operation. I would get to know it well as we performed it again and again.

The HLS was located immediately south of the school on a patch of bare ground that used to be a football pitch. We would wait until after dark. One ANA platoon would form an inner cordon directly around the pitch. Other ANA troops kept watch from the three smaller bases on each side of the school. At the same time, one of Harry's platoons would patrol the local area, scouting for enemy snipers. My guys, plus more ANA, would unload the helicopter when it landed. We had a quad bike with a trailer, which we'd use to transport the supplies back into the base. Anything that we couldn't fit in the trailer we ended up humping back ourselves.

That first night, the helicopter turned up right on time, about three hours after nightfall. It was a Chinook, a big aircraft with twin rotors that provide it with the power to lift enormous loads. I watched from the edge of the football pitch as the helicopter swooped in low from the west, banking sharply in a virtuoso display of flying that made it as difficult a target as possible for the enemy to shoot. The pilot touched down right in the centre of the pitch and my men and I ran in to drag off the cargo. As we reached the helicopter, a man walked down the rear ramp dragging with him a mountain of equipment in

126

various bergens and crates. I assumed he was one of the helicopter crew but as we helped him unload he told me that he was staying with us. There was too much work to be done for me to question him further and I just nodded a brief acknowledgement and went on with the task at hand.

We were done in less than five minutes. The helicopter took off immediately, not stopping even to close the rear door. As it rose into the air a sharp burst of gunfire rattled out of the night. I heard the bullets whip overhead and threw myself to the floor. Just as quickly, I heard weapons opening up from the ANA position in the west and saw red tracer spitting in the darkness. The helicopter's rotors whined as the pilot increased the power and twisted away to the east, away from the incoming rounds.

A few seconds later, the helicopter was clear, and the attack was over almost as soon as it had begun. Harry ordered his platoon to push west to try and catch the attackers, but with the target gone they had spirited themselves away into the night. The platoon stayed on the ground for another twenty minutes and then withdrew back to the safety of our base.

Back in the schoolhouse I was able to get a better look at the man who had arrived on the helicopter. He was a short, dark-haired sergeant with a swarthy almost Italian look about him. Despite the somewhat dramatic manner of his arrival he looked utterly calm. 'I'm Phil,' he said. 'Your new JTAC.' I was glad to see him. JTAC stands for Joint Terminal Air Controller and it was his job to co-ordinate any air assets that Brigade sent to assist us. These were most often Apache helicopters but might also be fast jets or even unmanned drones. We shook hands.

'Glad you're here,' I said. 'It looks like we're going to need you.'

CHAPTER SEVENTEEN

IEDs are the scourge of modern warfare. In those final moments before a patrol, when my thoughts turned to all the guises death might take that day, it was roadside bombs that caused my throat to dry up and sweat to spring from my pores. I knew some soldiers who used to throw up before they went out, their stomachs cramping in fear that it might be their turn to tread in the wrong place. It was a game of pure chance. No matter how good your soldiering skills, no matter what experience you'd accumulated, the IED is a weapon that doesn't discriminate. There is nothing to be done. You can't shoot back or call in air support. All you can do is die or maybe bleed and hope the medics stitch you up in time.

It was the day after the patrol with Wadood, my first 'proper' patrol in Nad Ali – just my OMLT and an ANA platoon. Wadood was back in the schoolhouse and I was in command. We planned to head back out to Luy Bagh and see if we could find the enemy who'd kept themselves invisible the day before. I expected to be out for three to four hours but if we did get contacted I had no idea how long the fight could last.

There were just six of us from the OMLT on patrol, allowing three men to remain in the base to rest. We tried to rotate the personnel who went out each time to prevent exhaustion. Consequently there were two fewer British troops than I'd been used to patrolling with in Gereshk and I was still getting used to working with a new team. The first thing I noticed was how much extra kit we all had to carry with fewer men to spread the load between. In my patrol sack, on top of the radio, seven litres of water and personal ammunition that I was used to, there was extra link ammunition for the Minimi machine-guns that Charlie and Beattie used, four grenades and two spare radio batteries. With my body armour, webbing, helmet and rifle as well, I must have been humping 120 pounds of kit. To put that into context, the average baggage allowance on a long-haul flight is around 50 pounds, so this was like carrying two full suitcases on your back. My knees felt as if they were going to buckle before I'd even left the base. To add to my discomfort, the sun was already blazing down like a blowtorch.

Our smaller numbers also made it more difficult to keep control over the Afghan platoon. I found myself talking constantly to the platoon commander through the interpreter while Harry kept asking me for situation reports over the net. It occurred to me that it would be much easier if CSgt Mason dealt with the majority of the radio communication back to the ops room since he also carried a radio with him. Once this patrol was finished I suggested this to him and he eagerly embraced the idea. For now though I simply pressed on as best I could.

Without the talismanic protection of Col Wadood and his mysterious 'arrangements' with the Taliban, I was keenly aware that we were walking through hostile territory. Every sense seemed heightened as I scanned the horizon for the enemy. I thought I saw the Taliban everywhere, crouching in the shadows under the trees, crawling up the irrigation ditches and hiding in the rustling crop fields. My finger fiddled nervously with the safety catch on my rifle and sweat poured in sheets down my back.

We headed southeast of the schoolhouse, following the tracks down towards the orchard near the outskirts of Luy Bagh. The Afghan platoon commander was a new face to me and he seemed young and nervous. His inexperience was reflected in the way his sergeant shadowed his every move, quick to step in if he did anything stupid. Cpl Beattie was at the front on point with one of the Afghan privates. I was positioned a few metres back with the platoon commander and his sergeant. Colour Mason was further back still, making sure the guys at the rear of the formation were looking sharp.

We'd reached the crossroads opposite the orchard and had started to turn east down the road that led to Luy Bagh when Beattie raised the alarm. 'IED!' he shouted. We all froze. 'Get down!' I yelled in unison with Mason. The whole patrol fell on their belt buckles or climbed down into the ditch by the side of the road.

From ten metres in front, Beattie reported in to me. 'I'm not sure,' he said. 'I can see two wires running into the ditch and off towards the orchard. Could be command wires. I can't make out where they start.'

'Try and get a bit closer,' I said. 'It could just be some old rubbish.'

'Roger,' Beattie replied.

We all looked on as Beattie inched his way forward, crawling ever so slowly along the ditch, towards the wires. I held my breath. We were all in cover now but we weren't far away from the danger area and a big IED could still do some serious damage. Beattie, now just metres away from it, wouldn't stand a chance.

'Yeah. I can see them now,' he said. 'There's three of them. They're dug in just under the surface of the track.'

He paused, and then very deliberately said, 'I'm coming back now.' Delicately, he picked his way back through the ditch until he came level with me. His face was pale beneath its heavy tan.

I ordered the patrol to shift back up to the crossroads, a safe distance away from the bombs. Before I settled into the cover of the ditch I carefully scoured the ground around me for signs of booby traps. It was standard procedure to do this every time you stopped on a patrol but as the months had slipped past without encountering any bombs, so the rigour with which I conducted these searches had declined. Now Beattie's discovery brought the possibility of explosive evisceration crashing back home and I picked through the rocks and undergrowth with renewed zest. Looking around, I was pleased to see the other men combing their surroundings in just the same way.

While Mason and his opposite number busied themselves setting the men in a position of all-round defence, I reported the situation over the radio to Harry before moving with the Afghan platoon commander back towards the IEDs to get a clearer picture of what we were dealing with. It was just as Beattie had described. Three low, barely discernible bumps in the track and wires snaking towards the apple trees. The scary part was the obvious boot imprints in the dirt directly above the bombs. Yesterday's patrol had seen the entire kandak traipse down this path and not one man had spotted the danger.

The Afghan commander was clear what needed to be done.

'I'll send a couple of the boys across to dig them up,' he said. 'We can blow them up and be on our way.'

I wasn't sure. Going anywhere near an IED was dangerous and shovelling them out of the ground sounded like a shortcut to amputation.

'I don't want to hang around here,' the commander went on. 'If we wait too long, you know the Taliban will come. We're exposed.'

The radio crackled into life. It was Harry with our orders – stay put, secure a perimeter and wait for the ATO to arrive. Under no circumstances were we to touch the bombs ourselves. In the meantime, Harry wanted us to follow the command wires and see what they were attached to. The commander shook his head and swore, then jogged off to break the news to his sergeant. Much as I didn't want to hang around in the open, I was pleased that none of us would be prodding at unexploded bombs today.

I detailed Magoo, Griff and a couple of the ANA soldiers to go into the orchard and investigate the other end of the command wire. As I lay there in the ditch looking out across the fields I felt strangely at peace. It was as though I'd been transported back to the summer holidays of my childhood. Then too I'd spent long hot afternoons clambering in and out of ditches, searching for the enemy. In those days the bad guys had been as invisible as the Taliban were today and for a moment I almost found it hard to believe that I was no longer playing, that the enemy were now dangerously real. The Taliban were a strangely intangible enemy. Seven years after the Army had gone into Afghanistan, we knew them only a little. Who were the men who'd been busy here with their shovels and homemade bombs?

A short while later Magoo returned clutching a battered old copper pot.

'What's that you've found?' I asked.

'It's the Taliban's kettle,' he replied, grinning broadly. 'I've pinched it. We need something to brew up in. Besides if we can't shoot 'em, we might as well nick their stuff.'

Magoo went on to explain that they'd followed the wires all the way back but found they ended abruptly, attached to nothing, bare copper poking out of the rubber coating. Mason, who had moved up from the back, scratched his chin thoughtfully. 'I've seen this kind of thing in Sangin,' he said. 'They need to be connected up to batteries to work. Without power those pressure plates won't do fuck all.' It made sense – that was how yesterday's patrol had been able to walk right over them without setting them off.

A sudden buzzing in my trouser pocket startled me. It was my mobile phone, an essential bit of kit in the OMLT. The ANA often preferred them over radios even though British security protocol demanded otherwise. I answered the phone to an angry Afghan voice – Col Wadood. Wordlessly I passed the handset straight to Ash. Wadood wanted to know what we were doing sitting on our arses next to a pile of IEDs. 'Get them blown up and move on,' he ordered. Clearly my ANA counterpart had been talking to Wadood while I had been on the net to the British ops room. I explained that I was under orders from Harry to sit tight until ATO arrived to defuse the devices and hopefully gather some much-needed intelligence about the Taliban's bomb-making capabilities. So began a heated back and forth between Harry and Wadood with me stuck in the middle, along with an increasingly irate ANA sergeant who was getting more and more frustrated about the delay.

To be fair to the Afghans, Mason was pushing just as hard to blow up the IEDs and get moving. 'We're asking for trouble, sir,' he said. I saw their point but with a direct order from Harry my hands were tied.

As the debate raged on, Ram shouted over to alert us that a column of battered old cars was moving fast up the track from the direction of Nad Ali. As they came closer I could make out an ANP badge painted on the bonnet of the lead vehicle. I assumed they were from the police garrison based in the south of the DC. The ANA must have told them about the IEDs, I thought, and called them for assistance. As they approached, however, they showed no sign of slowing down.

The ANA sergeant stepped up out of the ditch and stood in the middle of the track holding up his hand until, with just feet to spare, the lead vehicle skidded to a halt. Other ANA soldiers swiftly surrounded the car and an animated conversation began. It started out as a belligerent exchange but quickly escalated as shouts erupted on both sides.

'What's going on?' I asked Ash.

He shrugged. 'The police want the soldiers to move out of the way and let them past. Important police business, they're saying.'

I recalled the stand-off in Gereshk with Major Haider of the NDS and with Haji Tor Jan's guards in Marjah; it seemed that every time two Afghan agencies met one another, trouble followed quickly behind. Here at the crossroads things were getting increasingly tense. Suddenly half the ANA guys raised their rifles, pointing them at the lead police car. The driver reacted instantly. Gunning the engine, he accelerated forward down the track, running straight over the IEDs. Anticipating an explosion the soldiers in front threw themselves sideways, narrowly avoiding being run over. Within seconds the other two vehicles in the convoy followed suit and they disappeared into a cloud of dust, heading for Luy Bagh. It turns out they were skipping town. After the violence of the last few days, the police had apparently lost their nerve. Perhaps they thought that with our patrol out on the ground, the road would be more secure and figured they'd make a break for it, leaving us to deal with the Taliban.

Off in the distance, we heard heavy small arms fire opening up. The ANP had been wrong; the road was not secure and now they were paying the price. The soldiers exchanged glances and smiled. So their so-called allies had cut and run? The Taliban were rewarding their cowardice with interest – it was no more than they deserved. But I found it hard to share in the ANA's mirth. All it meant to me was that there were fewer people on our side in Nad Ali, no matter how unreliable they might have been.

I wasn't the only one who wished the police hadn't left. My next phone call was from Harry. 'Why the hell did you let them go?' he shouted.

'What would you have me do?' I said. 'Open up on the Afghan police with a GMPG?'

'Don't you ...'

'Sorry, Harry, gotta go.' I hung up as more police cars careered towards us, going the same way as their colleagues a few minutes earlier. They blasted straight past us. Two minutes later, a fresh barrage of gunfire erupted down the road. I imagined bullet-riddled vehicles tipping sideways off the track and the Taliban pulling shattered corpses out of the cabs. Who knows? Maybe they made it through. Good luck to them. I never did find out what happened. All I knew was that Nad Ali no longer had a police force. From here on in, it was all on us.

We'd now been stuck at this crossroads for nearly seven hours and there was still no sign of ATO. The ops room didn't know when they might materialise. The ANA sergeant had had enough and persuaded his platoon commander to order the troops back to the patrol base. The platoon commander was no doubt dreading the roasting that awaited him from Col Wadood. If he had any sense, he'd blame it all on me. Now, unless I wanted to stay out here with just my OMLT for company, I had no choice but to follow the Afghans home.

We patrolled north up the track with the ANA, back towards the base, strung out over two hundred metres in staggered file formation, two staggered lines of troops, one on either side of the track. We struggled forward under the weight of our kit. It was hard work; everyone was hot and exhausted from hours in the relentless sun. My body armour had begun to chafe and every step was uncomfortable.

My thoughts were rudely interrupted by a sharp crack over-head. It's hard to describe what it's like when you realise someone is actually trying to kill you. I had never been shot at before but knew the sound a bullet makes. I reacted instantly, bringing my rifle up and squeezing off two rounds in what I thought was the right direction before hitting the floor and rolling sideways into the cover of the ditch.

Pandemonium was breaking loose as hundreds of rounds whipped past, biting into the track between the two irrigation ditches. Colour Mason was yelling at the men, making sure everyone was facing in the right direction and shooting back. It wasn't clear straight away where the rounds were coming from or how many men were attacking us. I took a deep breath and pushed down on the pressel switch to operate the radio. 'Contact.

Wait out.' Three words I'd been aching to say for my entire career.

The adrenaline was pumping freely and as the bullets flew, I felt the rising exhilaration I'd always dreamed of. I was in command here and now it was my time to marshal my forces and take the fight to the enemy.

I was in the ditch on the eastern side of the track. It was a deep, wide channel, with gently sloping banks. I had slipped down into the water up to my thighs. No one could see the enemy but it had become clear they were somewhere off to the south, possibly only 100 metres away, using the trees at the edge of the orchard as cover. Half the ANA men had reached the fork in the track that led back to the patrol base and had already turned the corner onto a tree-lined path that hid them from view. I was several hundred metres from the platoon commander and his sergeant, so trying to direct their troops into an offensive formation was proving hard work.

Over on the other side of the track I saw Mason's head pop up out of the ditch even as bullets pinged all around. He craned to get a look at the enemy. A few inches above his helmet, a green tree branch swayed gently in the breeze. I watched as a bullet narrowly missed hitting Mason, hitting the branch instead. It jerked upwards and drooped ever so slowly into Mason's face. He blanched and disappeared rapidly back into cover, like a rabbit darting into its warren.

I made a call. That was enough. There was going to be no glorious counter-attack today. Our position was weak. Better to bug out now and save the killing for next time when the odds might come stacked in our favour. I ordered a fighting with-drawal. Over the PRR I ordered Mason to move the men in his ditch first. 'We'll cover you,' I told him.

They moved straight away, legging it up their ditch, while we provided covering fire. Then after they'd made some ground, they'd stop, turn round and cover us while we splashed our way through the water. It was straight out of the training manual; 'pepper-potting' they call it. I experienced an odd sense of pride as my OMLT played out this textbook manoeuvre, pleased that in this, my very first contact, I wasn't fucking up. Even so it felt a little like running away.

Once we'd turned off the track, a thick treeline covered us from the enemy and the incoming fire stopped. There was still another 400 metres to go until we reached the safety of the base and now we had to worry about where they might hit us next. While we'd been extracting north, the Taliban could have sent men around our flank to launch an ambush. Speed was our best ally now and we swept on as quickly as we could. We kept watchful eyes on the fields to either side of the path, ready to put down a withering barrage should anyone stir among the corn.

We made it back to the patrol base without further interference from the Taliban. As soon as we were through the gate, men dropped to their knees, exhausted. I called everyone round for a quick debrief, only to find the ANA platoon commander had already slipped away and his soldiers were following his lead. The OMLT listened patiently as I went over what I thought we'd done right and done wrong. There were always lessons to be learnt and thoughts to be heard. It was an important chance for me to hear what the blokes had to say on the day's work. A short conversation and two litres of water later I moved off to the ops room to make my report.

Harry's mood had not improved since our conversation on the net. 'Why did you let the ANP leave?' he shouted. I assumed the question was rhetorical as he didn't pause to allow me to answer. It seemed that everything we'd done that day had angered him – the ANA wanting to remove the IEDs themselves, leaving before the ATO had arrived, failing to launch a counter-attack when we came under fire. I let it all wash over me. Harry could say whatever he liked today and I wouldn't care. Today, my war had finally begun.

CHAPTER EIGHTEEN

Day three in Nad Ali and we were under attack again. It was the morning after our first contact and we had headed straight back towards Luy Bagh on patrol, leaving the base at 0600hrs. We reached a T-junction and the lead ANA soldiers pushed forward into the field beyond. I followed with the OMLT and as we filed across the road bullets began to dance around our feet. The enemy had been watching. They'd held off until they saw British uniforms. Afghan scalps were ten-a-penny, but kill enough of us and we'll lose our appetite for fighting and go home.

I span to my right and got off a couple of rounds. Ram and Magoo did the same. The three of us went backwards into the cover of yet another irrigation channel. This ditch had shallow sloping sides which enabled me to lie comfortably and raise my head into the danger zone for a quick look around without having to crawl forward. The water was just a trickle so even if we did end up running the length of the ditch we'd manage to stay dry.

The ANA men behind and ahead of us had managed to swiftly organise themselves and were putting down a heavy weight of fire. There was shouting on all sides as men tried to locate the enemy. We knew that they were off to the south, probably about 200 metres distant, in a couple of buildings close to the spot where we'd been attacked the day before.

As we focused our fire, so the number of rounds coming our

138

way began to lessen. We were winning. Now it was time to press home our advantage. Beattie had taken the rocket launcher from my pack and was aiming it down towards the enemy position. He pressed the trigger and the air around him split in a cataclysmic boom. I lifted my head to see the missile streak down the track, keeping only a few feet above the ground until, a second later, it slammed into the compound wall. A cloud of dust hid the building from view.

Once the air had cleared, we were able to see the havoc our missile had wreaked but, other than a neat hole in the compound wall, it didn't seem to have done anything at all. The enemy continued to fire at the same steady rate, unaffected by our delivery of ordnance. I hoped they were at least scared. If we couldn't kill our enemies then at least we might be able to make them think twice before tangling with us in the future.

Actually, I suspect that the only casualty that rocket launcher inflicted was on our own side. Stan crouched in the grass, dazed and unfocused. A thin trickle of blood ran from each ear, snaking down towards his jaw. He'd been right next to Beattie when the rocket had fired and the roar of the weapon had blown out both his eardrums. The pain must have been excruciating but to his credit he picked up his rifle and got on with things. He was completely deaf from this point on and we relied on sign language to communicate to him for the remainder of the patrol. This was to be the end of the war for Stan. Once we returned to the patrol base he would be straight on a chopper back to Lash before heading back to Britain to recuperate. I understand he recovered his hearing a few months later and subsequently left the Army to open the pub he'd always talked about.

Having managed to wrest the initiative back from our enemy, I was keen to push forward and assault their position. Our training encouraged us to favour aggressive action wherever possible and I began to work out how best to deploy my troops. I was worried that the enemy might try to flank us so I detailed eight ANA men to cover the ground to our left and right. With fields of thick corn on either side, however, it would be difficult for them to spot Taliban moving towards us.

As I wrestled with the tactical situation, I was interrupted by a far-off growl that signified the arrival of a helicopter in the sky above us. There's more than one way to skin a cat when you've got an Apache looking after you and I happily put off thoughts of a ground assault. I listened over the net to Phil, our JTAC in the ops room, coolly instructing the pilot where he might direct his cannon. I waited eagerly for the weapons to open up but, as I followed the conversation back and forth, it became apparent that the pilot wasn't going to oblige. He couldn't identify exactly where the enemy was and was thus unwilling to engage. All right for him to say, a couple of hundred feet in the air, in an air-conditioned cabin with no bullets winging his way.

All was not lost, however. I looked up to see the tiny black outline of an F-15 tracking across the sky.

Models of the F-15 have been in service with the US Air Force since the 1970s but even after three decades it remains a fearsome weapon of war. An F-15 can fly at over twice the speed of sound and they have a range of some 2,000 kilometres. Most important, though, were the munitions they carried. Each plane can carry up to 24,000 pounds worth of high-explosive bombs. An individual bomb could be as big as 2,000 pounds and is guided to its target by a sophisticated system known as a Joint Direct Attack Munition. We called them JDAMs and I hoped that I might get to see one of them in action now.

Over the net, I asked Phil to see if the newcomer might consider helping us out. The answer came back at once: 'We'll bomb the compound but only with direct authorisation from the commander on the ground.' Shit. That was me. Suddenly, with all the responsibility resting on my shoulders, I felt more sympathy for the Apache pilot who'd turned down our earlier request. Destroying the compound up ahead was now my choice alone. If there were civilians inside, their deaths would be on my hands.

I looked down the track towards the target, squinting through my rifle sights for a clearer view. I couldn't see our assailants but the earth in front of the ditch continued to explode in tiny puffs as the incoming fire continued. I'd seen no civilians anywhere these past two days but maybe they were battened down, hiding from the fighting in the very building I wanted to destroy. Perhaps the Taliban had forced their way in at gunpoint and even now a family cowered on the floor of their home.

I needed to make a decision. I could sit here for the next two hours, letting my imagination run amok while the enemy pushed up past our flank and prepared to end us all.

'Go ahead. Confirm compound as the target. Commander's ZAP number – EV1650.'

Now I was on the record. If I'd made a mistake, the buck really did stop with me. I pushed such thoughts from my mind and waited for the pilot to make good on his promise.

The plane circled round behind us and began its run in towards the target. Just a few seconds and it was directly over the compound. We lay there rapt, straining to catch a glimpse of the bomb as it fell. In fact we couldn't see it at all but heard the whistle. When it hit, the whole building was lost in a cloud that dwarfed our previous effort with the rocket launcher. It looked like a small nuclear explosion.

I shouted with delight. All around me the men were cheering too. It was exhilarating to see something so big blow up, but that wasn't what made us yell. Partly it was relief; we weren't being shot at anymore. But really we were celebrating. The bastards had tried to kill us. Instead we'd killed them. Good fucking rid-dance. Now was not a time for moral reflection. We'd been in a fight and come out on top. It felt wonderful.

Our euphoria didn't last for long. As we crawled our way out of the ditch, more bullets began to land around us. As I'd feared, the enemy had sent men creeping past us during the fight and now engaged us from our eastern flank. This time though, the Apache could see them, crawling through the crops with their guns. No problem with the rules of engagement here and the pilot made up for his previous caution, hovering low, emptying his cannon into the wheat.

The enemy were quickly finished. Those that were left alive in the field made good their escape and the battle was over. While Mason checked that everyone had made it through unscathed, I was back on the radio, letting Harry know that we'd dealt with the situation and now planned to return to the schoolhouse.

'Before you come back,' Harry said. 'Confirm enemy casualty numbers.'

'The Apache has reported that all enemy retreated with their casualties to the east,' I replied. 'And the building has been completely destroyed.'

'Advance forward to the building and check the rubble for casualties,' Harry went on.

'But we don't know what depth positions the enemy has. Our air support won't be able to cover us for the time it will take to get down there.'

'We must have an accurate casualty report on the enemy,' Harry insisted. 'Continue as instructed. Out.'

The conversation was at an end and I was left with no choice but to carry out Harry's order. It seemed ridiculous. Why risk our men's lives to sift through rubble looking for dead Taliban? What difference did it make if we'd killed two, five, ten or even fifty? We didn't know their strength anyway so our figures would add little to the intelligence picture.

Then it struck me. This was about the bomb. Brigade had recently issued very specific instructions that prohibited the destruction of buildings except in the most extreme circumstances. It was hearts and minds stuff – very difficult to win the support of the local population when you went around blowing their houses up.

Ordinarily I agreed with the Brigade's policy, but things look very different when bullets are whipping at you from a nearby rooftop. I thought again about giving my ZAP number in confirmation over the net and a shiver ran through me. Oh well. Nothing to be done about it now. Let's see how many bad guys we'd killed – perhaps a big body count might mollify my masters.

I called over Magoo and Beattie and rounded up an ANA section, leaving Mason with the Afghan platoon commander to look after the remainder. We headed down towards the ruined building, keeping off the track and pushing our way through the tangled undergrowth on the edge of the fields. If there were enemy depth positions, it seemed as well to keep ourselves hidden. While we'd been fighting, adrenaline had been pumping hard but now the immediate danger was gone I began to feel the after-effects. My legs and arms were leaden and the straps of my pack cut deep into my shoulders. It was approaching noon and the sun seared our skin and boiled our skulls in their helmets. I could see the others were struggling too. We had better get this done fast before we deteriorated much further.

We made our way to a small compound just 30 metres from the bomb site, separated from it by a patch of open ground. The rest of the patrol were now too far away for our PRR network to function and I was worried that they might mistake our movement for that of the enemy and open fire on us in error. I'd told them that we would cover our movement onto the target with smoke and I hoped that they'd see that as a signal not to fire. I also hoped that the smoke would cover us from the enemy as we crossed the open ground.

Magoo and Beattie were the ones who actually had to make the dash from cover and investigate the rubble. They looked distinctly unhappy. It was a simple task and it shouldn't take more than a few minutes but while they were doing it they would be cruelly exposed. If the enemy were watching, this could all go very wrong, very quickly.

'Good luck,' I said.

Beattie nodded silently but the unspoken reply, 'Sod off,' was written all over his face. The three of us pulled the pins from our smoke grenades and launched them out into the open ground. Green smoke ballooned into the air, creating a woefully inadequate screen. It looked like a scene from a Christmas pantomime; I half expected a fat genie in a loincloth and curly shoes to emerge from a trapdoor. Magoo and Beattie looked at one another and burst out laughing. The sudden absurdity acted as a valve, releasing the pressure that had been building.

Then they were gone, heads down and sprinting towards the bombsite. I tensed and waited for a hail of bullets to cut through the smoke. None came. The Taliban really had gone, I thought. If not they'd surely have fired blindly at the green haze on the off chance of hitting someone.

Five minutes later, Magoo and Beattie returned looking extremely relieved to be back in cover. Magoo shook his head. 'Nothing there,' he panted.

'No bodies at all?' I asked.

'It's a pile of rubble. There could very well be people trapped underneath but we're not going to spend hours digging through it, are we?'

'No. We've done what we were asked to do. Now let's get out of here.'

I gave Harry the bad news over the radio and reluctantly he agreed there was nothing more to be done. We headed back up the road and rejoined the rest of the patrol.

A few hundred metres short of the patrol base, half a dozen shots were fired somewhere off on our right flank. Hitting the dirt, I looked up and saw Griff dithering beside me. He looked exhausted, staring blearily around, unable to react to this new threat. I reached up and grabbed hold of his belt, dragging him to the floor. 'Wake up!' I yelled. Griff pulled himself together and crawled to the edge of the road. He was young and, despite his training, hadn't adjusted to the rigours of combat. He'd get there but right now, so close to the base, he'd let himself switch off. Mason took over, berating the youngster for his sloppy drills. It was kindly meant – a wandering attention could get a man killed out here.

The attack didn't last long, a quick 'shoot and scoot' and we hadn't had time to get off more than a few rounds in reply. Maybe they'd tracked us back here but it was just as likely that a roving group of fighters had happened upon us and taken an opportunistic pop before running off.

Back at the schoolhouse, the men flopped to the ground, utterly spent. I kept the debrief short – a few minor points for the ANA guys, picking up on some of their individual drills. All in all, I thought they'd done well. We'd achieved what we set out to do – find the Taliban and shoot them. And drop a bomb on them as well, let's not forget. I made my way to see Harry and face the fallout.

When I walked into the ops room, I half-expected a frenzy of blame and recrimination but instead all appeared calm. Harry was bustling about, making plans for more patrols while Woody sat in the corner talking to Phil, the JTAC who'd arrived by helicopter the first night. During the contact it had been Phil who'd been talking to the Apache and then the F-15 pilot, telling them exactly where we needed them to drop their ordnance. Sitting here now, puffing on a cigarette and chatting to Woody, he was a picture of relaxation. He had a corner of the ops room all to himself, set up with a bank of screens, radios and complex-looking consoles. He was ensconced in front of all the kit in a fold-up fabric chair, the kind you'd take along on a fishing trip. It looked more like the bedroom of a computer-obsessed teenage geek than the nerve centre of a military operation.

Woody glanced over at me as I approached and smiled. 'Hello mate. Interesting time out there today?'

'You're not kidding,' I replied.

'Made a bit of a mess of that compound.'

I tensed as I readied myself for the questions to come. 'Have Brigade been on to us about that yet?'

'Funny you should ask,' said Woody. 'Harry was on the net for some time. They didn't seem too happy.'

'I knew this was going to cause problems.'

'Well, Harry's explanation didn't quite cut it with the Brigade Ops Officer. If you listened to Brigade you'd think that there weren't any Taliban on the ground at all. Anyway, the next thing we knew, the Brigade Commander himself got on the net.'

This was worse than I'd imagined. I'd be lucky to keep my job at this rate.

'Yeah, he was pretty pissed off,' Woody went on. 'Asking who was responsible. He really went off the deep end.'

I was screwed. We'd taken no casualties. I couldn't prove that there had been enemy in the compound and, while civilian deaths looked like a remote possibility, there was no way to tell for sure. The Brigade Commander was going to make an example of me.

My misery must have been apparent to the others as Woody began to laugh. 'Yeah, it was looking pretty bleak,' he said. 'But then Phil here piped up on the net. "Hello Brigadier Mark," he says. "I was the one who called in the JDAM." Then the Brigade Commander is like, "Is that you, Phil? Oh I'm sorry, I didn't realise. Thought some clown had just got a bit trigger happy. You know what you're doing though." Then the two of them have a bit of a chinwag for a couple of minutes and off the Brigadier goes, happy as Larry.'

I couldn't quite take this in. Phil was a nice guy and a really slick operator when it came to calling in the air, but how come he was suddenly pals with senior officers and possessed with such influence as to be able to pull my sorry arse out of the fire?

I turned to Phil. He shrugged. 'Oh me and the Brigadier go

way back,' he said. 'He was my squadron commander years ago. And then of course he turned up later as the CO.'

'CO? Carleton-Smith's only been CO of one regiment hasn't he? And that's the SAS.'

'That's right,' said Phil and he reached for his cigarettes and lit up another one.

It suddenly all made sense. He was so self-assured, so competent and entirely unperturbed by the whole situation here in Nad Ali. Well, Christ. If the Brigade had sent an SAS man to look after us, then maybe they weren't quite as blind to our plight as I'd thought.

'So do you want to look at what happened today?' asked Phil. 'Eh?'

'We record it all you know. I had a drone up there above you for the whole patrol.'

Phil clicked a few buttons on his console and the screens in front of him flickered into life. On the screen we looked down at a fuzzy green and white image of the scene at the crossroads. The whole contact then played out in front of me, Phil fast-forwarding through the slow parts, until we reached the point where the F-15 dropped the JDAM. A flash of white expanded to fill the screen and then we lost the picture completely for a second or two. I heard Woody chuckling next to me. I stayed silent, detached from the whole scene. It was difficult to relate this footage to the raw elation I'd felt a few hours before on the ground.

I tried to imagine what it must have been like for the men in the compound, if there had been any there after all. Did they look up when they heard the whoosh of the jet passing overhead? Had they seen the bomb tumbling out of the sky? For a brief second did they stare at death as it rushed towards them? I put the thought out of my mind. My conscience was clear, I told myself. I had to. Tomorrow I'd be back out there again.

By the time I made it back to the accommodation, the men

had already sorted out all their administration and were variously sprawled on their beds, reading or clustered around Beattie's laptop. Magoo looked up as I came in. 'All right, sir,' he said. 'You've got to look at this. Ash had a camera out with him today and he filmed the entire contact. We've downloaded it to the laptop.' Here was the on-the-ground version of the film I'd just watched in the ops room. While Phil's images had been silent and clinical, Ash's were full of the intensity that had been present in the fight. I heard my own voice shouting orders and then roaring in fierce joy when we dropped the building. I turned to Magoo to share in the moment but he'd already wandered off. He'd seen the film before. It was always this way after a patrol. We'd come back and I'd head off to see Harry and Wadood, while the boys sat round and chewed the fat. I missed out on all the 'Did you sees?' and 'Can you believes?' By the time I caught up, everyone had moved on and were focused on other things. I felt oddly cheated by this, frustrated that I didn't get to unwind and get it all out of my system. Then again, these men weren't my mates – they worked for me and risked their lives at my command. I had no right to call on them for the emotional support one might expect from a friend.

I closed the laptop before the film ended. That was enough for today. I went outside and lit up a cigarette. This was war, huh? Everything I'd ever wanted.

CHAPTER NINETEEN

May 2009

'*Wellington Barracks, please.*'

As soon as the cabbie heard the destination, he was interested. Wellington Barracks is the home of the Coldstream Guards in London. It's next to Buckingham Palace. I was visiting as part of my new role organising expeditions for wounded soldiers. 'So, are you serving?' he asked.

'*Uh, yeah.*'

'*Right, right. That's great. So you been away anywhere?*'

'*Just got back from Afghanistan.*'

'*Jesus. Well done, mate. It sounds pretty bad over there. Take my hat off to you.*'

The conversation was proceeding down the same worn path I'd walked dozens of times over the past months with shopkeepers, bartenders and now cab drivers. Since I'd deployed there'd been a sea change in the public's opinion of the military. Before I'd gone, wearing uniform in public generally solicited no reaction at all, and occasionally even provoked anger and abuse. I'd been refused entry to bars just because the bouncer had suspected what it was that I did for a living. Now it seemed everyone wanted to be a soldier's friend.

I think a lot of it was down to Help for Heroes. A year before, it had been a little-known charity, set up to raise funds to build a new swimming pool at Headley Court, the MoD's rehabilitation centre for injured servicemen and women. Over the intervening months the charity, backed by the Sun, had grown enormously, becoming the fashionable cause of the day. Every second person seemed to be sporting one of their distinctive red and blue wristbands, showing their support for 'Our Boys' (and Girls). Of course they didn't believe in the war. 'Didn't agree with it myself,' said the cabbie. 'Should never 'ave gone in. Blair's a wanker and the new bloke's no better. Dunno what we're doing over there.' And then came the all-important caveat. 'Think you boys are doing an amazing job though. Got to support the troops even if I don't like the war.'

And there it was, the doublethink that had swept the nation. What did that statement mean? I'd heard it so many times.

'Why?' I said to the cabbie.

'Huh? Why what?'

'Why do you have to support the troops? We're fighting a war you don't like. No one made me do it. I went to Afghanistan because I wanted to.'

'Yeah, but you get ordered to fight there. Not up to you boys whether the war happens or not.'

I slumped down further in the seat. In the rear-view mirror I saw the cabbie looking baffled. He clearly thought I had a screw loose. He had offered me his support and now he thought I was saying I didn't want it. I was glad for every penny that had been raised to help injured soldiers but even though I was one of them I didn't feel like I deserved it.

There was no point having this argument. The cabbie was just trying to help. He didn't know what was going on in my mind.

We came to a stop. 'That's Wellington Barracks,' said the cabbie.

I got out and handed a ten pound note through the window.

'I dunno what you were talking about there, mate, but I meant what I said. You're doing a great job. Forget about the fare.'

I protested but he was having none of it and I was left standing in the street, clutching my money.

CHAPTER TWENTY

Over the next few days we carried on with our patrols, usually one in the morning as the sun came up and another around 1800hrs. As we'd planned, the second patrol was limited to the perimeter of the schoolhouse – ensuring our conscience was clear when we reported to Brigade that the kandak had carried out two patrols each day. The length of the morning patrols depended on the task at hand, be it reconnaissance, clearing IEDs, or an advance to contact, dubbed by Sgt Magoo, 'Going for a walk until we get shot at.' They could take anywhere between two and twelve hours, but as a rule we tried to get back before 1000hrs when it started to get really hot. The longer we stayed out, the greater toll it took on us all. We needed everyone to stay as physically fit as possible. If the helicopter resupplies were interrupted we would swiftly start to run out of food and water and be forced to move on to rationing. Under such circumstances our physical abilities would deteriorate rapidly. It was paramount that we husbanded our strength just in case.

The single most important factor that determined how long we spent on the ground was the Taliban. They attacked us almost every time we went out but we never knew what shape these attacks would take. Sometimes they'd fire a few shots and leg it, disappearing into the fields as quickly as they'd emerged. On other occasions they'd want to stay and duke it out. I couldn't help admiring them when they did this. Our firepower far outstripped theirs – not in terms of the weapons we carried on the ground, where we were more or less evenly matched, but rather the awesome fury we could unleash from the sky. To this, they had no response.

Every patrol we conducted, we now had something up above. Normally it would be an Apache but sometimes an RAF Tornado or an American F-15 would be kicking around, looking for some action.

I couldn't speak to the pilots directly – that was Phil's job – but I'd heard him at work in the ops room while other patrols had been on the ground. As soon as you heard the pilot over the radio it was obvious what air force Phil was dealing with. The RAF were entirely professional, going under sensible call signs like 'Blue 32' or 'Tango 19' and their delivery was straight out of a World War Two film.

'Roger,' they'd say in clipped, nasal tones. 'We have acquired your target. Three bravos on the edge of the cornfield 1,000 metres due north of your position.' Pause. 'Firing now.' Pause. Explosion. 'Target neutralised. Blue 32, out.'

And they'd be gone. Enemy killed, job done.

The Americans, on the other hand, had a strong flair for the dramatic. You'd get on the net to request some assistance and find some good ol' boy from Texas looking down on you, itching for a fight.

'Why hello there,' he'd drawl. 'You're talkin' to Thor.' They went under the most extraordinary monikers – Boss, Shooter and Rattlesnake were among my favourites. 'How y'all doin' today? What can Uncle Sam do to help out?'

'There's a unit under sustained effective fire from the farmhouse, one kilometre west of our position. Co-ordinates: 6478, 1325.'

'Uh huh. You betcha. Them boys ain't gonna know what's hit 'em. We got ya backs, fellas.'

The jet would roar overhead and right before the bomb dropped you'd hear a long, drawn-out, 'Yeeeee-haaaaaa,' 'Hell yeah,' or some other whoop of joy from a man who was having a good day doing something he loved. The bomb would plummet downwards and the target would simply disappear, engulfed in a gigantic cloud of dust and flame. On the ground we'd all get caught up in the moment and our delighted shouts would mirror those of the pilot. 'Fucking yes! Take some of that you fuckers!' It was only later, back at the schoolhouse, that I'd find myself dwelling on the carnage, imagining what it would have been like for the men on the receiving end of the ordnance. I liked to think they'd have known very little about it. When the JDAMs hit a mud-brick building, or a bunch of guys in a field, there was never much left to clean up.

When it went well, that was how it went down. All too often, though, we couldn't identify the Taliban position, or the pilots would spot potential civilians nearby and demure from pressing the button. When that happened, we'd be left trying to win the firefight on our own, slogging it out for hours until we pushed them back, or retreated ourselves.

Phil was probably the single most important person we had in Nad Ali, even though he never left the base. His uncanny ability to direct aircraft onto their targets was frequently the difference between life and death for those of us on patrol. On top of this Phil could seek out the Taliban when we had no troops on the ground at all. He could control all manner of drones from his corner of the ops room. They flew all over the surrounding area, often so high in the air that the enemy wouldn't even know they were being spied on. Over the coming weeks Phil would be responsible for killing more Taliban fighters than the rest of us put together. He maintained the quietest, friendliest demeanour you could imagine, drinking endless cups of tea and smoking his cigarettes while dealing death from above at the touch of a button. It was a little unnerving to think about and more than a little sinister. Well, he was in the SAS after all.

I suppose that the OMLT was lucky in those first few days. We miraculously took no casualties despite a string of fierce, drawn-out firefights. The Jocks weren't so fortunate though: two of them were shot while on patrol. They were evacuated out on a MERT. Both survived but it put the rest of us under even more pressure. There were now only fifty-three British soldiers left in Nad Ali.

Our daily routine was structured around twice-daily patrols. Reveille was at 0500hrs, around half an hour before first light and a mere four hours after we'd gone to sleep. The Jocks would all stand to, taking up defensive positions on the perimeter wall, watching for a Taliban dawn attack. They never tried this but it was a real threat and British Army doctrine dictated that this is what we should do. The same procedure was carried out at sunset as well. In between times the Jocks had to provide sentries in the sangars – a tedious, energy sapping jobs, but vital to our security. On top of this they were conducting their own patrols, there was almost no time for them to recuperate. While we were getting ready for the morning patrol – sorting kit out, going over orders and trying to make sure the ANA knew what they were doing – the Afghans would take a few minutes to pray, setting out their prayer mats to face southwest towards Mecca. None of them talked much about religion but in this one aspect they seemed particularly pious, praying five times a day, unless patrols or enemy action intervened.

Once we got back from our patrols, the OMLT would sort out their kit and do any jobs that CSgt Mason required of them, such as organising the stores or maintaining the generators. I would head to the ops room for a debrief with Harry and then move on to Wadood's office to do the same with him. The sessions with Wadood were usually shorter as he'd already heard it all from his own platoon commanders.

From lunchtime onwards the blokes would try and rest, sleeping or sitting around drinking brews or playing on their laptops. My own contribution to morale was the iPod that I'd brought with me from home. When I'd arrived back from R&R

in Lash, I'd given it to one of the other officers while I was being briefed about Nad Ali, and he'd taken the opportunity to upload his entire music collection. Unbeknown to me at the time he had also added an eclectic selection of adult films to the device – quite against regulations, which prohibited soldiers from bringing such material into theatre – and it was now the only source of porn in camp. Word swiftly went around and the iPod, in its distinctive red case, frequently went missing as someone took it away for a few minutes alone-time.

During the afternoons I had reports to write and plans to make for our next patrol. There would still be a couple of empty hours to fill though, which I'd usually spend chatting with the other officers, Woody or DB, although they were frequently engaged in the organisation or conduct of their own patrols. In that case, I often found myself talking to the senior company medic in the ops room or the small improvised medical centre next door.

Other than Gee, there were four medics in Nad Ali, three of whom were women. Sgt Taylor, or Chantelle as the soldiers often called her, was in charge. She was a pretty, blonde woman, about thirty years old. I thought it must be hard for her, operating in such a masculine environment, but she was tough as nails and an exceptionally competent soldier. She held the distinction of being the first woman to have killed an enemy fighter in Afghanistan, a feat she had achieved a few weeks before coming to Nad Ali while out on vehicle patrol with the company somewhere near Marjah. Woody had told me the story. Sgt Taylor had been acting as top cover when the patrol got ambushed. She saw one of the enemy fighters standing up, firing at her vehicle. Reacting immediately, she'd returned fire and put rounds into him until he dropped. Like I say, tough as nails. I'm not sure she liked me at first, probably thinking me a stuck-up Guards officer, but I think I won her round eventually. Although she was a soldier, she was outside my chain of command, so I felt able to relax with her more than I could with the OMLT.

Before I arrived, the Jocks had discovered a litter of kittens that had somehow made their way into the base. Straight away these were adopted as pets and de facto base mascots. Harry initially took a dim view of this, citing the risk of disease that the tiny creatures might pose. Even he soon crumbled, however, in the face of the kittens' overwhelming cuteness and the cats were frequently to be seen curled up in a corner of the ops room. Sgt Taylor took responsibility for one of them, feeding it and allowing it to sleep on her bed. It was christened 'Ali Cat'. This was a joke that worked on a number of levels. Obviously we were in Nad *Ali* and there was the play on words with alley cat, but in the military there was a third meaning too. It comes from the slang phrase 'alley' that is used mostly in the Parachute Regiment to describe something that is cool or particularly warlike. Anyway, we all found this hilarious. There wasn't much to do in Nad Ali so we had to find our laughs where we could.

A couple of the soldiers had rigged up an improvised shower outside the OMLT accommodation. It was a simple affair, consisting of a rubber bladder, with a tube attachment, hung from a wooden pole that was driven into the ground. A poncho was draped over the top to provide some privacy. We filled the bladder from a water bowser that was replaced every week by one of the helicopter resupplies. Just leaving the bladder hanging in the sun for a few minutes was enough to make the water piping hot.

These comforts raised the quality of life on base a little above hellish but it was still hard living. Flies infested the entire place. Fat, dirty, bluebottle types that buzzed constantly and crawled over your skin as soon as you sat down.

In one corner of the base were a couple of long-drop latrines – pits into which we would shit. Visiting the latrines after dark made things even worse as your sense of smell was heightened and the hot stench would fill your nostrils and make you retch. They were originally intended for use by just a few dozen schoolchildren, so with over a hundred men in camp, these fetid holes soon filled up and we would have to burn the waste, which sent clouds of foul-smelling smoke billowing into the air.

Five days after I arrived we'd just returned from our morning patrol when a single shot rang out from the west. The sentry manning the .50cal on the roof of the schoolhouse answered with a burst of fire and all went quiet. We didn't know from precisely where the shot had been fired but clearly the machine-gunner had done enough to make the shooter think twice about sticking around for another effort.

For a few minutes we all waited nervously for a follow-up. None came. Ram decided that it would be safe enough to take a shower. He disappeared beneath the poncho but instantly re-emerged and ran straight to the ops room with just a towel wrapped around him.

'Sniper!' he panted. 'Bullet . . . shower.'

He paused and pulled himself together. 'That shot we heard – it's gone straight through the shower.'

Harry and I went to investigate and sure enough, right at head height, was a neat hole straight through the middle of the wooden pole, almost snapping it in two. A brief search of the camp turned up the offending bullet embedded in the front seat of one of the WMIKs. Mason took a closer look at it. '7.62,' he said. 'Looks like a Dragunov round.' A Dragunov is a kind of sniper rifle produced by the Soviets. It's an old weapon but a deadly one that in the hands of a skilled marksman can accurately hit a target over 800 metres distant. The implication was clear. The enemy could shoot directly into our base from a long way away.

Suddenly any sense of security was shattered. We'd thought that within the perimeter walls we were safe. It hadn't been much of a home but it was all we'd had. Now the Taliban had penetrated it, physically and psychologically. The base had effec-tively become an extension of the battlefield. From here on we would be looking over our shoulders every waking hour.

No unnecessary movement around camp was allowed. Whereas previously we had made use of the courtyard to cook, wash and smoke we now found ourselves stewing in sweltering rooms. Living at such close quarters, conversation soon dried up. Tension built and tempers flared. Within days it got to the stage where we were thankful to go out on patrol. What difference did it make when the Taliban were everywhere?

Another new rule came into effect: all personnel must wear helmet and body armour whenever they were outside their own accommodation. This had an immediate impact on morale. Our body armour was punishingly heavy. You started sweating as soon you put it on. Just moving around camp became a physical hardship in itself. Little wonder then that the ANA troops chose to ignore this directive. I tried to bring the issue up with Wadood, but he brushed off my concerns.

'They are used to danger,' he said dismissively, turning away to pour more tea.

Meanwhile conditions inside the crowded accommodation quarters became increasingly dark and claustrophobic after we built up sandbags against all the windows. Harry ordered his snipers to join the sentry on the rooftop to look for likely firing points in the surrounding area. They were equipped with the L115A1 sniper rifle, a specialist weapon with a range of over 1,000 metres. If we were attacked this way again the enemy sniper would not find retribution long in coming. Still, despite these new countermeasures, the sniper attack was a stark reminder of just how precarious our position in Nad Ali really was.

I briefed Wadood on the situation. He reacted with his characteristic sangfroid and merely shrugged. I suppose that he had lived with this kind of threat many times and was forced to adopt a fatalistic attitude just to keep sane. The same was true of the rest of the Afghans and it was rare that I ever saw them don helmet and body armour unless they were going on patrol.

Wadood invited me to come back for dinner later that evening. Remembering my stomach trouble following our last meal together I tried to demur, but he was not to be refused.

Following the stand to at dusk, I returned to Wadood's office. It was just the two of us and Ash, so it was an opportunity to get to know one another better, open up a little and build a relationship outside of the formalities of our official liaison. The Colonel had brought his chef with him to Nad Ali and the food was just as delicious as I remembered. I only hoped that the gastric repercussions were less severe this time. The prospect of coming under fire while suffering from food poisoning was not a nice one.

I needn't have worried; the limited supplies now reaching us meant that the ANA had run out of meat the day I'd arrived. The meal this evening consisted of a meagre helping of white rice and a few vegetables. The cook still had a few spices left in his stores though and the concoction laid out before me was a good bit tastier than the ration packs I'd grown so sick of.

The lack of supplies reaching the ANA was becoming a serious problem. It wasn't just food; ammunition was also running low. They didn't use the same weapons systems as us so they couldn't share ours. After the first helicopter resupply I'd alerted the quartermaster in Camp Bastion who managed OMLT logistics across Helmand but he was unsympathetic. 'The ANA have their own supply chain. We can't hold their hands the entire time.' The ANA may indeed have had their own logistics set up but what they didn't have was helicopters. With the roads destroyed they were reliant on the same British Chinooks as we were. I don't know where the breakdown in communications was occurring but someone was stopping most of the Afghan supplies getting onto the choppers. I was outraged. It wasn't just that the ANA were our allies. If the kandak ran out of food and ammunition, they wouldn't be able to fight. If that happened we'd all be sitting ducks for the Taliban. I vented my frustration over the mobile phone.

'I've got teams all over Afghanistan to keep supplied,' stonewalled the quartermaster. 'It's not our job to wipe the ANA's arses for them.'

'Look,' I said. 'Men are going to starve here if we don't start getting more supplies. On top of the food they need, they also require wood so they can cook.'

'Wood? There's no code for that in the logistics manual,' said the quartermaster. 'Quite impossible.'

'Well, we really need it. As a stop gap we can start burning the pallets that the rest of the stores are packed on.'

'Those pallets all have to be accounted for. We've got limited stocks and need them back. You'd bloody well better return every single one or I'll come down on you like a ton of bricks. You tell those Afghans to ration their supplies.'

I passed on the quartermaster's message to Wadood. A raised eyebrow was the only response I got.

The conversation at the dinner table ranged widely. We found that as we relaxed over our meal, we could get away from a discussion of the day-to-day running of our mission here in Nad Ali. Wadood asked me about my religion; he assumed I was Christian but was fascinated when I explained to him that I belonged to the Church of England. He'd never heard of it and begged me to explain how the Church had come into being. I decided not to get bogged down with the details of the Reformation but took him quickly through a potted history of Henry VIII's split with Rome. Wadood was fascinated. 'So you're saying that your King changed a whole country's religion just so he could sleep with a different woman?' the Colonel roared. 'And you think Islam's a strange religion!'

We went on to discuss the religious fault lines in Afghanistan that had contributed to the Taliban's rise. 'They are godless men,' said Wadood, 'and they will ruin this country.' His hatred of the Taliban was heartfelt. 'Your politicians talk about reconstruction and give millions of dollars in the hope of making Helmand a better place. What nonsense! Until the Taliban are defeated, all this is for nothing.'

The Colonel went on to point the finger at Pakistan, blaming the government in Islamabad for supporting the Taliban. 'They don't want stability in Afghanistan. As long as there is chaos here, they believe we won't side with India against them. Until your government and the Americans stand up to Islamabad, we'll never end this war.'

My grasp of geopolitics was shaky at best but Wadood's words had more than a ring of plausibility about them. 'So you think we're wasting our time in Afghanistan?' I asked.

'No,' he said. 'We need to fight the Taliban here as well. But tell me – what are all the British troops doing now? They're moving a great big turbine a few miles up the road because the Americans told them to. Meanwhile, the Taliban run amok. That's why we're stuck here, fighting for our skins, without enough food to eat. The men in Kabul, in London, in Washington – they have a very strange sense of priorities.'

The Colonel was right. As a captain I didn't often get to see the bigger picture. I was told where to go and what to do. Asking questions wasn't encouraged. That was my job and I'd been more than happy to do my commanders' bidding, especially if it meant I got to fight. Hell, I'd spent my whole life looking for combat but now I'd found it I realised that I needed more. That sounds blindingly obvious to most people, I'm sure, but for me it was a revelation. To think that soldiers were spilling blood, that I was risking my own neck, for nothing more than a photo opportunity next to a dam and some fluffy stories about development in the *Guardian* newspaper seemed suddenly grotesque.

'Don't worry,' said Wadood. 'We're soldiers. That's why they pay us.'

The evening drew to a convivial close and I took my leave of the Colonel, feeling that I understood the man and Afghanistan itself a little better. From that point on I spent almost every evening in his office, enjoying his gruff hospitality and slowly questioning more and more what I was doing fighting another man's war in this remote corner of the world.

CHAPTER TWENTY-ONE

Three days after the sniper's attack on the shower, the Jocks took another three casualties on their afternoon patrol, all of which were evacuated by helicopter. The whole OMLT was on edge as we went out for our evening patrol.

We were only 50 metres outside the gate when I heard the crack of an incoming round. I dived down as the earth kicked up around me. Caught in the open with no immediate cover, I pressed my body into dirt, shouting for someone, anyone, to tell me where the bullets were coming from.

Charlie identified the firing point on the roof of a small compound, 400 metres to the west. It was Compound Green – the building that Wadood had pointed out to me on the first patrol. Distant muzzle flash sparked bright in the dusk, throwing out a challenge to our marksmanship. Our weapons screamed their reply, sending red tracer arcing towards the horizon while the Jock snipers on the roof also swung into action. As they found their range, the distant light show flickered and died.

The enemy seemed so far away and the safety of the patrol base so close. The effort it would take to reach the Taliban position scarcely seemed worth it, to say nothing of the risk. In any case, they would almost certainly be gone by the time we got there. I ordered an end to the patrol and, keeping the compound in our sights, we withdrew to the schoolhouse.

At my post-patrol debriefing with Harry we discussed the threat from Compound Green. The obvious solution would have been to permanently base troops in the building and so deny it to the Taliban. Unfortunately we lacked the manpower to do this but Harry came up with a possible short-term solution. If we couldn't physically deny the Taliban access to the compound then we could at least discourage them from going there.

'We can set a deliberate ambush,' he said. 'The next time they try to move into Green we'll hit them hard. It will put them off using the place so freely in the future.'

Over the next couple of hours we worked up a plan. The concept was simple – an ANA platoon, with my OMLT, would move into the compound during the night and wait for the enemy to put in an appearance. When they did, we'd kill them all.

Wadood liked our plan. Whenever we gave him the opportunity to kill the enemy his support could be relied upon. It was only when he perceived that his men were being unfairly treated or used as pawns to achieve British objectives that his ardour for battle cooled.

At 0400hrs we filed out of the gate and headed for Compound Green. As the crow flew our destination was a mere 400 metres away but the direct route would take us through irrigated fields where the soil had turned into cloying mud that sucked at our boots, leaving us heavy-footed and slow. Instead we took a narrow dirt path that looped around the fields for a mile before joining a track that led to the compound.

The air was still warm but the searing heat of our daytime patrols was absent and for this we were thankful. Patrolling without sweat cascading down one's back was a sensation to be savoured and prompted the question of why Afghanistan didn't become entirely nocturnal during the summer months. Received wisdom was that the Taliban didn't often come out at night as, like the ANA, they lacked night-vision capability. Well, more fool them. This was surely the way to fight a war in the desert.

We walked in single file. I was second, a few metres behind Beattie whose outline was just visible through the dark. Without the streetlamps and headlights that illuminate even rural Britain with an ambient glow, the darkness of night-time Helmand could seem oppressive. Tonight, however, was cloudless, the quarter moon just allowing us to pick one another out as we walked. I still worried that I might miss the turning towards the compound and push us further into Taliban territory.

To our left and right corn grew tall and dense, shielding us from anyone who might be watching. Of course, the crops might equally have been camouflaging the enemy's movements, a possibility that gnawed at me as we moved towards the target. Would we ourselves be ambushed?

The threat of IEDs was ever present. Since being blown up by the mine in Gereshk I'd been haunted by visions of the ground exploding. However, as we'd never patrolled down this path before there was no particular reason to suspect it had been mined. In addition, the enemy had been spotted using the same path on several occasions themselves. Fixated on the greater threat of ambush, I paid little attention to the earth beneath our feet.

So the explosion, when it came, was a surprise. I heard the roar behind me and straight away assumed it was the beginning of an attack. We hurled our bodies to the dirt and scrabbled for the cover of the irrigation ditch that paralleled the path. Straining in the dark I looked for the flash of weapons and braced myself for the crack of rounds whipping over my head. More than that, I listened for the screams.

CHAPTER TWENTY-TWO

May 2009

I had just finished another spell on guard at Windsor Castle. My fingers slipped on the fiddly brass studs, letting my collar fall to the ground for the sixth time. Once a year I had to wrestle with these ridiculous things and it always took me an age to get ready. It was Black Sunday, my regiment's annual day of remembrance for Coldstreamers who have fallen in combat. Like everything in the Guards, the event was governed by traditions, chief of which being the dress code. We were obliged to parade in dark suits, complete with the aforementioned shirts with detachable stiff collar, bowler hats and clutching tightly furled umbrellas. The umbrellas were particularly important – they must be carried at all times but never opened through even the heaviest downpour.

My collar was causing me particular trouble because I was trying to get dressed in a hurry. I called to my orderly to give me a hand. Orderlies are soldiers assigned to officers when they are on public duties and are responsible for making sure all their uniforms are properly pressed and their boots immaculately shined. It might seem like laziness but officers are expected to concern themselves with the business of command instead of spending hours on their kit. Actually I think that we simply weren't trusted to do a good enough job.

I had only twenty minutes to catch a train into London for the memorial parade. The whole weekend seemed to be passing in a series of last gasp efforts to make it to my appointments on time. Twenty-four hours earlier I had been racing towards Windsor in the back of a cab. My resentment at having to give up another precious weekend for an Army I increasingly felt less a part of had pushed me into a mammoth Friday night drinking session. I'd woken up on the floor of a friend's living room twenty-five miles from Windsor and had forked out a small fortune on the cab fare to get to work on time. When I arrived, I would have only to clamber into my uniform, which a guardsman had laid out for me at the barracks, and I'd be ready to go – just a few minutes late. As the driver had turned the final corner, a policeman stopped him. 'Can't let you through, sir. The Guard's about to march down the street. Actually,' he said, checking his watch, 'it looks like they're running a bit late.'

'No shit,' I replied, leaning out of the window. 'And they're going to be even later if you don't let me through.'

The officer looked unconvinced, but he relented. In the end Her Majesty's Guard stepped off towards the castle just two minutes late but we were nevertheless required to march quicker than was customary in order to make it to Windsor Castle in time for the handover with the outgoing guard shift. I was sure that I would hear more about this from my superiors in due course.

I made it back to London just in time for the Black Sunday parade and formed up with the other officers and soldiers on the parade ground at Wellington Barracks. Together we marched down Birdcage Walk and swung left onto Horse Guards Road before we came to a halt opposite the Guards Memorial, which stands on the edge of St James's Park. The padre stood in front of us and intoned the traditional words of remembrance before we removed our hats and observed the obligatory two-minute silence. I'd done this every year since I joined the Army and usually I searched my imagination for the faces of men who had fallen in the First or Second World Wars. I felt some faint kinship with these dead men but it had never been deeply personal for me. Today though, my thoughts went elsewhere. Instead of the trenches of Flanders or the beaches of Normandy, I found myself dwelling on my own war. The images of the corpses I'd seen there flooded my mind. They weren't Coldstreamers but they'd fought and died on the same side as me. How many more Afghan soldiers had been killed since I'd left? Around me, everyone else looked silently ahead, lost in their own thoughts. I wondered where they'd gone and whom they saw there.

Afterwards, a number of us repaired to the Grenadier pub in Knightsbridge where I embarked upon the familiar endeavour of becoming as drunk as I could, as quickly as I could. Before I could travel too far down this road, however, my Company Commander tapped me on the shoulder. 'I see you made it on time today,' he said. News of my late start in Windsor yesterday had travelled fast. My sentence was thankfully not too onerous. I was to travel down to Warminster the following day where I would assist in playing host to a group of potential officers who were interested in a career in the infantry. It was a mildly tedious task that no one really wanted to do, the sort of shit job senior officers love to dole out to subalterns who step out of line.

At whatever time the pub finally kicked us out I decided that I wanted to see Sophie. When I'd phoned her earlier in the evening she had hung up but I was not discouraged. I hailed a cab and headed to her flat in Battersea. She lived on the third floor of a block, accessed via a communal hallway. To gain entrance without a key one was obliged to select the appropriate flat number and ring the corresponding buzzer. Two things conspired against me here. Firstly, I was too drunk to read the numbers next to the buttons. Secondly, Sophie was an extremely heavy sleeper – capable of slumbering through the loudest alarms or ringing phones. Her neighbours did not react well to me disturbing their sleep early on a Monday morning, first by pressing all the buzzers in the entire block, and then yelling up at her window from the street below. When that earned me nothing but abuse, I gave up the struggle and curled up to sleep on the doorstep.

I awoke several hours later, being nudged in the ribs by someone's shoe. Through bleary eyes I saw that it was Sophie. 'You'd better come up,' she said. Apparently one of her neighbours had recognised me on their way out in the morning and had phoned Sophie. She made us both a cup of coffee and we sat down at her kitchen table. I obviously expected that a certain amount of grovelling would be required to repair the damage here but I hadn't expected her to end our relationship over it. Consequently, the news hit me like a train.

'This isn't working,' she said.

My heart flipped over. 'Listen, I'm sorry about last night. I was incredibly drunk.'

'It's not about last night. Well, not just about last night. It's you.'

A tear ran down her cheek.

'It's been fun, Mark. I've loved the crazy nights and the not giving a fuck about the future, but I can't live that way. You're out of control. I think you know that. You need help and I can't be the one who gives it to you. I don't want to be dragged into your world.'

She was now crying openly but I had nothing to say. With her rejection I felt the crumbling of all hope. Without Sophie to distract me and provide a reason to keep away from the abyss, I felt I lacked the strength to hang on.

'That's ok,' I remember saying. 'Bye.'

I left her crying and caught a train to Warminster.

There were around ten potential officers on the visit, mostly sixth-formers. The first activity was an assault course – not something I relished with my hangover but by the end of it I felt refreshed. I could tell straight away that maybe half the group were never going to end up joining the military. To be an Army officer you don't have to be exceptionally bright, you don't even have to be that fit but you do have to enjoy a physical challenge. As I watched these youngsters crawling through mud and scrabbling at the face of an eight-foot wall, I could see the enthusiasm dimming in their eyes; see them deciding then and there that an Army career wasn't for them. I pushed them harder still, not out of cruelty but rather because I wanted to ensure that the ones who made it past this stage were made of the right stuff. If they made it all the way to Afghanistan they'd need to be.

Later that day we let the kids loose on the SAT range. One of the British Army's more impressive facilities, the SAT, or Small Arms Trainer, is a virtual reality simulator where troops can practise with various weapons, shooting at enemies that appear on a giant video screen.

A huge range of scenarios can be played out in the SAT and today we decided to give our visitors a taste of what it's like to go on patrol in Afghanistan. The desert flickered into being on the screen in front of us and the boys on the range squinted through the sights of their rifles. The images of Helmand already had me on edge but the first volley of fire triggered a more fundamental response. As surely as Pavlov's dogs began to salivate at the sound of a bell, so was I conditioned to throw myself on the ground when I heard gunfire.

I slowly got to my feet and dusted myself off. Thankfully, the visitors were too engrossed in their shooting to have noticed. Looking around, I saw one of the sergeants, also recently returned from Afghanistan, picking himself up from the floor too. We caught one another's eye and smiled nervously. I suppose we shouldn't have been embarrassed; if we hadn't developed these reactions then we quite possibly wouldn't still be alive.

Over lunch I saw a news bulletin on the television, announcing the death of another soldier in Afghanistan. Lt Mark Evison of the Welsh Guards had been shot while on patrol somewhere near Nad Ali. I'd tried not to pay too much attention to the death notices; this was the first time since I'd come back that I'd heard about someone getting killed in Nad Ali. It turned out that one of the other officers supervising the visit with me was a close friend of the dead man, having gone through Sandhurst with him. He was understandably cut up about it and had little to say to anyone for the remainder of the visit.

What an impression we must have made on these youngsters in the bar that night. One man grieving for his dead friend and me sullen, withdrawn, going over the same old ground in my head. 'What's it like?' they wanted to know. They weren't asking about the big picture, the training, life in camp or what career prospects were on offer. They wanted to know about Afghanistan. As the only officer present who had been, it fell to me to fill them in. It was odd; I'd hardly talked about this to anyone and, now I had a good reason to do so, wasn't sure how to pitch it. I was supposed to be advertising all the benefits of a military career but today it seemed harder than ever to remember what those were. I wasn't even sure that it was right to try and convince these boys, still too *young to legally buy a beer, to sign up to a career that might cost them their lives. It occurred to me that when I was their age I'd have found it hugely patronising if an Army officer had thought to protect me in such a manner. I decided to play it straight. I span a few stories about the early days in Gereshk, chasing after the Taliban in Saidan and Marjah and my audience sat politely, interested but not captivated. Then I told them the bloody truth about Nad Ali. Suddenly I had them; they leaned in, wide-eyed, fascinated. This was why they wanted to join. When I came to the end, they begged for more but I was done. I went to bed certain that however unpopular the war in Afghanistan became, there would never be any shortage of men and women willing to fight it.*

CHAPTER TWENTY-THREE

After the explosion there was only silence. This was ominous. Screams meant life, but their absence suggested we would be taking a body back with us at the end of the morning's work. An explosion that big meant at least amputation. There was no way someone could trigger an IED that size and escape unscathed. But who was it? To whose mother would I be writing a letter when we got back to the schoolhouse?

The hush was broken by CSgt Mason yelling down to Beattie to number off. Beattie, Sir, Charlie, Magoo, Ram, Gee. All there. How was this possible? The explosion had come right behind me. The Afghans were too far away. It was the New Zealander, Charlie; had to be – he was the next man along from me.

'Charlie?' I shouted into the darkness.

'Yes, boss?'

'You all right?'

A pause, as though Charlie wasn't quite sure he knew the answer.

'Yes, boss.'

OK. There wasn't time to get into the whys and wherefores. We had to get to Compound Green before the sun came up. The path could no longer be considered safe. Where there was one mine, there could be more. There wasn't far to go so we left the path behind and pushed into the cornfield. The explosion had spooked me and I wasn't prepared to take chances. I ordered the men to initiate 'Op Barma', our IED clearance drill. It was a painstaking process that called for Beattie to go out in front of the patrol with hand-held metal detectors and scan every bit of ground before they moved forward. The rest of us followed in single file.

We carried on in this manner for fifteen minutes before I realised that dawn would come long before we'd reached our destination. I made a decision. 'Forget Barma, there's no time,' I ordered. 'We'd have to be really unlucky for them to have mined the field as well.'

From then on, it was a short walk into the compound and we arrived with half an hour still to go before first light. This left us just enough time to get set up before settling down to wait for the Taliban's arrival. Compound Green was a fairly typical structure – two single-storey buildings on either side of a courtyard, all surrounded by a high mud-brick wall. In the centre of the courtyard was a patio made up of white and blue tiles. It was covered in dust, but otherwise the place was well kept and free of rubbish. There were, however, dozens of spent cartridges on the floor, left behind by the Taliban snipers.

Our plan was simple. We placed sentries on the roofs at either end of the compound, overlooking the track. They would alert us when the enemy approached. The bulk of the force would wait hidden behind the wall until the sentries triggered the ambush by setting off Claymore mines placed at the side of the track directly in front of the compound. The main force would then spring up from behind the wall and engage what was left of the enemy. The aim was simple and brutal – kill as many Taliban as possible.

Claymores are a devilish piece of weaponry, designed to kill and maim dismounted enemy troops. They are essentially anti-personnel mines which, despite having signed the Ottawa Treaty banning such weapons, we are still allowed to use because they are not set off by the victims themselves. Each device consists of a green convex plastic case with metal spikes protruding from the bottom, allowing it to be fixed into the ground. On the relevant side of the case is inscribed the legend, 'Front Toward Enemy'. It is as well to heed this message. Each mine contains a layer of high explosive that sits behind some 700 steel ball bearings. The whole thing is detonated by a soldier, concealed somewhere on the 'safe' side of the device, pressing a button connected to the mine by an electrical wire. When this happens, the ball bearings are spewed out at around 1,200 metres per second, ripping into the flesh of anyone unlucky enough to be standing within a 300 metre radius. Like I say, a nasty bit of kit.

Claymores were one of those weapons I'd heard a great deal about during training but had never actually had the chance to use in practice. I was secretly excited by this opportunity to try them out. Unfortunately CSgt Mason felt the same way. In no uncertain terms he told me that laying Claymores was not an officer's job and that he and Beattie would take care of it while I marshalled the troops within the compound. Reluctantly I conceded. Mason, with a smile on his face, moved stealthily out of the gate to play with his deadly toys.

I turned my attention to the placement of the troops. It became apparent that we were going to have problems setting up the ambush as planned. The wall was about nine feet high and even by improvising steps out of tables, crates and other detritus we found in the compound, it was only just possible for the men to reach over the top to fire their weapons. The flat roofs at either end of the compound were only wide enough for one man to lie there, so for now, only our two sentries were in position to shoot accurately at the enemy once the ambush began. The other men would just have to do the best they could. I hoped that by sheer weight of fire they would hit something.

When Beattie returned from setting up the Claymores, I sent him to take up the sentry position on the roof at the southern end of the compound while Wali, who was commanding the ANA, put one of his men on the northern roof. I preferred it this way round as I expected the enemy to be coming from the

173

south, walking up from their semi-permanent base in the orchard. Beattie was a reliable man and I wanted his keen eyes in the prime position to spot our guests before they arrived.

There was nothing to do now but wait. I sat down beside Magoo and lit a cigarette.

'All right, sir,' said Magoo.

'Magoo, I'm not going mad am I?' This was a foolish sort of thing to say to the Irishman. Before he had time to reply, I continued, 'That explosion earlier – I didn't imagine it?'

'No, sir. There was an explosion, right enough. A big one too. Charlie's one lucky bastard.'

So it was Charlie.

'Do you know where he is now?' I asked.

'He's inside the building,' said Magoo. 'Colour Mason sent him for a sit down. Thought he might need to recuperate.'

I walked over to the low doorway at the south end of the compound and peered into the gloom. There, crouched in a corner was Charlie, his lanky frame folded up like a deckchair. As he heard my footsteps, Charlie stood up.

'Hello, sir.'

'I just wanted to check up on you,' I said. 'That was a hell of a big explosion on the way over. I thought you were a goner.'

'Yeah, I don't remember too much about it,' he said. 'I felt it more than heard it. One second I was walking along and the next I'm flat on my face in the dirt.' He shrugged. 'Not much more to say really.'

Charlie walked forward into the pool of light by the doorway and I saw him properly for the first time. The back of his uniform had entirely disappeared, from his boots, which now flapped open at the heel like slip-on loafers, to the bottom of his body armour. His trousers were held up by the ragged remains of his belt. Even his boxers were torn. Miraculously, his skin was unbroken; a faint redness on the back of his legs was the only indication that anything had happened to him at all.

'Fuck me, Charlie!' I said.

'I know,' he replied. 'Pretty lucky, eh sir?' He smiled a funny sort of half-smile that spoke less of luck than it did of fear.

'You all right to carry on today?' I asked. This was rhetorical. When the enemy arrived, he'd be carrying on whether he was ready or not.

'Yes.'

'Good man. Go and take up position by the wall next to Ram.'

As Charlie shuffled off, the PRR crackled into life in my ear and Beattie murmured in a low voice, 'Eight of them. Moving on the track north to south towards our location. All carrying AKs.' He later told me that the Talibs had been sauntering casually down the path as if out for a country stroll. They seemed entirely relaxed and unprepared for an encounter with the enemy. This revealed the inadequacy of our presence in Nad Ali. Taliban soldiers could walk within 400 metres of our base and yet still be surprised when they ran into a hostile patrol.

We'd hit our third snag of the morning – they were coming from the wrong direction. We'd assumed that they'd be moving from south to north, walking away from their hideout in the orchard. I hoped they wouldn't see our sentries, would keep on coming and walk into the arcs of the Claymores at the southern end of the compound. At that moment the ANA soldier on sentry at the northern end of the wall opened fire. Thinking he'd been spotted, he preferred to start the fight on his terms.

I couldn't see the enemy as they scattered but I heard the roar of the Claymores as Beattie detonated them. The rest of the ANA soldiers rushed to their improvised firing points as the Taliban began to shoot back.

The wall of the compound was raked with fire. Beattie and the ANA soldier on the other roof, our only real eyes in this battle, were driven from their positions. We were blind. The enemy knew where we were but they were now hidden from us, just a few metres away on the other side of the wall. With the weight of fire flying over the top of the wall no one was willing to jump up on the improvised firing points and so expose their heads to the enemy. Some of the men began to toss grenades over the wall, hoping that they landed somewhere near the enemy. While I didn't blame Beattie and the ANA sentry for taking cover, I had to know what was happening beyond the compound walls.

I shouted for Sgt Magoo and he ran over.

'Magoo, get up on the roof and tell me what's going on.'

Looking up, we could see rounds as they ricocheted off the edge of the roof. A wave of nausea washed over me. I was ordering this soldier to toss his life into the lap of fate. If Magoo died, the responsibility would lie with me. Moreover, if he refused the order I knew my only choice was to climb onto the roof myself.

Two seconds passed as Magoo stared mutely back at me. A bead of sweat slowly made its way past his right eye, pausing on his cheekbone before sliding down to his chin. His gaze was expressionless.

'Magoo!' I shouted.

And then he was gone, hoisting himself up onto the roof into the unrelenting barrage. The flat surface offered him no cover and bullets pinged viciously around him. He flattened himself against the rooftop, trying to force himself into the concrete surface. Any one of those bullets could have eviscerated him in an instant. It was an act of bravery beyond anything I'd seen before. The sickness came upon me once more as I wondered if I'd killed him.

As Magoo began to return fire the other men took heart. The ANA soldiers clambered onto the platforms by the wall and began to fire as well. Judging by the explosions on the far side of the wall and an increased volume of incoming fire, the enemy had brought in reinforcements armed with RPGs and heavy machine-guns. Magoo's position became even more dangerous.

With a man back on the roof I had a clearer picture but the Taliban fighters had disappeared, hiding themselves in the cornfield on the other side of the track. Only by judging the direction of their fire could we guess at their positions.

I felt trapped inside the compound. Without knowing the enemy's location I feared they would send fighters around the back of the buildings and assault us from behind, overrunning our position. We didn't have enough troops to defend the compound from simultaneous attacks from all sides. Doctrine dictated that I should be aggressive, moving troops forward to take the fight to the enemy. I wanted to send a section around the northern edge of the compound, flanking the enemy, but to do so I would have to split the OMLT, sending British soldiers with the Afghans in order to maintain control. The situation was already chaotic enough without spreading my troops more widely across the battlefield. In any case, we had only one interpreter with us, so communication would have become nigh on impossible.

We stayed where we were – a decision that pleased my soldiers but one that nagged at me. Should be doing more? Was I doing the 'right thing'? Was my fear getting the better of me?

Mason spoke to the ops room over the net, asking Phil to call in fast air. Just five minutes later the jets sped in from the east. The F-15s could obliterate the enemy at the press of a button but until we could provide a clear target indication the pilots refused to oblige. As the Taliban remained among the corn, hidden both from Magoo on the roof and from the air, the planes were powerless to help. They bellowed their impotence from half a mile above and we cursed them. Maybe if I made up the enemy's location, told the pilots we'd seen the fuckers, maybe then they'd do their job. But something inside my head, an inbuilt and quite unexpected respect for 'the rules' perhaps, stopped me from going ahead.

From the improvised firing points we'd constructed against the wall, the men continued to pour fire in the general direction of the enemy. I couldn't see if their bullets were finding their way to the target but the sheer weight of our fire suggested that we must be having at least some effect.

Magoo's voice crackled over the PRR: 'I think they're beginning to withdraw.' Although our wall continued to take a battering, the intensity seemed to be lessening and it became apparent that the enemy fighters were firing from further and further away as they retreated through the field.

Eventually, after maybe an hour or so, the incoming fire dwindled away entirely and I was able to order the ceasefire. Before we left, however, I needed to be sure that the enemy really had departed and weren't lying up in cover, hoping to lure us out from the security of the compound and turn the tables on us. I grabbed Ram along with five ANA soldiers and together we left the compound and pushed out in an extended line into the cornfield. As we crossed over the track, I saw signs of the carnage we'd inflicted. Where the Claymores had been, the earth was scorched and blackened. Scraps of torn clothing showed that at least one fighter had been caught in the blast. More tellingly, scraps of bloodied flesh had been hurled into the branches of a beech tree, a welcome feast for the crows.

The field told its own story too. Broken, trampled corn showed where the enemy had scrambled to get off the path, out of the killing zone which we'd filled with burning lead. The blood daubed on the green stems marked the passage of the wounded or dead as they'd been dragged away by their comrades. Piles of spent bullet cases told me where they'd stopped to shoot, covering their withdrawal. Once we'd gone maybe 50 metres I concluded that the enemy really had departed, so we turned about and headed back to the compound.

Clambering up from the field onto the raised path, I suddenly saw a movement off to the north. About 200 metres down the track stood another compound, almost a carbon copy of Compound Green. There in the gateway I saw a figure standing stock-still and staring straight back at me. I signalled the others to stay down and remain in the cover of the crops. I lay on my front, my upper body resting on the track, while my legs trailed into the field. My rifle extended out from my shoulder in a straight line pointing directly at the figure to the north. Squinting through my sights, I studied the form of the individual, trying to make out their features and if they were carrying a weapon. Instinctively, my finger tightened on the trigger as a discordant chorus struck up a blazing row inside my head.

'It's a man,' said the first voice. 'Has to be a man. Too big to be a boy and it's bareheaded so not a woman.'

'Is it a man though? He looks small. What if you're wrong?'

'There are no civilians here. They all cleared out weeks ago. He's got to be a fighter.'

'But where's his gun?'

'What's that in his hand? I'm sure he's holding something.'

'Is he? I can't see anything.'

'Yeah. Right there; it's just behind his robe at the moment. He's definitely got something.'

'Fuck the rules of engagement,' said the angriest voice. 'These bastards want you dead. You've killed plenty already so what's one more anyway?'

It was true. Collectively we had killed perhaps a hundred men over the past few days. Phil with his aircraft had probably accounted for the lion's share of these. But this was different; I could see the face hovering above the glowing spike of my rifle's sight. This was all me. I was the one with the finger tightening on the trigger.

'This is war. You kill the other guy. It's your job. What are you? A coward?'

Deep down I wanted to do it. Wasn't this really why I'd come to war, why I'd joined the Army at all? This person's life was in my hands and mine alone. Apply a little pressure with my finger and it was all over for them. The power was exhilarating.

I never made a decision – a cardinal sin in the Army. The

figure turned and walked back into the compound, out of sight. I exhaled for a long time, although I hadn't even been aware I'd been holding my breath.

I ordered the men to move back into Compound Green and slowly followed them, all the time watching the building to the north.

Back in the relative safety of the courtyard I began to wind up the operation, organising the move back to the schoolhouse. Sgt Magoo slipped down from his rooftop position and walked slowly over to me. He stopped and removed his helmet. His hands shook as he fiddled with the clasp on his chinstrap. 'Sir, if you ever make me do something like that again, I'll fucking kill you myself.' His face looked gaunt and his eyes were wide – the eyes of a man who'd been staring at death for over an hour. I stared back at him, saying nothing. What could I say? Another leader might have put him in his place, told him to buck up and take whatever order I gave him. After all, there was every chance I'd have to tell him to do the same again, or worse, tomorrow. But I couldn't bring myself to do it. He'd risked his life because I'd told him to. He'd acted utterly selflessly when it counted, so by what right would I now assert my specious authority? He held my gaze for a second and then walked away.

We patrolled back to the schoolhouse taking the most direct route across the field. As we walked, I suddenly felt a sharp tug on my leg and pain shoot up my thigh. I cried out. Up ahead, Beattie, now on point, turned around.

'You OK, boss?' he asked.

'Pulled muscle!' I shouted back. 'Keep going. It's fine.'

Ridiculous. I'd spent the morning being shot at and end up getting crocked walking in a straight line through a field. I gritted my teeth and hobbled forward.

Within twenty minutes we were back and the men set about their admin while I reported in to Harry and then the Colonel, both of who seemed pleased with the outcome. Harry, of course, asked for a body count, but as ever I had no good answer. 'Three?' I hazarded. 'And a few more wounded.' It was mostly guesswork but it was good enough for Harry. Three it was, and that is what Brigade would be told. And so was the success of the war measured.

Once I was done with my verbal reports I headed over to the med centre to see what Sgt Taylor could do for my leg. The pain had now subsided to a dull ache but my mobility was reduced to a shuffling limp and running was quite out of the question. Sgt Taylor was able to help with a soothing massage, conducted under the watchful eyes of DB from his bed. The small size of our base meant that there weren't enough rooms to go around so some of the officers had improvised their sleeping quarters as best they could. DB had bagged a spot in the corner of the medical centre. The constant round of medical procedures carried out in his bedroom never seemed to faze him, but on balance I think I preferred my own spot with only the occasional rustling of a masturbating Irishman to interrupt my downtime. The massage eased some of the discomfort but Sgt Taylor reckoned it would be a couple of days before I'd be fit to patrol.

That evening I went over to the blokes' accommodation to see how everyone was getting on. Sgt Magoo stopped me by the door. His usual exuberance had been replaced by a look of shame. 'I just wanted to apologise, sir,' he said. 'I was bang out of order, saying what I did earlier on.'

'Don't worry about it, Magoo,' I said. 'That was some of the bravest soldiering I've ever seen. Anyone would have been shaken up by what happened. You were fucking brilliant. Thank you.'

Sgt Magoo looked down at the floor. 'Aye, well, that doesn't excuse what I said. You gave me an order and that's where it ends. I'll do the same again anytime you say so.'

He walked away, eyes still fixed on the ground.

CHAPTER TWENTY-FOUR

After the ambush we felt like we'd managed to take the fight back to the Taliban. It was a relief to feel back on the offensive. Over at Brigade, however, they wanted more. Harry's immediate boss, Lt Col Sandy Fitzpatrick, ordered him to gather more intelligence on the Taliban forces in Nad Ali. This meant more patrols for my OMLT and the kandak. My injured leg was still keeping me out of the action, so I was forced to sit out the next few patrols in the ops room, where I could only listen as Mason's sitreps came in over the radio.

The first patrol pushed out to the south of the schoolhouse. I tracked their progress on the map, picturing the ground in my mind and working out where the best cover was if they got hit. This was a fruitless endeavour. Stuck inside the base, I felt powerless. Harry didn't make it easier. 'Has it got too tough for you?' he asked. 'You've got your blokes taking all the risk while you stay tucked up safe in here.'

Harry's words were accompanied by a mocking smile so I wasn't sure how seriously I should take him. Nevertheless, his words stung.

The patrol had gone only 300 metres when Mason sent in a contact report. The enemy were firing at them from what seemed like prepared positions in a compound further to the south. Such was the weight of enemy fire that our men were forced to withdraw.

I went out to meet the patrol as it came back in. The team

looked ragged and exhausted and for the first time I thought I saw a glimpse of fear in Mason's eyes. He shook his head. 'There's just too many of them,' he said. 'It'll take two whole kandaks to dislodge them.'

Over the next two days there were more patrols, which probed out in all directions. Each one got hit hard. Five ANA men were wounded in one contact and three Jocks the following day. Once more the RAF flew the casualties out but each time the helicopters came under fire and it became clear during Harry's conversations over the net that Brigade was increasingly worried a chopper might be shot down. There were some successes – DB's platoon managed to kill four armed men as they moved towards our position and Beattie gunned down two more, caught in the act of laying IEDs by a road. We couldn't escape the truth though. The Taliban had us surrounded and had built up at least four defended positions which, lacking either sufficient troops or the permission to destroy buildings from the air, we couldn't take.

It was hard to tell exactly how many fighters were ranged against us but there was no doubt we were outnumbered. One of our unmanned drones spotted a funeral ceremony being conducted in a cemetery on the far side of Luy Bagh. On the screen in the ops room we saw more than fifty men with guns watching their comrades being buried. Phil immediately started looking for a way to initiate an airstrike but as soon as he spotted a handful of women and children among the mourners the opportunity was lost. I felt gutted. Of course I didn't want to kill civilians but if we'd been able to kill fifty enemy fighters in a single attack it would have gone a long way to evening the odds in our ongoing fight.

It felt like there was nothing we could do. Whenever a patrol left the schoolhouse the Taliban knew it. We couldn't walk more than a few metres in any direction without coming under fire. The only way around this was to move under the cover of darkness and set up ambushes, the way we had at Compound Green.

After three days of restless inactivity, my leg had recovered sufficiently for me to start patrolling again. I began to make preparations for the following morning. It was supposed to be a straightforward defensive patrol through the area immediately surrounding the schoolhouse but late that night Harry gave us new orders. Brigade was still unhappy about the continued lack of detailed intelligence on the Taliban. In order to rectify this we were to push further into enemy territory than we ever had before, through Luy Bagh and beyond. The staff at Lashkar Gah wanted to know exactly how many enemy fighters there were and how heavily they were armed. DB's platoon was to go out first, before the sun came up, and occupy a compound over-looking the track that ran from east to west on the northern edge of the orchard. They would watch for Taliban movement and ambush any force that came within range. The OMLT were to accompany Wali's platoon, leaving just after dawn and moving directly towards Luy Bagh, find the enemy and engage. Supposedly this would give us a clearer picture of the enemy's intentions.

The plan was clearly nuts. 'You want us to walk straight towards the enemy's strongholds?' I asked Harry. 'In broad day-light?'

'You've got your orders,' Harry replied. 'Now go and do your job.'

Harry looked away as he spoke to me, unable to meet my gaze. He knew the danger he was putting us in but he was under orders himself. I caught DB's eye and opened my mouth to speak but he just shook his head.

Once Harry was finished, DB, Woody and I all filed out onto the veranda and lit up cigarettes. DB was the first to speak. 'It's been nice knowing you,' he said. Neither Woody nor I laughed.

'It's suicide,' said Woody.

'What choice have I got?' I asked.

Woody shrugged. 'What do they think this patrol's going to achieve anyway? The best we can hope for is that we kill a few Taliban but we're not going to find out anything we don't know already.'

Mason emerged from the accommodation and joined us on the veranda. I quickly briefed him on the plan. He swore under his breath. 'You trying to get us killed, sir?' he asked.

We sat there for an hour, chewing it over and trying to decide what to do. To top it all off we'd heard reports that the Taliban had moved a Dushka into the area. The Dushka is a Soviet-manufactured heavy machine-gun, similar to our .50cals. It was originally made to shoot down aircraft but was now being used to tear infantry patrols to pieces. If we walked into the path of this weapon we would be in serious trouble.

At various points during the conversation I resolved to tell Harry to get stuffed. Screw the plan. Change it at least. I'd be doing him a favour; the truth was he was as much caught between orders and reality as me.

I have no idea what would have happened if I had. I suppose I'd have been sacked. In any case, we all decided to soldier on and obey our orders. I still wonder if we did the right thing.

CHAPTER TWENTY-FIVE

The following morning I found myself patrolling south across the fields towards Luy Bagh. DB's platoon were already in place. The trap was set; now it was our job to make the Taliban spring it. Wali's sixteen soldiers were ranged in an arrowhead formation ahead of us. I followed fifty metres behind, with five men from the OMLT. Magoo and Beattie were both left in the base nursing minor injuries. We had desperately hoped to get close to the orchard before the enemy engaged but the first rounds came in before we'd got 300 metres beyond the DC. The drills were now an instant reflex and I got straight on the floor.

I lay on my belly and breathed deeply. It was a relief not to be walking. The gunfire was sporadic and seemed a long way off. I was tired. I didn't want to fight today. I closed my eyes. I wanted to drift off some place where people didn't want to kill me. Maybe Fiji. Sun on my face, beer in hand. Perhaps I'd go for a dip in the ocean later.

The shooting grew closer and a voice on the radio demanded a sitrep. 'It's a sunny day over here, down by the sea,' didn't seem like an adequate response but at this stage I actually didn't know what was going on. I had to find out. It was time to push forward once more.

Kneeling up, I peered cautiously out across the field. I could make out the shapes of our Afghan allies, all lying prone and firing their weapons at some unseen target.

By now the enemy were laying down a heavy rate of fire. Gouts of earth spurted high into the air where rounds ploughed into the wet loam. The only hard cover was a lone building about 50 metres distant, further towards the enemy's location. I had to get up there, hope that I could spot the enemy and then call in the Apache that was on stand-by 10 minutes away.

I shouted at Charlie to follow me and made for the building. Fifty metres doesn't sound like a long way but when bullets are flying, one's perception alters considerably. It was a long crawl on our bellies but not once did it occur to me to stand up and make a run for it.

Finally we made it to our destination, a small building made up of two rooms with mud walls already scarred with bullet holes. I clambered in through a window, tumbling in a heap on the other side. Ten Afghan soldiers had already taken refuge there and were firing out of the windows on the opposite side. The enemy's location was still uncertain but it seemed likely they had occupied a compound 200 metres beyond the building we were in.

Charlie piled in after me and I set him the urgent task of finding the enemy, looking for the telltale muzzle flash that would give away their position. In the meantime I called the rest of my men forward to join us.

Immediately in front of the building was a dirt road, running from west to east. The incoming fire originated from a point somewhere beyond that track. I decided to call in air support with a clear instruction not to fire at anything north of the road. Anything to the south it was 'weapons free'.

When I heard over the net confirmation that the Apache was headed our way, I began to relax a little. With luck we might even be back at the base in a couple of hours.

My optimism was short-lived. After just ten minutes I heard the roar of the Apache as it arrived above us but the pilot refused to engage, due to the proximity of our troops to the target. He told us that he wouldn't fire until all friendly troops were inside the same building as me. This scared me. It meant that all our men would be squashed together in one place – a juicy target for the enemy. In addition it made it harder for us to manoeuvre and to return fire. The noise in the room was already deafening as men fired their weapons. The pilot wouldn't budge though, so I was forced to agree to his plan.

I realised then that Ash hadn't joined me in the building, so I couldn't reach Wali over the radio. I was forced to relay a message through the ops room to Wadood who then ordered Wali by mobile phone to move everyone to my location. It took a few minutes before the ANA men began to move. Just as I received confirmation that they were on their way, the ground seemed to lurch sideways beneath me. The building shook, showering dust down upon us. Overhead, the air ripped apart in the loudest thunderclap I'd ever heard.

'What the fuck was that?'

Charlie's shouted question sounded faint against the screaming tinnitus in my ears. I had no answer. Then the Dushka popped into my mind. I'd never been around when one had been fired but perhaps this was how it sounded. I looked at the wall in front of me. A round from a Dushka would tear straight through it. We had to get out of there. Fast.

A shadow by the window made me look up. Falling through the empty frame was an Afghan soldier. He hit the floor hard and lay there, his legs twitching in tiny, rapid spasms. I knelt down next to him and then saw the blood pooling on the floor beneath him. Quickly turning him over, I looked for the source of the bleeding. It wasn't hard to locate. From the crown of his head down to the base of his skull, there was a gaping hole. I could see the man's brain, exposed, crimson and wet.

Mechanically, I reached for my first field dressing, an emergency bandage used to staunch bleeding. I ripped open the packet and clamped the absorbent pad against the soldier's head. I pressed down, not knowing how hard to push after I felt the spongy softness beneath my hand.

A wave of despair rolled over me. This man was dying. Perhaps he was already dead. But I couldn't let go.

'Sir! Sir!' Gee was crouching next to me. 'Sir, this is my job. Let him go!'

I stared uncomprehendingly. Why was he shouting at me?

'You have to let me do my job. You've got to get us all out of here!'

I nodded dumbly and staggered to my feet. What next? What was my plan?

In my ear I heard the radio crackle and Mason's voice scream, 'Stop! Cease fire! The Apache is firing on us!'

As I heard his voice I saw him stumbling through the door into the building. The uniform down one side of his body had been entirely ripped away and he was covered in filth and blood. His right arm dangled limply by his side. He'd been shot. A freshly lit cigarette was perched at the corner of his mouth. He sucked in one long drag and then with trembling fingers plucked the fag from his lips.

'The Apache,' he said. 'It was the Apache. It hit us.'

I stared at Mason, unable to comprehend what he was saying.

'The fucking idiot's got it wrong. He thinks our guys are the Taliban and he's ripping us apart.'

I heard the thunder above suddenly stop as Phil relayed our message to the Apache pilot. What the hell had the pilot been thinking? I expected another burst to come at any time.

The radio crackled. 'The Apache has ceased fire. What's going on?'

I looked around. The truth was I didn't know what was happening. Here in this building I was blind. There was no way of telling how many dead and wounded were lying in the field outside. All around me there was screaming. English and Dari mingled together in one huge cry of terror.

'Where are the rest of the men?' I asked Mason.

'Our boys are off to the right of this building. The ANA are still pushed forward near the road.'

'Right. Get the rest of the OMLT inside now and we'll consolidate our position. I need a casualty state.' I knew that most of my men had been hit and god knows how many Afghans.

Although the Apache had halted its attack, the Taliban were still firing. I had to know what kind of shape we were in and find out if we had any troops left standing to hold off the enemy.

Gee looked up at me from where he crouched next to the bleeding Afghan. 'I've lost him, sir,' he said.

The body lay quite still in its puddle of blood. Unexpectedly, relief washed over me. Gee was now freed up to look after the other men and there was one less critically wounded soldier to drag through the rest of the firefight. Perhaps my humanity had drained out with the Afghan's blood but I had no time for sentiment now.

A steady flow of wounded men began to arrive in the small room. Most were on their feet but three of the Afghans were dragged in, their legs shattered and bloody. Of the Brits, Mason, Ram and Griff were all walking wounded. The ANA had taken twelve casualties, including the dead man. Ram and Griff took it in turns to fire out of the window, and dress one another's wounds.

When a man gets wounded on the battlefield, the rule is that you have sixty minutes to get him treated at an aid post. The statistics show that if you make this 'Golden Hour' then you've got a very good chance of making it all the way. If you miss the deadline survival rates fall off a cliff. My main job now was getting these men back to the schoolhouse. The clock was ticking and we were still under fire.

We'd been stuck in this shack too long. The enemy knew exactly where we were and had started hammering the walls with small arms fire. All it would take was an RPG through the window and it would all be over. The Apache could yet be our salvation. I asked the ops room to order the pilot to re-engage – this time targeting the enemy. Inevitably, the pilot asked for co-ordinates. 'For fuck's sake,' I screamed down the radio. 'They're somewhere beyond that track to our south. Tell the pilot to take out those compounds.' No. Of course it was impossible. The pilot was now suddenly gun-shy and couldn't possibly fire without clearer direction. 'Didn't stop you five minutes ago, did it?' I yelled up towards the sky.

The ops room came back online. 'Topaz 32 are going to move in from the north-east and engage the enemy to cover your withdrawal.'

This was DB's platoon, currently holed up in their compound some 500 metres away. Thirty Jocks piling into the Taliban's flank should be more than enough to distract them and allow us to break contact. I set to work marshalling the men into some semblance of order, ready for the long trek back to the schoolhouse. Out of the twenty-two soldiers that had come on the patrol, only five were now free of injury. We had one dead man and three that couldn't walk, all of whom had to be carried or dragged along with us when we moved. Mason was doing his best to organise the soldiers and oversee the construction of improvised stretchers for the wounded and the dead man. I was on the net and trying to keep an eye on the action through the window, wary that the Taliban might rush us before the Jocks arrived.

Suddenly, over the net I heard DB's voice. 'Contact. Wait out.'

I peered through the window, trying to glimpse what was happening but bullets were whacking into the wall beside me and I was forced back into the room. Fifteen minutes had now passed since the Apache had attacked and we hadn't moved a metre towards the patrol base. Gee popped up beside me. 'Sir, we've got to move,' he said. 'One of the Afghans is losing consciousness.'

On the net I started to hear casualty reports coming in from DB – they had two men down and would have to carry those men with them when they moved. They were being hit hard from their front and couldn't move anywhere fast. There would be no cavalry riding over the horizon to save us now. If we were to get out of here, it was going to be under our own steam. To compound our difficulties, the Apache suddenly announced its withdrawal from the scene, having run low on fuel. I didn't know whether to feel disappointment or relief at this news.

I had to make a decision. This was what being an officer was all about. Everyone was looking to me for direction. I had to keep my nerve and get us all out of here.

I turned and addressed the men. 'The Jocks can't provide us with fire support. We are going to conduct a fighting withdrawal. We're on our own now.' There was no dissent. In any other circumstance what I was suggesting would have sounded like madness but we all knew that it was the only thing to do.

There was a shallow ditch running northwards, away from the enemy positions but it was at least 100 metres away. Reaching that ditch was our only hope of salvation. I just prayed that we would get there before the entire patrol was cut to ribbons.

I divided the men into three groups which would move separately, one at a time, to ensure that the group moving would always be covered by fire from the other two. Charlie went first, taking five Afghans with him. After several agonising minutes, the first group dropped out of sight into the ditch. The plan was working. Through the terror, a flash of pride ran through me. We were in a tight spot but we were going to come out the other side.

They sprinted for the ditch while the rest of us kept up a rapid rate of fire to keep the enemies heads down.

Mason went next with Gee, Griff, six more ANA soldiers, including the most heavily injured men and the corpse, taking up a position on the right-hand side of the building. Someone lobbed a few hopeful smoke grenades out of the front window and under a green and red haze we began the long slog to safety.

I was the last man out of the building, Ram and the last four ANA men exiting immediately before me. Ram's arm was bleeding but he could still run and fire a weapon. As soon as we left the building, we were under fierce and terrifyingly accurate fire. We hit the floor immediately, trying to duck under the maelstrom of lead whizzing a few inches above the ground.

We scrambled towards the ditch in short bounds as the wounded men couldn't cover ground quickly. Most couldn't use their weapons and so it was up to the rest of us to put down as much fire as we could. We fired in short, controlled bursts. Our ammunition was running low. Once it was gone we really were fucked. From the weight of fire coming our way, I estimated there were maybe fifty of them – easily outnumbering us, even before we'd taken casualties. We had neither the strength nor the time to crawl our way out of this. We were already thirty minutes into the 'Golden Hour'. Each metre towards the ditch was gained at a run, bent double to make the targets we presented to the Taliban a little smaller. The soil was filled with sharp rocks which tore at my skin every time I put my hands on the floor, ripping open a hundred tiny bleeding fissures. The sweat ran down from inside my helmet and stung my eyes. When I wiped them with the back of my hand I pushed in grit that half-blinded me.

An ANA man collapsed beside me, blood spewing from his arm. He screamed as he went down, a high-pitched cry of pain that chilled me. There were more injured men than able-bodied now. Over half the patrol was struggling to move, let alone fight. I ripped a first field dressing from my trouser pocket and clamped it over the bloody gash in his arm. Grabbing him by the shirt, I forced him to look into my eyes. 'You're all right,' I shouted. 'It's just a flesh wound! Can you still move?'

The man found his focus and met my gaze. He may not have understood English but he knew what I was asking. He nodded.

'Good! Now move.'

I hauled him with me by his good arm and we were up and scrambling again, just 20 metres from the ditch now. Thankfully it was his left arm that was injured and he was able to shoot just as effectively as before. A minute later we were in the ditch.

This irrigation channel was not substantial – about two metres wide and perhaps one deep with a few centimetres of water running along the bottom, just covering our boots. We still couldn't stand up straight and the bullets continued to wing through the air above us.

Astonishingly I saw that it was just the British soldiers who had taken cover in the ditch. The ANA soldiers continued to run along beside us, fully exposed to the incoming fire. 'Get in the ditch!' I yelled but they didn't even look my way.

Fuck it. If they wouldn't take even the most basic precautions to stay alive then that was their lookout. In any case, things inside the ditch suddenly became just as hairy as they were outside. Bullets began to sizzle past me, plucking at my sleeves. I dived into the water and peered forward, trying to see where the fire was coming from. At least one enemy fighter had managed to get into the ditch 200 metres further down and was now firing directly upon us. I shot back and yelled at Ram, 10 metres further up the ditch, to join me.

Because of the width of the ditch, only two men could lie side by side and shoot straight back along it. This wasn't enough to suppress the wall of lead coming our way. The enemy must have got one of their PKMs into the ditch. We needed our machine-guns to put down a heavier rate of fire but both our Minimi and the ANA's own PKMs were at the north end of the ditch. Over the PRR I ordered Charlie to bring them down towards my position where they'd be able to fire directly onto our pursuers.

It was slow. Too slow. Bullets bit into the side of the bank. It was only going to be seconds before they found their mark and more men died. Then, just as I began to contemplate utter disaster, one man altered the course of the battle with a single feat of reckless bravery.

An ANA soldier with the PKM came charging, firing as he ran. The air around him fizzed with death but still he stormed forward, sending a stream of rounds straight over our heads. Within seconds, the incoming fire slowed and we were up and running, crouched double to stay below the PKM's fire. As I heaved my way past him, I saw that he was laughing. I couldn't hear it over the noise of the weapon but his mouth was open and his shoulders heaved. He wore a look not of fear but of strange, mad, joy as he blazed away. More power to you, I thought. Whatever crazy, fucked-up emotion you need to tap into to do what you're doing – just keep doing it.

We ducked and weaved our way back up the ditch, which became deeper the further up we ran. As we put more distance between us and the enemy, the incoming fire grew less. PKM man, as he would ever after be known to me, caught up with us and we gritted ourselves for the last stretch. By now we were strung out, one hundred metres separating the front of our column from the back. The injured men were the furthest forward, while me and those best able to cover our withdrawal were at the back.

I heard Woody's voice in my ear over the radio. 'Wadood's sent ANA Toyotas down to the edge of the field,' he said. 'When you reach the end of the ditch you're in, you'll find them waiting for you. They are going to move the injured men first and then the rest of you.'

I could hear the vehicles now, their mounted PKMs chattering away, firing above us and driving back any pursuing enemies. Physically shattered, I was running on adrenaline alone. My lungs burned and each step was like wading through a swamp.

Finally, we made it and clambered out onto the track. I flopped against the side of the lead Toyota. I heard Harry's voice over the radio. 'I need you to secure the southern edge of the football pitch,' he ordered. 'We've got a MERT flying in to pick up casualties.'

I looked around. Out of the twenty-two men who had gone out, only five remained uninjured. One of them was Wali. To my relief I saw Ash kneeling beside him. We didn't have enough men to put together a proper cordon but we would have to do the best we could. I quickly explained the situation to Wali. He just nodded, too exhausted to do anything but agree.

The vehicles moved out and sped back with their cargo of wounded men while I set off with Wali, Charlie, Ash and the remaining four ANA men towards the football pitch. It took us ten minutes at a shambling dogtrot to reach our destination and we barely had time to deploy into some semblance of a defensive line before the MERT swooped in.

The helicopter was only on the ground for about five minutes while the wounded men were bundled aboard. I was crouched in the dust on the edge of the football pitch and couldn't see who was being taken.

Once the chopper was clear, we quickly collapsed the cordon and returned to base. Sgt Taylor, the medic, was in charge, striding purposefully about, dealing with the minor casualties that had not been evacuated. Her calm professionalism had prevented the base from tipping into chaos. I interrupted her as she prepared to inject a stricken Afghan soldier with morphine and asked her where I could find CSgt Mason. 'Oh. He's gone,' she replied. 'All the OMLT wounded went out on the helicopter. They're on their way home. They were badly banged up but they'll be all right.'

I didn't hear what else she had to say. Over half my men were gone and here I was, still standing, not even scratched. I thought back to the explosion in the desert outside Gereshk; miraculous survival was becoming a habit of mine.

The butcher's bill was long. From the OMLT we'd lost Mason, Gee, Ram and Griff – all wounded. I hadn't even realised that Gee had been hit – he'd carried on doing his job, helping the other casualties even though he'd been bleeding too. Once again I was humbled by one of my soldiers' professionalism and devotion to duty.

From the OMLT it was just Beattie, Charlie, Magoo and I left in Nad Ali. The ANA had lost thirteen men – one of them had died on the battlefield and another on the medevac helicopter. Of the eight wounded, three would never walk again. When DB's platoon finally made it back in, they'd taken two casualties who were also flown back to Lash. Numbers were dwindling and there was still no relief. I began to wonder whether we were going to make it out of Nad Ali at all.

That night I stayed up late out on the veranda, chain smoking. I couldn't sleep. DB came over and sat down next to me. He nodded a curt acknowledgement and lit his own cigarette. We sat side by side like that for a while, saying nothing and staring up at the night sky. His face was blank, his dark-ringed eyes devoid of all emotion.

DB broke the silence abruptly. 'Did you hear the dog barking last night?' he asked.

'No,' I replied.

He just nodded and went on smoking.

'Any particular reason?' I asked.

Slowly, haltingly, he began to tell me. As per our orders, his platoon had gone out a few hours before me to covertly occupy a compound while it was still dark. The move in had gone without a hitch. They'd made their way straight to the compound and begun to establish their position. 'It was all going like clockwork,' he said. 'Then all of a sudden a dog started barking.' The animal was clearly a stray that had made itself a home in the compound after the owners had left. DB's men had woken it up and it was naturally upset at the intrusion. 'Once it started, it wouldn't stop. I mean this thing was going crazy. It wasn't big. About the size of a border collie.'

We regularly saw these mongrels roaming around the deserted streets of the DC. They were normally quite unafraid of us and soldiers would often stop and pet them as they passed by.

'It wasn't aggressive. I mean it wasn't trying to bite us or any-thing. It just wouldn't shut up. You could have heard it all the way over in Luy Bagh. Are you sure you didn't hear it?' I just shook my head. 'Well if it had carried on the Taliban would have been all over us. We had to get it to stop. One of the boys tried to calm it down, talking to it and stroking it. But the damn thing kept barking.'

DB paused and lit another cigarette before continuing.

'It just wouldn't stop,' he repeated and then fell silent.

'Go on.'

'So I ordered one of the boys to make it stop. We couldn't shoot it − then the Taliban would really have been onto us. A couple of the men held it down and then another used his bayonet. Stuck it right in the dog's throat. He had to stab it in. And then again. And again. I thought it'd be quick but the dog wouldn't die. It stopped barking though so that was all right. Started making a sort of bubbly, wheezy, whining noise. I can't describe it. It was horrific. A lot of blood came out too. Place looked like a slaughterhouse by the time they were done.'

I stared at him, not saying anything.

'Anyway,' he went on. 'Just wondered if you'd heard anything.' He got up and flicked his cigarette butt onto the floor. 'Good night then,' he said and walked off towards his accommodation.

CHAPTER TWENTY-SIX

The morning after the Apache had ripped apart my team I took stock. With just four of us left in the OMLT, we no longer had enough men to patrol. The Army's rules said that we couldn't deploy alongside the ANA with fewer than six men. Without reinforcements we were effectively grounded, and if we couldn't patrol then neither could the kandak. As Wadood had said when I'd first arrived, the ANA wouldn't go on the ground without air support and without British troops patrolling, but the Brigade refused to provide the Apaches. Harry reported the new state of affairs to Brigade but the reply came back that they couldn't spare any extra troops for at least a week. I asked Harry if he could lend me two of his men in the meantime to put us back up to patrolling strength. He looked at me as though I'd just asked to spend the night with his wife. 'My men can't patrol with the ANA,' he said. 'You're used to it but it would be bloody dangerous to send anyone else out with them. Besides, with sentry duty and our own patrols, I haven't got any men spare.'

I couldn't believe it. 'But Harry,' I said, 'the alternative is that we don't patrol at all. We'll be left with just your men doing one patrol a day. The Taliban will have the run of the place.'

Harry's face reddened. 'Well that's how it's going to be. Anyway, I'd have thought you'd have enjoyed a few more days with your feet up.'

I fought to keep my temper under control. 'What's that supposed to mean?'

'You were happy to let Mason take command of the OMLT for a few days when your leg went. And where were you when your men were being shot up by the Apache yesterday?'

Harry walked away, leaving his question hanging in the air. I sat in the ops room and fumed. How dare he? He hadn't been there. I went back to my accommodation, gripped with fury. I smashed my fist into the sandbags piled against the window and recoiled as pain shot through my hand. Was Harry right? Had I put my men in danger and then run for safety? Is that why I was still alive while they got flown out on stretchers? Wadood, the only man in Nad Ali with greater authority than Harry, couldn't exonerate me. He hadn't been there either. Before I'd spoken to him I'd been sure that he'd be furious with me. It had been a British Apache that had killed his men after all. In fact he was gracious. 'It's war,' was all he'd said. No, there was only one person who could tell me it wasn't my fault. That was Mason and he was gone. I was left alone with my fear and doubt.

For the rest of the day I avoided Harry. Content to clean my rifle, I took up my usual spot just outside the OMLT accommodation, as far as I dare go into the open. On the far side of the courtyard a group of Jocks were doing vital maintenance under the bonnet of a WMIK. The vehicles had a tendency to develop minor engine problems when they weren't used regularly. Outside the Afghan dormitory an ANA soldier sat making tea.

The crack of the bullet as it passed through the air was loud. There was only one shot. I jerked instinctively, and searched around wildly for the gunman. The sentries on the rooftop were ahead of me and once more the .50cal thundered a deadly response. The ANA man fell forward and crumpled to the ground. I rushed forward. Reaching the soldier, I could see a neat hole in his T-shirt just below the neckline. He lay there, his breathing shallow and measured. There was no screaming and his eyes betrayed no hint of pain. Some blood trickled out through the hole, but only a little. It wasn't pumping out like it does when an artery gets cut. He's going to be all right, I thought.

'Medic!' I yelled.

Sgt Taylor came running over and began to examine the wounded man. 'Help me carry him,' she said. 'We need to get him into the med centre.'

I looped my arms beneath his while Sgt Taylor took his feet and together we lifted him and shuffled towards the medical centre. He was a small man but as a dead weight he was difficult to carry. The medical centre was empty save for DB. He was sitting on his bed, plugged into his iPod and eating a bowl of noodles when we burst in. We laid the man down on the makeshift operating table and Sgt Taylor and her team got to work. I didn't know what to do; I had no further part to play in this drama but stood there rooted to the spot, unable to tear my eyes away.

The door banged open and half a dozen Afghan soldiers piled into the room shouting all at once. They crowded forward, reaching towards their stricken comrade. Sgt Taylor ripped open a packet of HemCon, a kind of bandage that works to stop haemorrhaging when stuffed into an open wound. I thought his bleeding had been minor but looking down I saw that my sleeves were soaked crimson. The bullet had made a much bigger exit wound as it came out of the man's back. Sgt Taylor found her path to the patient blocked by the crowd of Afghans.

'Get them out the way!' she shouted.

I screamed at the men to move and when that had no effect physically grabbed a couple of them and pushed them towards the door. Their eyes were wide with panic and I had to man-handle them all the way outside. The Company Sergeant Major arrived and helped clear the rest of the room, giving the medics the space they needed to work. DB very calmly pulled his legs up onto his bed and continued his meal, apparently unperturbed by the sight of a man fighting for his life on the other side of the room.

With the audience reduced to manageable levels, the room became quiet. Only Sgt Taylor's terse words of command broke the hush. I'm not sure how long this went on but it can't have been more than a few minutes before Sgt Taylor looked up and in matter-of-fact tones declared, 'He's dead.'

I couldn't believe it. It was hard to imagine that such a small wound could kill someone. 'He was bleeding internally,' she said. 'He didn't have a chance.'

'I'll tell them outside,' I said and Sgt Taylor nodded. She looked suddenly drained. She had a terrible job. Seeing men die up close was the lot of a medic and I'm sure they bore the responsibility heavily.

By the time I walked out of the medical centre, the crowd by the door had swelled dramatically. It looked like half the kandak had gathered there. Ash was among them and I spoke to him, telling him what had happened. The rest didn't need to wait for his translation. My expression told them what they needed to know. One of the Afghans fell to his knees, weeping. 'He's his cousin,' Ash told me. Two soldiers helped the grieving man to his feet. I turned away. There was nothing more I could do to help and I had no wish to watch another human go through such pain. Instead I walked to the ops room.

Harry accosted me on my way in. He'd clearly already heard the news.

'Why the fuck wasn't he wearing body armour?' he asked me, his face uncomfortably close to mine. 'Might as well have had a target pinned to his chest.'

I backed away. 'I know. God knows how many times I've told them. The Colonel ...'

He cut me off with a dismissive wave of the hand. 'I'm not after excuses, Mark. It's just such a fucking waste.'

After he'd stormed out I slumped against the wall, running

back over my meetings with Wadood. If I'd done something different, been more persuasive, would that guy still be here, laughing off his near miss?

Harry was right. It was a fucking waste.

The immediate problem was what to do with the body. Islamic custom dictates that burial should take place within 24 hours of death. The man's family, save for his cousin, were all hundreds of miles away to the north. They didn't even know that he had died. It now fell to his other family, the ANA, to make the funeral arrangements. Up until now, the dead Afghans had been taken back to Lash along with the wounded but this time no one needed medical attention. The ANA were adamant that Nad Ali was not a suitable location for a burial so Woody raised Brigade on the net. He outlined the situation, requesting a helicopter to pick up the body and take it to Lash, where a ceremony could be carried out. The answer came back: a resounding no. We weren't due a resupply for another two days and the RAF wouldn't risk an extra flight just to fetch someone who was already dead.

The Afghans were furious. As far as they were concerned, disposing of a body in the correct manner was just as important as saving the life of a wounded man. These soldiers had become much more accepting of their own mortality than we were. The idea, however, that they might not be accorded the proper respects once they'd departed this world was horrifying to them. I feared they were close to mutiny.

Three hours later I was called to Wadood's office. The Colonel looked tired. The death had been a shock to us all, but no matter how close we became as allies we would never feel the same raw grief when the dead wasn't one of our own. Wadood gestured towards the chair in front of his desk and I sat down. He launched straight into a long harangue about the importance of respect for the dead and how this was yet another example of how we didn't understand Afghanistan. I felt conflicted. On the one hand

I understood the RAF's decision – with the man already dead, it would be wrong to risk more lives to deal with the corpse. On the other I believed that we ought to consider the strategic implications of offending the Afghans. This 'insult' was likely to put us at loggerheads with the ANA, handing an advantage straight to the Taliban. Of course my feelings didn't really come into it. Any decision was out of my hands. I was merely an intermediary, shuttling back and forth between Wadood and Brigade with increasingly vitriolic messages. It was a delicate position. To maintain the Colonel's precious goodwill I had to make him believe that I disagreed with Brigade's decision, but at the same time I didn't want him to think I had no influence, or he might stop talking to me altogether.

Wadood's tirade gradually ran out of steam and he sank back into his chair. I took my chance to state my case but the Colonel cut me off with a dismissive wave of his hand. 'Don't bother,' he said. 'I know you can't change their mind. Anyway, we've found a solution.'

'You're going to bury him here in the patrol base?' I asked.

Wadood looked scornful. 'That is unacceptable.'

I didn't understand why burial here would be so improper but the Colonel's tone brooked no further questioning.

'We've arranged for the body to be taken away by road.'

'By road? How? We're under siege. How will a vehicle get out past the Taliban?'

Wadood scowled. 'I've spoken to the Taliban. They understand our problem much better than you do. They realise that we cannot delay a man's funeral and so they have agreed to pick up the body themselves. It will be driven to Lashkar Gah where our comrades will collect it.'

'But the Taliban?' I said. 'They're the enemy. They killed him in the first place. Why are they helping you?'

'The Taliban are dogs,' said Wadood. 'But they are Muslims nonetheless and in this matter they know the right thing to do.

Don't look shocked. You have been here only a few months. As an army, just a few years. We have lived alongside these Taliban our whole lives. In many ways they are more like us than you are.'

'When will they come?' I said. 'Have the sentries been warned?'

'It is done already. They made the handover outside of the camp. There was no time to delay.'

The only positive thing to come out of the shooting was that it prompted Harry to overcome his reservations and agree to lend me two of his soldiers, enabling the OMLT to patrol with the ANA once more. The Jocks found the seemingly haphazard approach of OMLT patrolling somewhat unsettling compared to their more orthodox experiences. After each patrol, they would come in looking astonished that they'd made it back at all.

Looking back, it occurs to me that I never knew the dead man's name. I hadn't known it before he was killed and now he was gone I didn't think to ask. That doesn't mean the man's death didn't affect me. He'd lived and fought beside us, shared the hardship and the dangers. It hurt us all. The fragile illusion of security in the patrol base had been dealt yet another blow.

CHAPTER TWENTY-SEVEN

July 2009

It was the Coldstream Guards' Summer Ball, held at our base in Aldershot. The party was in full swing now that dinner was over. People were mingling on the dance floor or perching haphazardly around the white circular tables that were strewn with empty bottles and wine glasses. The band was on stage, ripping into another Johnny Cash cover, and the drunken masses twisted and shuffled to the country rhythm. It was fancy dress. Here a Roman gladiator rocked unsteadily, entwined with some lissom girl in a tight green ball gown; there a pirate threw back his head and guffawed as Elvis, the Commanding Officer, reached the punchline of his joke. For my part, I was dressed in a skin-tight rainbow catsuit and blonde wig. Drag was de rigueur for junior officers at most fancy-dress events, or even at normal parties come to that.

I was alone at last. This was my event, or at least I'd organised it. Funny job, being in the Army – one minute you're calling in an airstrike and the next you're a party planner. There wasn't much to it. Food, drink, more than everyone could handle, and some music courtesy of a live band. The Commanding Officer liked music. 'Spare no expense,' he'd said. Which was why I had splashed out £1,000 on the band's fee. I had the money in cash stuffed in an envelope, zipped in the side pocket of my gym bag which I'd stashed under a table in an empty room. It was worth it – especially because it was the Regiment's money and not mine. The music really was good.

The singer reached the end of his second encore and glanced over at me. 'One more,' he mouthed over the applause from the dance floor. I nodded back and went off to get his money.

The Commanding Officer clapped me on the shoulder as I went past. 'Great party, Mark,' he said. 'First class. Well done.'

I acknowledged his praise with a quick smile and slipped out of the room. Well done – what a joke. Throwing a party – that's worth acknowledging. Fight a war, kill a bunch of people and no one gives a shit. Where was my well done for Nad Ali? We'd taken everything the Taliban could throw at us over the summer and come out the other side. But did anyone give a fuck about that? Had anyone told Mason, Magoo, Gee, any of the boys that they'd done a good job? I had no idea. I hadn't seen or spoken to any of them since they'd been taken away on the choppers. Whatever. I'd get the band paid and then I could start drinking properly.

I found the bag right where I'd left it, underneath the table, but now the side pocket was unzipped and gaping open. A sliver of dread slipped down my spine. Fuck. I reached into the pocket and felt around. Empty. I opened the main compartment of the bag and tipped it upside down, scattering the contents on the floor. Not there. The thousand pounds was gone.

What had I been thinking? Leaving the bag unattended with all that money inside. I was an idiot. I was screwed. I'd signed for the money from the Regimental Clerk. It was my responsibility. The band had to be paid but now it was to be with my money. With the lifestyle I'd adopted since I'd been back, my bank account, once fat with unspent Afghan wages, was looking positively malnourished. I couldn't afford this.

I briefly considered confession. Laying my foolishness bare in front of my boss and begging for leniency. I imagined his face, the stony contempt-filled stare, followed by the slow headshake of disappointment. Then would come the dismissive shrug and the, 'Sorry, your problem.' Christ, we wasted enough money on operations. Every Javelin anti-tank rocket cost twenty-five times as much as the cash I'd lost and people in Afghanistan were popping them off at blokes in flip-flops just for the hell of it. But it was different rules back here and I was bang to rights. My screw up. I had to sort it out.

I still had my chequebook. After a brief argument with the band, who obviously preferred cash, I managed to sweeten the deal with a couple of crates of booze from behind the bar. Now I could drink.

My own guests were here somewhere but I didn't care to seek them out. I squirrelled away a bottle of vodka and went and found a private corner to give it my full attention.

Half an hour later, I was back and feeling a lot better. The world made a lot more sense when I was pissed. I could actually see more clearly. When I was sober there was too much noise, too much going on inside my head to see what was really important.

I took a seat at an empty table and watched a clutch of women on the far side of the dance floor. They'd been abandoned by their dates; it had reached that stage in the evening where many of the officers were drunk enough to forget about being chivalrous. A group of young officers were gathered in a tight circle by the bar, staring inwards, their backs to the world. I couldn't hear them but I knew from their intensity that they were talking about killing. I recognised the same fierce desire that had burned in me a year before. I wanted to go over and tell them that it wouldn't be like how they thought but realised at once the futility of such an act. No one could have dissuaded me from going after the war and so it was for these men. Since they were being so boorish, I wondered about taking the opportunity to approach their neglected girlfriends before I became too drunk for speech to be possible.

My plan was scuppered by the arrival of my company commander, who sidled into the chair next to me just as I was about to make my approach.

'Hullo Mark,' he said. 'Sorry to talk shop with you this evening but I wanted to catch you while you were over from London. We've got a couple of Guards we need you to cover. The battalion's off to Afghanistan in a few weeks. We're a bit short-staffed for the ceremonial stuff. You don't mind do you?'

I thought furiously for excuses while he listed the dates he wanted me to fill. They were all weekends.

'Actually, I've got quite a bit on over the next few weeks,' I said.

The company commander's expression hardened. 'Well, there's no one else. You'll just have to move some things around. It's not like you're going on tour so you really ought to be a bit more willing to help out.'

Considering the matter settled, he walked away, breaking into a sort of half-hearted jig as he reached the dance floor. Prick.

I was by now thoroughly sick of the Army. In all walks of life one has responsibilities and irksome duties to perform, but it seemed to me now that no part of my job was worthwhile. None of it – from the life or death stuff in Nad Ali to the absurd pantomime of public duties. Well I was fucked if I was going to play any more. I was done with orders.

Over by one of the other tables, a man in a Roman legionnaire's costume leaned to reach a bottle. He stumbled as he did so, knocking a glass onto the tiled floor where it smashed. By now, no one was sober enough to bother about a bit of broken glass and it was left on the floor. I stared, fixated by the shards that glinted red, yellow, green and blue as the disco lights strobed. I don't think I was in full control of myself, or even fully aware of what it was I was doing, as I unlaced my shoes and slipped them off. It was in a kind of slow motion that I made my way across the room. I paused briefly, resting my hand on the table top, before slowly, deliberately, pressing my foot hard onto the broken glass and twisting it.

I don't remember the pain. Perhaps I was too drunk to feel any or perhaps it was down to the nerves I severed. I do remember the blood running out from beneath my foot and thinking that there seemed to be an awful lot. Then my focus went. I lost my balance; hit my head on the way down. The last conscious thought I had was one of triumph. Good luck ordering me to do guard now.

CHAPTER TWENTY-EIGHT

The morning after the ANA soldier was shot, the weather set in. Dust storms are a common hazard in Helmand and they wreaked havoc on our operating capability. You could see them moving in over the horizon, great orange blobs drifting out of the desert.

When the storm arrived, the air thickened with tiny sand particles, making breathing difficult and stinging any exposed skin. The sky turned a sickly yellow colour and the weak sunlight strained to get through. Before going outside I would wrap my shemagh around my face and then dash quickly to the safety of another building, my eyes streaming with tears by the time I arrived. It wasn't the discomfort or poor visibility on the ground that put the kybosh on patrolling though. Aircraft couldn't fly through the storms and without air cover we didn't leave the base.

So we stayed in. At first this was a relief from the relentless pressure of patrolling and combat, and I welcomed the opportunity for some downtime. I wrote some overdue reports, had the men clean their weapons thoroughly, shaved for the first time in a week, enjoyed a shower. So far, so productive, but by the time the sun went down I realised that was it. I had nothing left to do but I still couldn't relax. My body was stuck on high alert and my mind kept racing, processing all the violence I'd seen over the past days.

The next day the storm still hadn't lifted – sandstorms in Helmand could last three or four days. I asked Capt Wali if he wanted to run some small training exercises in camp but he was unenthusiastic. It was hard to blame him. The storm was a god-sent opportunity for the ANA to get some rest and my own blokes seemed happy to ride out the storm, spending it asleep or playing video games.

For me the enforced rest was a sentence. I moved restlessly between the ops room and my bed space, occasionally calling in on the interpreters for some variety. I couldn't settle. The truth was I had no one I could really talk to in camp. The remaining OMLT blokes, Magoo, Beattie and Charlie, were a likeable group and the long hours out on patrol had welded us into a tight-knit unit. But the soldier–officer divide remained and I could never truly relax when I was around them.

Not only did the sandstorm stop us patrolling, it also pre-vented the resupply helicopters from reaching us. Wadood's S2 took me to see their storeroom to show me how dire the situa-tion was becoming. It was practically bare – just a few sacks of rice. There wasn't more than four days' worth of food left for the entire kandak. The ammunition state was little better. They were almost entirely out of PKM ammunition and they were down to the last few AK-47 rounds. If the Taliban launched a frontal assault on the base it wouldn't be long before the ANA were reduced to using their rifles as clubs. Still my pleas for Brigade to send more supplies continued to fall on deaf ears. I prayed that the sandstorm was keeping the enemy inside too.

Everyone was on edge. Woody was an old friend but being confined to the ops room while I went out on the ground had bred a distance between us. As the days slipped by he had become increasingly frustrated. It can't have been easy being stuck next to a radio, sitting in a chair, listening as the bullets flew. Since the Apache attack, DB had become even more tac-iturn and spent most of his spare time sitting on his bed in the medical centre, reading a book or staring into space. As for Harry, I avoided him at all costs, not trusting my temper to hold if we spoke.

On the evening of the second day of the sandstorm Woody came into the ops room looking even more curmudgeonly than usual. He'd been taking his turn to use the one satellite phone we had to call back to the UK and speak to his family. Contact with the outside world was infrequent and the pressure of making up for weeks of estrangement in one ten-minute call placed a great deal of strain on relationships. From Woody's face I could tell his conversation had not gone well. The Company Sergeant Major was the first to make a remark. 'Trouble on the estate, sir? Servants misbehaving?' Distinctions of social class may be blurring fast across Britain but in the Army the old order struggles on. It was a stock joke among the soldiers that all officers are members of the landed aristocracy and they rarely missed an opportunity to take the piss. In fact Woody's father was a soldier himself and he had grown up as a so-called 'pad brat' on a succession of military bases around the world. It didn't matter; he was an officer now, a Rupert, and the joke still worked. The soldiers in the room all chuckled. Woody merely glowered.

'Everything all right?' I asked.

'It's my ex,' he replied. 'She's getting married. Wedding's tomorrow.'

Some might have been sympathetic to Woody's anguish as he dealt with what was clearly an emotive subject. None of those people joined the Army though. 'Got fed up waiting for you to come home?' one soldier asked.

'Or was your cock too small?' quipped another.

Even Harry joined in. 'We should have a party,' he said. 'Celebrate the wisdom of another girl who's realised she can do better.'

With nothing more suitable to hand we raised our bottles of lukewarm water and toasted our comrade's inability to keep hold of a woman. 'They're probably shagging right now,' chimed in the Company Sergeant Major. 'Sealing the deal.' We all found the humour in Woody's pain but it wasn't really about that. It was just a rare opportunity for us all to relax and forget about where we were for half an hour.

I excused myself from the festivities to attend my regular dinner engagement with Wadood. The S2 joined us this evening, for which I was glad, as I wasn't sure how well disposed the Colonel would be towards me after the twin setbacks of the Apache and Brigade's refusal to fly out his dead soldier. I apologised again for Brigade's intractability but Wadood refused to dwell on it. 'It is done,' he said. 'The man is buried now but you and I will continue to fight alongside one another.'

I remarked that Wadood's soldiers had seemed to react more emotionally to the prospect of the dead man not being buried on time than they had to his death.

'Death is part of life,' said Wadood. 'It comes to us all and we can't control when that will be. If there's nothing one can do about something then there is no point in worrying about it. Everything is in God's hands. *Insha'Allah* – God willing.'

I thought of the Afghan soldiers refusing to take cover in the ditch as we'd retreated under fire the day of the Apache strike. They'd seemed to think themselves impervious to the Taliban's bullets but maybe they just trusted God to keep them safe until it was their time to go. I put this hypothesis to the Colonel and he agreed wholeheartedly. 'That is the true embodiment of *Insha'Allah*.'

Across the table the S2 began to chuckle through his large beard. Wadood turned and glared at him. 'Have you got something to add?' he asked.

'Well, Colonel,' said the S2. 'That's not the only reason they prefer to stay out of the irrigation ditches.'

Wadood raised an eyebrow.

'It's their boots,' the S2 continued. 'They don't want to get them wet. Unlike you British we only get one pair of boots a year. The army won't issue a second pair. Once our boots fall apart we'll be walking round in bare feet.'

'Your soldiers would rather risk death than damage their shoes?' I asked.

The S2 laughed. 'Death comes to us all. Good shoes are harder to find.'

CHAPTER TWENTY-NINE

July 2009

I was taken away from the ball in an ambulance. The doctors dug the glass out of my foot and stitched me up but they told me I'd sustained extensive nerve damage and that I'd eventually need an operation. In the meantime I was on crutches and in a substantial amount of pain. My father came to pick me up from the hospital. We were due to visit my grandad that afternoon, who was by now in hospital himself.

In the car Dad made a few solicitous inquiries about my foot but over the years he had picked me up from various casualty departments and had become blasé about my capacity to bounce back from injury. Besides, he was more worried about my mother, since her dad was not expected to last much longer.

When we arrived at the hospital we went straight in to Grandad's room. My mother and grandmother were both there sitting by the bedside. Grandad was asleep on his back and his breath came in short gasps. His head looked small, lying among an array of vast, over-plumped pillows.

I kissed my mother and grandmother hello. They were both tired, with drawn faces and dark circles ringing their eyes. 'Why don't you go for a cup of tea while he's asleep?' I said. 'I'll stay with Grandad.' They agreed and my father went with them, leaving me alone with my grandfather. I sat down in one of the chairs next to the bed and watched him as he slept. He seemed to have deteriorated since the last time I'd visited and I knew this would likely be the last time I would see him. It was difficult to believe this was the same vigorous man I'd known growing up, who had spent most of his visits to my parents' house outside in the garden, doing battle with weeds and digging through flowerbeds like a human JCB. It was harder still to picture this frail, parchment-skinned old man fighting in a war, hurling himself into the dust and crawling through a hail of bullets, in just the same way that I had a few months ago.

After a few minutes my grandfather stirred and slowly opened his eyes. His gaze was unfocused and he raised a hand to block out the sun streaming through the window opposite his bed.

'Hello Grandad,' I said.

He opened his mouth and tried to speak but a coughing fit intervened. When he recovered he looked directly at me and for a moment his gaze was clear. I was sure that he recognised who I was. His hand appeared over the top of the covers and fluttered unsteadily towards me. I stood up and reached down to grasp it — it was almost weightless. I caught his eye again and almost imperceptibly felt his hand squeeze mine. I squeezed back. We held each other's gaze for two or three seconds. Then I felt my grandfather's grip relax once more and his eyes shut.

Later that day, while my father and I were on the motorway back to London, I received a phone call from my mother. My grandfather was closer to the end than we'd thought. We should turn round and come back. We didn't make it. I tried to feel something but no emotion came. It wasn't that I hadn't loved him. I had, deeply. I was just relieved his suffering was over. After seeing young Afghans die painfully, the natural passing of an old man seemed somehow all right, how death was meant to be.

Exactly a week later, we had the funeral. The ceremony was extremely well attended. The small church wasn't large enough to accommodate all the mourners. For such a quiet man my grandfather had an enormous number of friends. My mother cried. I wished that I could comfort her but found myself unable to respond with any warmth. I stood up when everyone else did and bowed my head when the vicar called for prayer. I had no prayers to offer.

After the service we went across to a hotel opposite the church for a few sandwiches and cups of tea. I skulked in the lobby while everyone else stood around in the lounge and talked about my grandfather. I was *wondering how long I could stay out here before someone dragged me back to the crowd when my grandmother walked in.*

'Oh, hello Mark,' she said. 'I thought you might be out here.'

'Hi Grandma. I just came to find a bit of space. It's a bit crowded through there.'

'That's all right, dear. Wherever you feel most comfortable.'

She was holding it together remarkably well. Apart from a few tears during the service, my grandmother was composed and managed to smile at me like she really meant it. It was the smile I found hardest to bear. I felt like a real shit. Here was a lady who had just lost her husband of nearly sixty years and she was the one putting on a brave face. It was supposed to be the other way around. I should have been supporting her but could think only of myself.

'How are you?' she asked.

'I think I'm supposed to ask you that,' I replied.

Another heartbreaking smile.

'I've been worried about you these past few months,' she said. 'You've not been yourself.'

'I'm fine, honestly.'

My grandmother carried on looking at me with that same expression of kindly concern and I felt my own pain well up inside.

'No. I'm not. I'm not fine, actually. Ever since Afghanistan I've not been fine. Some things happened to me over there and I can't stop thinking about them. I want to forget but I can't.'

My grandmother reached down and placed a hand on my shoulder. 'I thought so,' she said. 'You know your grandad was the same when he came back from India after the war. He'd wake up in the night screaming. He wouldn't tell me what it was he'd been dreaming about. He wouldn't tell me what had happened to him either. He'd just go out into his allotment for hours on end. He wanted to be on his own.'

'What happened? Did he have any help?'

'Oh, no. That didn't happen in our day. Every second person was going through the same thing. Wasn't done to talk about it. People just got on.'

'I think I might need some help, Grandma. I'm thinking about going to see a doctor.'

Those words coming out of my mouth shocked me. I wasn't thinking that, was I? I hadn't seriously considered this since the doctor in Windsor prescribed me sleeping pills and sent me on my way. My friend Steph had suggested once that I get help but she thought you needed psychiatric help for joining the Army in the first place. I looked over at my crutches and remembered the blood leaking out of my foot. That hadn't been the behaviour of a man in control. Shit. Now my grandma was going to think I was weak. Or she'd be embarrassed about the stigma. The world would think she'd got a grandson who'd gone raving mad. I couldn't believe I was laying all this on her, the same day that she'd buried her husband.

'Quite right too,' she said. 'Good for you.'

'Don't you think I should just get on with it, the way Grandad did?'

'Of course not. That was sixty years ago. The world's moved on since then. I hope it has, anyway. If you've got a problem then get it fixed.'

I was amazed by my grandmother's pragmatism. Perhaps her generation really was made of sterner stuff than mine.

'Anyway,' she went on, 'take your time out here. Come back through whenever you feel like it. And if you don't then that's quite all right too.'

Left on my own, my thoughts turned again to my grandfather. He was probably the only person I was close to who might have understood what was going on inside my head but I didn't regret not having seen him more after I'd got back. I didn't want lots of memories of him flat on his back, struggling to breathe. There wasn't even anything for us to really talk about. It wouldn't have helped either of us to have unpicked the sordid realities of each other's war. The only thing I really wanted to know was if he thought it was worth it. What he went through, all the death he saw and meted out, all the physical suffering, did it mean anything? He hadn't fought his way across Europe, didn't repel the Germans and stop them invading his homeland. His war was fought halfway around the world, protecting an empire that was almost dead anyway. When he got home, the war had been over for months and people were *already moving on. His was the Forgotten Army. Or maybe none of that mattered. Perhaps, as my grandmother had put it, he'd just got on. I had found no logic to justify the war I fought. It seemed that we'd achieved nothing in Afghanistan other than ratchet up the death toll. But I'd been a soldier and I'd done my duty. Now I just wanted to get on too. If that meant I had to see a doctor, then so be it.*

CHAPTER THIRTY

It wasn't until the fourth day that the weather cleared, by which time I was desperate to get back out on patrol once more. As we made our preparations to go out, Harry called me over to the ops room.

'Mark, I want you to bin your plan for the patrol this morning. There's a new task for you.'

It transpired that Col Wadood had reported that an IED had been planted in Compound Green, the building from which we'd ambushed the Taliban patrol. The enemy hadn't been scared off by our ambush and still went there to shoot at our base.

'Are you sure?' I asked. 'Why would the Taliban booby-trap their own firing point?'

Harry scowled. 'Don't argue the toss, Mark,' he said. 'Get a patrol over there and find out what's going on.'

I left the ops room and went to brief the guys on the new mission. We were only going a few hundred metres. Provided the enemy behaved themselves, it should be a quick patrol.

Capt Wali was coming along with his platoon. I asked him why he thought the Taliban would mine a compound that they used so frequently. He looked momentarily confused, began to say something but finished up simply shrugging.

As we prepared to leave I caught sight of Ash. He had an AK-47 slung over his shoulder.

'What are you doing with that?' I asked.

'What? This?' Ash said, all wide-eyed innocence. 'One of the ANA lads gave it to me.'

'You do know that you're a non-combatant? You're strictly not allowed to carry a weapon.'

'After what happened last time I went out with you, I thought I'd be safer if I had a weapon.'

'Do you even know how to use it?'

Ash looked sheepish. 'I just point it and pull the trigger, don't I?'

'I think we'd all be safer if you left it behind.'

Ash gripped the weapon tightly. 'Those Taliban keep shooting at me,' he pleaded. 'It's my right to defend myself.'

I sighed. I could see his point. The threat was as serious as ever. The Jocks had come under heavy fire that very morning. 'Well, don't point it anywhere near me.'

Ash grinned nervously.

We took the most direct route to the compound, straight through the fields. We were now just weeks away from the harvest, although there was still no sign of any farmers and the crops were at least eight feet tall. It was hot work, pushing through the thick green foliage, but at least we were hidden from any prying eyes that might have been out there.

It took us around twenty minutes to reach the compound and my heart grew heavier with each step. I knew that the job of identifying the IED would fall to me. It was going to be like the market-place in Gereshk all over again, except the chances of it being a false alarm this time seemed remote.

I crouched next to the gate at the entrance to the compound and tried to compose myself. Now that I'd experienced combat, one might expect that I'd have discovered new reserves of courage, that being under fire and surviving would have infused my soul with steel. Apparently not. If anything I felt even more cautious than the last time I'd gone to investigate a bomb.

Capt Wali walked over. 'You coming?' he asked.

'Just a minute,' I said. I waved a pack of cigarettes in his direction, hoping he'd accept and buy me a few more minutes. Wali shrugged and took one. I was struck by the change in him. In Gereshk he'd been careful not to go anywhere near the bomb, happy to marshal his troops manning the cordon. Today he was leading the way, impatient to get down to business.

We finished smoking, stood up and, with no more excuses proceeded through the gate, as ever accompanied by Ash. It looked just as it had the last time I'd been there to set the ambush. The makeshift firing platforms we'd built against the wall were still there.

Our enemies hadn't bothered to conceal their trap. There, at the edge of the patio, perched atop a water butt was the bomb. I had never seen anything quite like it. The outer casing of the device was an enormous earthenware cooking pot and from out of the top sprouted a mass of tangled wires hanging down towards the floor like spindly jungle creepers. My heart was in my mouth. The bomb looked huge.

Aware that there could be a pressure plate on the ground to trigger the device, I swept the ground thoroughly with a metal detector before I approached. I took a dozen hurried photos on my digital camera, moving nervously around the bomb to capture it from all sides. Then, screwing up my courage I moved slowly forward to get some closer shots.

Boom!

I catapulted backwards landing heavily on the tiles, convinced the world had just ended. Then, through the fog of terror, the sound of laughter broke through. Wali loomed over me, clutching two cast-iron cooking pots. He swung them together and a loud bang echoed again around the courtyard. Ash was sprawled in the dust next to me, looking as terrified as I felt. I thought he might take a swing at Wali as he scrambled to his feet. Tears of mirth streamed down Wali's face. He wiped them away and extended a hand to help me to my feet.

'That's not funny!' I yelled. 'Let's get the hell out of here before that thing really does go bang.'

Still chuckling, Wali followed me back out through the gate. I'm quite sure this was the funniest thing he had seen since the war began. Stony-faced, I told Wali to get his men together and we headed back to the schoolhouse.

Once we were safely back at base, I made my report to Harry. He took a look at the photos and agreed with me. 'Looks like a bomb. Looks like a big bomb.' I wrote up a brief report to go with the photos and we emailed it back to Brigade. They shared our opinion and in due course an ATO was dispatched to check it out.

An ATO arrived by helicopter the following evening and with her came several crates of ammunition for the ANA. It wasn't enough but if it continued to trickle through we might stave off disaster. We arranged another patrol to escort her to the compound. This time I was only too happy to remain outside the wall while she went and looked at the bomb. When she emerged, she looked quite perplexed. 'It's a bomb, all right,' she said. 'But not like anything I've encountered before. I wouldn't really know where to begin taking it apart.'

Since Compound Green was stuck out on its own and not on any particular patrol route, we were in no hurry to have the bomb defused. Instead we strung tape across the gate as though it were a crime scene and left it alone. On our maps we blocked out the area immediately around the compound and ordered all patrols to keep their distance.

Following the ATO's inspection of the bomb and her subsequent report, we received a message from Brigade HQ, telling us that experts at Permanent Joint Headquarters (PJHQ) in the UK had taken an interest in the device and planned to send a specialist team to investigate. They feared that it represented a hitherto unknown type of bomb, a next-generation IED that could be more dangerous than anything seen before. When I heard this latest intelligence, the backs of my hands began to sweat as I thought about how close I'd been. Wali really wasn't a funny man.

CHAPTER THIRTY-ONE

I'd been in Nad Ali for four weeks. Days had passed since the Brigade had delivered the turbine to the dam at Kajaki but there was no sign of any troops being sent to help us lift the siege. We couldn't just leave. If the Taliban took Nad Ali then Lashkar Gah would be in danger. The Brigade Commander and his staff, who had been directing our operations from Lash, were coming to the end of their six-month tour and their thoughts had turned to an orderly handover of command to the incoming 3 Commando Brigade, the unit that would be in charge for the next half a year. The Taliban, meanwhile, had stepped up their campaign against us. Snipers were taking pot shots at the base up to five times a day now and only through a combination of luck and our own sentries' marksmanship had no one else been shot. On top of that we received word through Wadood's mysterious intelligence network that the Taliban were bringing a mortar team into the area. There wasn't much we could do to defend ourselves against this new threat and we mentally prepared to deal with more casualties over the coming days.

Then, out of the blue, we received a message from Brigade that a small team was going to be arriving in Nad Ali by helicopter and would stay with us for several days. Woody, anxious about our limited food supplies, asked for more details. He was told by Brigade that the mission was classified. Just secure the HLS and find space for the newcomers to sleep, they told him. It was all most mysterious but Woody just found it frustrating.

In due course the helicopter arrived. The new arrivals turned out to be two corporals from the Special Forces Support Group (SFSG), a recently formed infantry unit made up of Paras, Marines and a few RAF Regiment guys whose job it was to provide assistance to the SAS and SBS on their missions. With them were four Afghans who described themselves as Special Forces. Straight away the corporals managed to annoy Woody.

'I can't tell you what we're doing,' said one, leaning against the wall of the ops room, arms folded and sunglasses set at a jaunty angle on his head. 'It's need to know, I'm afraid.'

'Need to know?' Woody gripped the armrest of his chair to keep his temper in check. 'Well, this is my fucking AO and we've been knocking back the Taliban here for nearly a month now without any support. We're fighting for our lives right now so who runs around town and what they do here falls very much into the category of things I need to know.'

The corporal smiled and shrugged. Technically, he was in the right. What the Special Forces and their supporting units get up to is their own business. They didn't report to the normal chain of command and were tasked directly from London, but the arrogance of these men was infuriating. Woody sent them over to stay with us – well away from his own accommodation. 'Thanks,' I said.

I suppose it was nice to have a few other people around the place. It made us feel a little less isolated and if the Taliban attacked in force then at least there would be seven extra rifles manning the wall. But we didn't understand them and they didn't appreciate what we'd been through these past weeks. The SFSG thought they were the gnarliest motherfuckers who ever picked up a gun and that they were the only ones that ever got in a real fight. The reality was that in Afghanistan the regular infantry was seeing some of the toughest combat since the Second World War. Griff, nineteen years old, with a year's service under his belt and now lying in a hospital bed in Birmingham, had seen as much combat as the most grizzled Cold War veteran of yesteryear. Actually this was beginning to cause a problem with special forces recruitment. Before Afghanistan caught fire in 2006, soldiers had seen service with the SAS as the only way to experience real war-fighting. Now they were getting more than their share of bloody mayhem without having to subject themselves to the rigours of SF selection. Why would they bother? We'd won our spurs here in Nad Ali and weren't about to be impressed by a couple of alley-looking dudes with flash sunglasses. For their part, the SFSG guys weren't much interested in us anyway, spending most of their spare time hanging around the medical centre, trying unsuccessfully to chat up Sgt Taylor.

The kandak received the new arrivals with even less warmth than we had. The four ANA Special Forces men were persona non grata in the kandak lines from the start and soon learned to keep to their corner of the OMLT accommodation block. I didn't understand the cause of the friction, and just assumed they had similar issues with their new arrivals as we did with ours. At dinner with Wadood that night, I learned that there was a little more to it.

'They aren't to be trusted,' said Wadood. 'Those people don't believe in Afghanistan. They are traitors. Always have been.'

'The ANA Special Forces?' I asked.

'No, not all ANA Special Forces. These men are from a particular tribe. They've always betrayed us to the enemy. For hundreds of years.'

Wadood went on to relate a complex history of politics and betrayal that at face value had little bearing on our situation today. Afghans have long memories though and their blood feuds can span generations. It was yet another facet of this country which eluded me and, I suspect, all the men and women who shaped our policy here.

The following morning I was in the ops room, briefing Harry on our latest patrol, when one of the SFSG men burst through the door. Harry broke off from our conversation. 'Can we help you, corporal?' he asked.

'Your bloody Afghans have been stealing our kit,' he said, pointing a finger at me. 'We've lost a pair of night-vision goggles.'

'What's that got to do with the ANA?' I said. 'Maybe you just dropped them.'

'We don't just drop valuable equipment. I'm telling you that they've been lifted from the accommodation.'

The back and forth went on for a while, the corporal refusing to budge from his position. Reluctantly, I agreed to get Wadood involved. I knew how he'd react. The ANA were our colleagues. They risked their necks alongside us every day. And now we were accusing them of petty theft.

Sure enough, Wadood was furious. He prided himself on the discipline of his troops. Suggesting that they would steal from their allies was incredibly insulting. I reassured him that I personally didn't believe his men were to blame, but this did nothing to dispel the frosty atmosphere.

'Why are you taking orders from a corporal?' he wanted to know. It was quite baffling to him why we wouldn't just accept his word, but eventually he gave way and agreed to investigate. 'Mark my words though,' he said. 'It's not my men that will be the source of the trouble.'

Having effectively insulted the Afghans' honour, my role as intermediary between Harry and Wadood became nigh on impossible. Even ANA soldiers, men I'd fought alongside, now refused to make eye contact with me or my men, turning coldly aside when we passed them in the base.

Two days later I was sitting in the ops room, having a brew with Woody, when Ash jogged over to us, sweating and clearly agitated. He glanced around furtively. Only when he was satisfied the coast was clear did he launch into his story, which he told in hushed, conspiratorial tones.

The interpreter's delivery may have been comical but what

he had to say was deadly serious. 'I was just passing by the room where those ANA Special Forces guys are staying,' he whispered. 'The door was open and I could hear two of them talking. They are bad men. I heard them say how they were planning to break into the rooms where the British soldiers sleep and kill them. They are planning to do it tonight! It's just two of them though. They said they had to keep their plans secret from the others.'

It was a plot that sounded at once quite fantastical but also terrifyingly plausible. There had been two such attacks – Afghan soldiers turning on British or American troops – in the last year alone. I didn't know the details but had heard the horror stories third or fourth hand. It was a chilling thought that the men who you patrolled alongside, and on whom you relied to have your back, could in fact be waiting for just the right time to put a bullet through your head.

We had to act quickly. Woody went off to find Harry, while I went in search of Wadood. If we were to foil this plot, we would need the Colonel's support. Given the contempt in which he held these Special Forces soldiers I was sure he'd quickly get on board with these latest developments.

Twenty minutes later we convened a council of war in the Colonel's office. We couldn't yet know if the interpreter's tale was accurate but it was a risk we couldn't afford to take. Harry and Wadood were for once in complete agreement. The suspects had to be arrested. It was agreed that the British would take the lead on this. That way, if we'd got it wrong, Wadood would be less likely to face repercussions from the ANA Special Forces leadership. It was really the only course of action open to us, yet it felt strange to be moving against men who we'd considered allies.

Firstly the S2 separated the two innocent Afghan special forces men from the two under suspicion by inviting them to his office for a chat. The job of taking the suspects into custody was given to a squad made up of the biggest soldiers on camp, headed by the Company Sergeant Major. Harry, Woody, Wadood and I loitered in the courtyard while the squad went into action. The six soldiers crept slowly towards the accommodation block, taking a circuitous route around the back to avoid being seen from the windows. The suspects were heavily armed and if they realised what was happening they might open fire.

Our men were in position. At a signal from the Company Sergeant Major, one of the corporals smashed open the door with a kick and the rest of the squad piled in behind, pistols drawn. The element of surprise was total; it was all over in minutes. The Company Sergeant Major escorted them out, wrists bound together with plastic handcuffs. The kandak hadn't been informed of the impending action and soldiers stopped and stared as the prisoners were marched across the schoolyard. We'd got them as far as the schoolhouse, the most substantial building in the base, when we realised that there was actually nowhere secure to keep them. The plan was to fly them back to Lash as soon as possible but a helicopter wouldn't be arriving for another day. It was Woody who came up with the idea of locking them in the back of a Snatch. They were pushed in and a couple of Jocks were posted outside as sentries. As midday approached, conditions were far from ideal, and although they were given water, the temperature inside the makeshift prison must have been unbearable.

We had no way of telling if justice had been carried out or whether we'd arrested two innocent men. The interpreter could have been lying, or simply got the wrong end of the stick; it could have been a scheme concocted by Wadood, fuelled by tribal prejudice. But we simply couldn't afford to take the risk. I supposed they'd sort it all out in Lash. I was more inclined to dwell on the possibility that there were more traitors in our midst. If there were two potential murderers, then why not more? Although I trusted the ANA implicitly, I really didn't know them that well. Even Wadood, despite all our conversations over dinner, remained an enigma. Helmand politics were extremely murky; all manner of motives and alliances bubbled away. We British just floated along hopefully, blind to monsters lurking beneath the surface.

My contemplation was rudely shattered by a thunderous explosion. The mortar team we'd heard about were making their first attack. Two more bangs followed in quick succession and I sprinted for the hard cover of the schoolhouse. Soldiers across the base crammed into whatever shelter was nearest and hunkered down, waiting for the barrage to end. We could hear the thud of each round as it hit. The walls of the concrete building shook. There were perhaps only three or four explosions but spaced out, so just when I thought the attack was over, another round would land. I imagined the shrapnel spraying across the schoolyard and was glad I'd made it in here, rather than getting stuck outside near the sangars. Mortars might struggle to penetrate a concrete wall but anyone caught in the open was likely to be ripped apart.

After maybe quarter of an hour, the explosions stopped completely. There seemed to have been no casualties and in fact no rounds had landed inside our perimeter – a lucky escape.

It was one of the Jocks who'd been on sentry duty by the Snatch who raised the alarm. The back door of the vehicle was wide open. There was no sign of the prisoners. The hapless soldier was quite distraught. 'I ran to take cover,' he pleaded. 'The door was locked. I dunno how they can have got out!'

A small crowd formed around the vehicle and a loud debate kicked off. Should we give chase? We needed to sort our kit and mount a patrol.

While we in the British contingent were making our plans, the ANA moved with lightning speed. Before we'd even started to issue orders for a patrol they were out of the gate. Four Toyotas tore down the track into the DC. Wadood watched their departure from the steps outside his office before disappearing inside to co-ordinate the hunt. No worries about air cover now.

The decisive action taken by the ANA made me proud. For months I'd been lecturing Wali and the other ANA commanders on the importance of quick thinking. Now they'd put it into action.

Despite my admiration for the kandak's reactions, my money was on the fugitives to make good their escape. They could have been gone for up to twenty-five minutes before we'd discovered their disappearance. That was ample time for them to have found a well-concealed hiding place in the deserted DC or to have travelled several kilometres in any direction.

As it turned out, my faith in the cunning of the escapees was misplaced. It was only a few minutes before the first one was dragged back through the gate, followed not half an hour later by his comrade. Instead of handing them straight back into the care of the Company Sergeant Major, both men were hustled inside the schoolhouse. Harry was indignant, insisting that they should be returned to British custody at once. He ordered me to arrange this with the Colonel.

Walking with Ash along the corridor towards Wadood's office, I could hear shouting from behind the closed door. When I opened the door there was a man lying on the floor. Wadood and the S2 stood on either side. Another two men were kneeling, facing the wall, covered by a pair of sergeants with pistols. Wadood looked over at me as I entered but didn't speak.

I took a look at the man lying on the concrete. He looked like someone had recently given him a serious kicking – entirely against the rules but any one of the Afghan soldiers on base could have been responsible. As I peered down at him, I realised that I didn't recognise him. It wasn't either of the two men who we'd thrown in the back of the Snatch. They were the men kneeling by the wall.

'What's going on?' I asked. What else could I say?

Wadood paused for a moment, standing with his hands on his hips, staring down at the man in front of him. 'This is the bastard who let them out,' he said. 'One of my men.' Wadood spat on the floor. 'One of my own fucking men! He's from the same tribe as these other two traitors. I warned you about them.'

I was shocked by the vehemence in the Colonel's voice. I'd rarely heard him raise his voice before. He was a man normally in such control of his emotions that to see him like this, gripped by rage, was a profoundly disturbing experience. I realised that the usual latitude he granted me to speak my mind was probably absent today. I'd have to pick my next words with care.

'You're right. They're traitors and once we've got them off the base they'll be prosecuted. But for now, we should look after them properly.'

Wadood just stared at me.

'We can take them off your hands until the helicopter gets here tomorrow night,' I said.

'We'll give them back to you later,' Wadood said. 'Just before the helicopter arrives. Until then, we'll keep them. Safer that way.'

One of the sergeants opened the door behind me. I hovered for a moment but the implacable gaze of the Afghans told me everything I needed to know. These were Wadood's prisoners now. As I turned to go, the S2 stopped me. 'These are yours,' he said and handed me a pair of NVGs. 'We found them on one of the prisoners.'

I nodded and then walked back out of the office with Ash. The door was closed behind us. The ethical implications of what I'd witnessed consumed me.

Although the traitors had been caught, I couldn't help feeling nervous. If there were two such men, how many more might there be? From now on, no one slept easy in their bed.

233

CHAPTER THIRTY-TWO

August 2009

I went to see the doctor; it was easy in the end. The medical officer at Wellington Barracks was much more sympathetic than the one I'd seen in Windsor. I told her what I was feeling and straight away she told me I had PTSD. I'd suspected as much for a while but hearing someone else say it floored me. On the one hand it was a relief to hear that there was something legitimately wrong with me, something that made sense of all my mixed-up feelings, but at the same time I was suddenly terrified as to what it meant – was I really mentally ill? I lost my self-control and began to cry. The doctor had seen it all before and pushed a box of tissues across the desk. Embarrassed, I grabbed one and pulled myself together while she outlined my options for treatment.

I was lucky. I had private health insurance – my parents had insisted on it years ago because I was so accident-prone. Now it came into its own. With no particular hopes or expectations, I rang BUPA. They picked a specialist for me and sent me over to Harley Street for my first appointment.

I'd never really been convinced of the benefits of psychiatry, believing it to be the province of self-indulgent hypochondriacs and Americans. Consequently, my first few sessions didn't go that well. I spent most of the hour trying to convince Christina, my shrink, why someone would want to go to war in the first place and what doing so actually entailed. Surprisingly, I found myself on the defensive, desperately trying to justify to this stranger why it was OK to harbour a desire to go overseas to kill people. More than anything, perhaps, I was trying to convince myself, to recreate that belief I'd felt before I went away. Contrary to what I'd been told by the first doctor, talking about my problems didn't help at all but rather seemed to bring up more and more painful memories. Three sessions in, I went back to the doctor to report on my progress, or lack thereof, and she suggested that it might help if I attended an Army-run group therapy session with some of the other officers with whom I'd served in Nad Ali. Privately I thought that this was an absurd suggestion but the idea of seeing the others again was appealing. I agreed and the arrangements were made.

Two weeks later, I met Woody in a pub around the corner from Wellington Barracks. He'd come over from Colchester, where he was now based. He looked OK and had put a bit of weight back on but his eyes were sunken, telling a story of many sleepless nights. After the initial pleasantries, catching up on girlfriends – he had one – and moaning about our respective jobs – he was lobbying to go back to Afghanistan – we started talking about our tour. I hadn't seen him for nearly a year now and had no idea how he'd been getting on. It turned out that, like me, he'd been struggling. He'd had a few sessions with a psychiatrist but it hadn't done much to improve matters.

'Was it really that bad?' I asked about our time in Nad Ali. 'Or am I imagining it?' We talked about the contacts, the Apache and the Afghan soldiers we'd left behind.

'Yes,' he said. 'It really was that bad.'

It was fascinating to hear Woody's take on things. Especially his thoughts on Harry. They'd had a close relationship. As far as Woody was concerned Harry had done everything in his power to help us – all I had seen was him causing me problems. The truth was probably somewhere in between. It was the first time in almost a year that I had spoken to someone else who had been at Nad Ali. I realised then that my memories were simply that, my memories, not the whole picture.

Woody also had fresh news for me about the aftermath of the Apache incident. 'There's been an inquiry,' he said. I was astonished. How could they have an inquiry without a member of the patrol present? I had been the senior commander on the ground, so why hadn't I been asked to give evidence?

'Only Harry went along,' Woody continued. 'He told me about it afterwards. Not that there was much to tell. Sounded like they'd made up their minds before they started. They said that it was down to the "fog of war". No one to blame.'

I'd have taken a shot at apportioning blame. The bloke who pulled the trigger and shot up my patrol, surely that was a good place to start. I couldn't believe that the Army didn't want to hear my side of the story. Perhaps it was too embarrassing, the sort of thing best swept under the carpet and never spoken of again. It seemed like another 'Fuck you, Captain Evans' from the Army.

The following morning DB joined us for the therapy session. It was the first time I'd seen him since Nad Ali. The three of us took a cab together to Woolwich, where the Army had one of its psychiatric centres. According to Woody, DB was finding it hard to readjust. After the no-nonsense pragmatism of war fighting, DB had struggled to come to terms with the boot-polishing, knife-edge-creased bullshit of military life in the UK. He claimed that all was well but he had the same dead-eyed look I saw in Woody and, I had to admit, in the mirror.

When we arrived at the centre we were ushered through into a large office with a sofa and comfortable armchairs. Dotted around the room were unmistakable signs that the psychiatric nurse whose office we were in was an Army officer. A Barbour jacket hung on the back of the door and wellington boots stood next to the desk. Webbing pouches were heaped on the floor next to an army-issue bergen. Most tellingly of all, an elderly cocker spaniel snoozed on a dog bed in the corner.

The psychiatric nurse rose from behind his desk to greet us. 'Please take a seat,' he said. We ended up sitting in a circle, me and the nurse in the two armchairs while Woody and DB perched side by side on the sofa. I was wearing a suit, as were the other two. It was oddly formal attire for a therapy session and not one that lent itself to opening up and discussing our innermost thoughts. To make matters worse the nurse was wearing combat uniform, the crown insignia on his chest reminding us all that we were in the presence of a superior officer. Together we presented a perfect picture of discomfort. We all sat in identical poses with straight backs, our hands on our knees, staring straight ahead. The penalty for a wrong move in this room was a devastating loss of face in front of friends and colleagues, as well as a superior officer. None of us were going to risk it.

'So how are you feeling?' the nurse asked Woody.

'Fine.'

'And you, Mark?'

'Yeah, not bad.'

DB just yawned.

I knew the others were lying but then so was I. None of us were going to be the first to crack, to admit weakness.

The session meandered on, the nurse pushing us to talk about what we'd done in Nad Ali. We told him exactly what had happened while simultaneously saying nothing at all. 'I took my call sign on a patrol towards Luy Bagh. 200 metres from the base we were contacted. We returned fire and advanced towards the enemy position.'

'How did you feel?' the nurse asked.

'Tired.'

Eventually, he gave up and declared the session over. I walked out, proud not to have cracked but also acutely aware that any victory we'd scored here was over ourselves.

I had seen in the other two a reflection of my own troubled state and it didn't look pretty. Perhaps I had been underestimating what therapy might be able to do for me. I realised now that talking to military personnel about my problems wasn't going to help so it seemed that my private therapy sessions represented my only way out of this mess. I resolved to go back to Christina and try again with a renewed sense of purpose.

CHAPTER THIRTY-THREE

The next day was the second day of October, a month after I'd arrived in Nad Ali, and the Afghans celebrated the festival of Eid al-Fitr, which marks the end of Ramadan. I woke that morning to the sound of bleating. Outside, I was met by the incongruous sight of a dozen sheep milling around the courtyard. 'What the hell is going on?' shouted someone behind me. I turned to see Harry standing in the doorway of the ops room. He looked furious. 'Mark, who let these animals in here?'

'I don't know,' I said. 'I'll go and ask the Colonel.'

'It's a health and safety nightmare. Who knows what diseases they've got.'

I found the Colonel in excellent humour. '*Eid Mubarak!*' he greeted me as I walked into his office. 'The fasting is over at last.'

'*Eid Mubarak* to you too, Colonel,' I replied. 'Do you know what all these sheep are doing outside?'

'They're for the feast, of course. I had them brought in this morning. I hope you and all the other officers will join me for lunch today and we will celebrate the end of Ramadan in style.'

I was taken aback. It was astonishing that the ANA had enough food to be able to put together even basic meals, let alone a feast. 'I'd be delighted to. I'll pass on your kind invitation to Harry and the others. Where did you get the sheep from?'

'I phoned up some people I know round here and had them delivered.'

'But there's no one around here except the Taliban.'

Wadood inclined his head to one side. 'I've told you before. We may be enemies but we're all Muslims.'

I went back to Harry and passed on Wadood's invitation. 'Out of the question,' he said. 'We'll all end up with food poisoning.'

'I think it'll be all right. The meat couldn't be any fresher. It's still bleating now. Besides, it would be incredibly offensive if we turned down the invitation. You know that the ANA have been running out of food for days. They're offering to share what little they have with us. I don't think we can refuse.'

Harry sighed. 'If the entire company goes down vomiting then I'm going to hold you responsible, Mark.' He vanished back inside the ops room.

A few hours later, all the officers and SNCOs gathered in the Afghan dormitory where the beds had been cleared away and replaced with a number of wooden tables and benches. Wadood sat at the head and welcomed us all to the feast. He apologised for the frugal repast – just rice to go with the mutton. It was a timely reminder of how parlous their situation had become. I was glad that Ramadan was over. The ANA soldiers had been growing weaker by the day and were patrolling with less and less enthusiasm. I hoped that with full bellies they'd have renewed energy for the fight. On the other hand, it meant that the Afghans would start to go through their remaining rations even faster than before. We had to solve the supply chain problems before they actually began to starve.

The food was ladled into bowls and passed down the tables – hearty chunks of mutton on steaming white rice. It tasted delicious. I'd listened to the screams of the sheep as they'd been slaughtered in the northeast corner of the compound under one of the sangars. The noise had reminded me of DB's story about the dog he'd killed.

Harry sat beside the Colonel at the head of the table. I was between the S2 on my right and Ash on my left so he could interpret what the Afghans were saying. 'We're expecting an expert from the UK in a couple of days to look at that IED in Compound Green,' I told the S2. He looked at me in astonishment and leaned over to say something to Wadood. The two men began to smile. Wadood said something in reply which sent both men into fits of laughter. Whatever joke he'd made was swiftly passed around the rest of the Afghans until the whole room was in uproar. I looked round at the other British officers, who looked as bemused as I felt. The only Afghan who wasn't laughing was Ash. 'What's the joke?' I asked him.

'It's not really a joke,' he said. 'They are laughing about you bringing in an expert to look at the bomb.'

'Why's that funny?'

'It seems that there is no bomb in Compound Green. They're saying that there never was. Wadood sent some soldiers there to plant a fake bomb. He thought it might scare the Taliban and stop them using the compound as a place to shoot at us from.'

I stared at Wadood who was laughing harder than ever. 'I'm sorry,' he said, gasping for breath. 'I forgot to tell you. I thought you'd figure it out on your own. It's just an old cooking pot stuffed full of wires.' He collapsed into fresh gales of laughter.

I caught Harry's eye. He was trying to look stern but the absurdity of the situation had caught his imagination. His lip began to twitch and then he too was laughing. I couldn't help myself either. After the tension of the past month it felt so good to let go like this and made the whole joke seem much funnier than it really was. We laughed until tears ran down our faces and we fought for breath. The only person still straight-faced was Ash, who'd been by my side when we'd gone to investigate the 'bomb'. 'I thought I was going to die,' he said. Somehow, that just made me laugh even harder.

That night the helicopter arrived on schedule. Thirty minutes before, the ANA handed the three prisoners back over to the Company Sergeant Major. They limped as they walked but other than that looked in reasonable shape. The British SFSG corporals and the other, innocent, Afghan Special Forces men followed them onto the helicopter. We never did hear what happened to them or what their mission had been in Nad Ali.

Perhaps I ought to have felt guilty about what had occurred. I was a British officer and we had standards to uphold. I'd seen a prisoner who had probably been physically abused and done nothing. Was I complicit? What else could I have done? I'd asked Wadood to give up the men and he'd refused. He was fighting his own war and I was fighting to stay alive. The man on the ground had conspired to kill me and my soldiers. Wadood had my back. As the siege dragged on, my moorings were coming loose and I felt myself beginning to drift in a sea of moral ambiguity.

The same helicopter that took away our unwanted guests delivered to us another outsider, in the form of Captain Nick Bridle. Nick was the Battalion Ops Officer, right hand man to Lt Col Sandy, Harry's immediate boss. After a quick briefing with Harry he wandered out to find me and Woody smoking outside. He was tall and broad shouldered but months spent in the ops room in Lash had done nothing for his fitness – he had a pudgy, well-fed look about him. He dumped his kit down and treated me and Woody to a broad grin. 'All right, boys. So what's going on?'

It seemed that the reports we were sending to Lash had finally provoked a response, but not one we had expected. Our constant requests for more resources hadn't been taken seriously at Brigade. 'Well, it never looked to us like you were going to be overrun,' Nick explained. 'We thought that you were hanging on OK.'

Woody, always on a short fuse, erupted. 'Hanging on? We're fighting for our fucking lives and you cunts in Lash won't even send us enough food or ammunition.'

Nick was wrongfooted by the passion of Woody's response. He held up his hands in supplication. 'Hang on,' he said. 'We couldn't believe that things were that bad out here. That's why I've flown out. Col Sandy wanted someone to go and take a look; get a bit of perspective on the situation.'

I placed a consoling hand on Woody's shoulder. 'Nick,' I said. 'You've got to understand we're all a bit tense here. It's been a tough few weeks.'

'Right. Yeah, I see that now. Listen, it's getting late. Why don't we get our heads down and pick this up in the morning. Harry's said I can come out on patrol with you tomorrow, Mark – get a sense of the atmospherics out there.'

'If it's atmospherics you want,' I laughed, 'you've come to the right place.'

The following morning we started our patrol at 0600hrs. Beattie, Charlie and Magoo were all carrying minor, niggling injuries and so I decided to rest them. They didn't question my decision, perhaps glad of a bit of space after what we'd been through together. In order to go out I latched on to a patrol with DB's platoon. Wali's platoon was out as well. With sixty soldiers on the ground we looked a formidable force as we stepped through the fields. It worked well, having another British unit on the ground with us. While DB commanded his men, I led the ANA. The two of us kept in close touch over the PRR and managed to keep an impressive degree of order over the operation. Nick stuck close to me; although he was the most senior officer on the patrol he kept a strictly watching brief, a passenger just along for the ride.

We were headed north from the patrol base. The plan was to check out a couple of the compounds one kilometre away, searching for signs of Taliban activity. I felt particularly edgy. There were all the usual fears of IEDs, ambush or snipers but it was more than that. It was due in part to Nick's presence – I felt his eyes on me as we walked. I was conscious that he was judging me, drawing his own conclusions about the accuracy of our sitreps. If we didn't come under fire then would he think we were all fantasists? 'Yeah, it's pretty rough and ready down at Nad Ali,' he'd tell them back in Lash, 'but hundreds of Taliban? Nah, they're panicking over nothing.' I found myself praying for a quick and dirty contact, nothing too serious but enough to give Nick a good scare.

Then there were the Afghans. I'd felt a great many things, patrolling alongside these men during the past five months. Exasperation was commonplace, incomprehension and confusion were old friends. I'd even been properly angry a few times. But never before had I been frightened of them. Sure I'd been scared on patrol but only by what the Taliban might do to us. Now I looked around at the ANA men, my comrades, and felt an icy chill. No one could be trusted completely. We'd learned that the hard way. We were strangers in a foreign land and no matter how many battles we'd fought alongside one another, no matter how many brews we'd shared or what friendships we thought we'd forged, there was really no telling who might turn against us. This was the power of treachery. It was an insidious weapon and the Taliban knew it. Turning just one Afghan soldier against us had planted a cancer in our ranks. Instead of looking off to the horizon for trouble, my eye was drawn ever inwards, searching for an invisible danger.

Incredibly, we made it to our destination without incident and the search of the compounds turned up no hint of Taliban occupation. Plotting a different course home, we were moving along a rough track that looped into the DC from the east. Things were now so bad we no longer patrolled down roads or obvious routes, but moved tactically through the crops and long hedgerows. The point man spotted two figures standing in a field about two hundred metres to our front. We halted and took cover until we could assess the situation properly. Not since that first patrol with the Colonel had we seen civilians out in the fields. Our only encounters since then had been with the enemy but they didn't normally show themselves so brazenly. I checked in with Phil on the net, asking if he could see what they were up to on his screens. 'Can't see much,' he said. 'But one of them seems to be talking on a mobile.'

They could have been dickers – Army slang for unarmed enemies who spy on our movements for the enemy – calling their comrades to encircle us. The Taliban had become experts at exploiting our rules of engagement. They knew we weren't permitted to fire on people who weren't carrying weapons, no matter that they might be fully-fledged enemy combatants. If possible we wanted to talk to these men and find out exactly what they were up to.

It appeared that our suspects had failed to notice us from a distance as now they had left the field and were walking straight towards us down the track. We were all crouched low in the ditches on either side of the thoroughfare and we pushed ourselves further into the undergrowth for better concealment. Wali's platoon was in front, while DB's men were strung along the track a bit further back. If we wanted to take them by surprise it would have to be the ANA who made the move. I tapped Wali on the shoulder and outlined a plan to him. He nodded and passed a whispered message up the line to the rest of his troops.

As the two men drew level, a whole Afghan platoon burst from the ditches on either side, weapons pointed straight at them. One of the suspects cried out in fear while the other froze. Up close, they looked quite ordinary. Nothing about them signified that they might be Taliban fighters. Mind you, nothing ever did except when they clutched an AK-47 or RPG launcher. These two were both wearing ragged navy cotton trousers and white shirts with flip-flops. They could have been anything between about eighteen and twenty-four years old, or what we called 'military-aged males'. Wali had a short conversation with them and explained that they were claiming to be farmers having a look at their crops. There was no way to prove their story one way or another, but right now just being around Nad Ali was evidence enough to question someone further. 'Bring them with us,' I told Wali.

Our new prisoners didn't complain much, but with their hands bound together in front of them and four rifles pointed at their backs argument would have been futile. Half an hour later we were back at the base, where Wali delivered his captives to the Colonel. After what had happened with the traitors, I'd have sooner turned the men over to Harry but ultimately Wadood was in command here. I didn't want to clash with him again.

I shouldn't have worried. In contrast to the treatment meted out to the traitors yesterday, the kandak's behaviour towards these detainees was exemplary. They were sat down, offered tea and generally put at their ease. Both Wadood and the S2 had questions to put to them but at no time did they try to intimidate the prisoners. I was allowed to sit in the corner of the office and watch.

The whole questioning can't have taken longer than about forty minutes, at the end of which Wadood motioned for me to join him outside. 'They're just farmers,' he said. 'Not Taliban. We should let them go now.'

'Really?' I was still sceptical. 'What were they doing wandering around here? All the civilians have gone. Are you sure they aren't lying to you?'

'It's the harvest. It's overdue. All the farmers are worried. These crops you see in the fields need to be reaped. People's livelihoods depend on it. If they don't harvest soon, they will lose everything. These men were checking up on their crops, simple as that.'

The men had looked scared. Maybe it wasn't just the shock of being arrested. It must have been terrifying for any civilian to be here right now but I could see how the prospect of financial ruin could have impelled a farmer to risk everything if they thought there was a chance to save the harvest. Crop failure could easily equal starvation in this part of the world. The explanation was plausible. I went to find Harry. He found the prisoners' alibi much less compelling than I and insisted that they must be Taliban. Without a close relationship with the ANA, it seemed to me Harry was finding it increasingly difficult in Nad Ali. He wanted to fight the war on his terms but he found himself frustrated by what he saw as Wadood's perversity. I made an attempt to bridge the gap. 'Come to dinner with Wadood this evening,' I suggested. 'The Colonel needs to understand your priorities better.'

'There's no time for that,' said Harry and he turned back to his laptop. As I walked back to Wadood's office, the burden of being the one link between the Afghans and the British weighed heavily upon me. By the time I got there, the prisoners had gone.

I spent the next couple of hours talking to Nick, giving him my own perspective on the situation. His scepticism of the night before had been stripped away. 'I can see how tough it is here,' he said.

'Does that mean we'll get more troops?' I asked.

'Very unlikely. You have to understand that the Brigade's on its way home now. The staff have got half their mind back in Blighty. Your problem is that no one's been killed here yet.'

'Except for ANA soldiers,' I interrupted.

Nick smiled mirthlessly. 'You and I both know that's not the same. Don't look at me like that. You get what I mean. It's all politics. We could lose a battalion of Afghans and no one in London would pay the slightest attention. One Brit gets killed and it's a different story.'

He was right. If we'd started taking fatalities, we'd have had resources thrown our way immediately.

'Hey,' said Nick. 'Would you have swapped one of your dead Afghan soldiers for a British one? You'd have probably had two more companies down here if that had happened.'

I didn't know how to answer. Was an Afghan life worth less to me than a British one?

That afternoon I was sitting on the edge of my bed, cleaning my rifle. I found this necessary chore insufferably dull. It's an intricate business, stripping the weapon down to its component parts and digging into the tiniest recesses to scrape out the carbon residue that built up fast due to the huge number of rounds we were firing. The dust here made the task more arduous still, finding its way into every crevice. If you didn't clean your weapon every day the firing mechanism would stick, leaving you in a very dicey position come the next contact. I found myself longing for the AK-47 rifles carried by the ANA. You could rub sand all over those weapons, leave them to rust for a week and they'd still fire perfectly. Understandably the Afghan soldiers loved their rifles. When they heard that a deal had been done with the Americans to supply them with modern US-manufactured M16s they came closer to mutiny than at any other time.

I'd just about finished and was putting my rifle back together when there was a knock on my door. The S2 walked in. He pointed at my half-assembled weapon and laughed. 'What are you doing? You're an officer. Why don't you get a soldier to do that for you?'

I tried to explain that it was important for officers to carry out all the same basic tasks as soldiers. It set an example and meant that one's own skills remained sharp.

The S2 found this hilarious. 'When you get married, you will end up cooking like a slave while your wife sits and gets fat. Why aren't you married anyway? You're more than old enough. Maybe you like men more than women?'

This last sally sent him into fits of laughter and he clutched at the doorframe while he tried to regain the power of speech. When he recovered he remembered the reason he'd originally come to see me. The ANA had received intelligence that the

Taliban had moved a rocket launcher into the area and were planning a concerted attack on the helicopter when it flew in that evening. I was alarmed. The enemy attacked almost every helicopter that flew in, but so far it had been with small arms fire. Using a rocket launcher they'd have an even greater chance of shooting one down. Nick didn't seem to register the threat. I passed the information on to Harry and he agreed to double the number of troops on the ground that night.

Night drew in and we went into our pre-helicopter routine, setting out the cordon and putting patrols out to search for the enemy. The drawback of securing the HLS was that it flagged to the enemy that a helicopter was about to arrive. They knew that when we started these procedures after dark they had around 30 minutes to take up their firing positions.

I was on the football pitch, right beside the HLS itself. It was a clear night and the air was still. Everyone was in position. For a moment there was perfect silence. It didn't last long; it never did in Nad Ali. The buzz of rotor blades grew steadily until the whirling cacophony was directly above us, spitting grit in our faces. There was no sign of enemy action and I began to fantasise that we might get all this finished in the next twenty minutes and be back off to bed.

The chopper touched down fifty metres away, cargo door already open and the rotors kept on turning. 'Two passengers to pick up!' shouted the loadmaster. 'Get them on now!'

One of the interpreters was flying out tonight. He shuffled forward, bending low under the spinning blades. Nick was the second passenger. I shook his hand briefly before he too ran out towards the helicopter. As he did so, the scene was suddenly lit up. A ball of fire streaked through the darkness tracing an unerring path towards the rear of the Chinook. It struck the fuselage with a dull clang and all was dark again. 'RPG!' The shout went up on all sides. Nick was face down in the dirt, just two metres from the door. As he scrambled to his feet a huge explosion sounded somewhere off to my right. 'Incoming!' Machine-guns now joined in and bullets began to clatter against the sides of the helicopter. The Chinook does not have thick armour and these rounds were punching right through the skin. 'Fuck this,' the pilot thought and the rotors whined as he surged on the power. The chopper lifted straight up and headed north. Nick was left on the ground, trying to press himself even flatter into the surface of the football pitch.

At precisely the same moment as the Chinook tried to escape, the ANA to the east of the patrol base chose to start returning fire on the Taliban. Their tracer streamed over the top of the schoolhouse. The Chinook pilot had no time to change course and flew directly into the line of fire. It was moving so fast that it spent only a fraction of a second in the danger area but it was time enough for dozens of bullets to strike home. The helicopter leapt in the air as though it had been stung. I expected it to come tumbling out of sky right then. Instead it lurched to the right and accelerated off into the distance.

An Apache that had been standing by a couple of kilometres away was now on station and threw two Hellfire missiles into the darkness. I think they found their target – or if not, the Taliban realised that with the element of surprise gone this was no longer an equal contest and they fled.

Back in the patrol base, I walked into the ops room and put the kettle on. Nick sat in the corner, dishevelled and wild-eyed. 'So, how do you think things are in Nad Ali, now?' I asked him. He just stared and slowly shook his head.

The following day we received news that another helicopter would be flying in that night to pick up Bridle and take him back to Lash. It was most unusual for us to receive helicopters on successive nights and we were cheered by this, interpreting it as a sign that Brigade was finally beginning to take our predicament seriously.

'Make sure you tell them how bad it is here,' Woody told

Bridle. Bridle assured us that he would pull no punches in his report. He also explained that 3 Commando Brigade had now officially taken over command of Task Force Helmand from the 16 Air Assault and with the change of leadership he hoped there would come a renewed interest in our beleaguered corner of the province. The new battlegroup responsible for OMLT forces was 1 Rifles, a unit created by the merging of the Devonshire and Dorset Regiment and the Royal Gloucestershire, Berkshire and Wiltshire Regiment. From my first radio conversation with the new ops officer, I knew I was going to like them. Perhaps it was just the eagerness of a new bunch of guys yet to pay the bloody toll that Helmand exacts, but the new commanders were sympathetic and decisive where I'd found their predecessors obstructive and moribund. Perhaps that's not fair; we hadn't been the top priority for the last Brigade so it wouldn't have made sense for them to allocate us resources that were desperately needed elsewhere. Whatever the reason, it felt good to be finally getting a little love.

The first thing the Rifles pledged was a new team that would enable the OMLT to operate independently once more. In addition they were going to send an officer who would be able to take the reins from me when I finally left. His name was Iwan Williams and he was due to fly in that night on the same helicopter that would take Bridle away. I was introduced to him over the net. 'Have you got any questions?' I asked, once the formalities were out of the way.

'Could you tell me' he asked, 'if you're fighting a classic counter-insurgency operation in Nad Ali?'

Woody caught my eye and he started sniggering, biting onto the end of his pen to try and stop himself.

'Well, when we walk more than a few metres in any direction, people shoot at us. If you call that a counter-insurgency situation then yes, I suppose we are.'

There was a silence at the other end. Woody took the

opportunity to grab the microphone. 'We'll fill you in on the rest when you get here but for Christ's sake bring some cigarettes with you – as many as you can manage. Forget that and we'll put you on the next chopper back to Lash.'

The imminent arrival of the new OMLT in turn heralded the departure of the remainder of my team. Magoo, Charlie and Beattie had been on tenterhooks for days, waiting to find out when their tour would end. They now had just a few hours to pack up their kit and get ready to go.

Over the past few weeks, as we'd lived and fought together, I'd grown increasingly close to my team. Now that they were leaving I felt a profound sense of loss. They were leaving to go back to the real world, to wives, girlfriends, children. I was staying, for how long I didn't know. We only found out the precise time of their departure a few hours before the helicopter arrived to pick them up. A brief flurry of handshakes and then they were gone. There was no place for emotion, just a brief, 'See you on the other side,' before they grabbed their kit and left.

Later that night I picked up the book I was reading, some escapist sci-fi tale of intergalactic war, and there on the inside front cover was a short note scrawled in biro. *'Just wanted to say thanks for everything, boss. We've been through a lot. Good luck and keep your head down.'* It was signed '*Magoo*'. In Army terms that was the equivalent of a bear-hugging, tear-sodden farewell.

Fucker, I thought. This time tomorrow, he'd be drinking beer in Cyprus.

The helicopter arrived as expected. The Taliban launched another attack but this time we had two Apaches standing by to put a swift end to it. Bridle and my three men were safely dispatched. We greeted Iwan, along with seven gunners from the Royal Artillery, who would form the backbone of the new OMLT.

'Hello,' said Iwan in a friendly way as he walked into the ops room.

'Hello,' said Woody. 'Have you got those cigarettes?'

'Oh, I thought you might be joking about those.'

Iwan looked suddenly nervous as he registered the appalled expressions on our faces. 'I did bring a few, anyway though,' he went on, hurriedly. He fished in his bergen and pulled out a carton of 200 Marlboro Lights.

'Hmm. Won't go far,' said Woody, snatching the box. It had been days since we'd run out and the two of us sat in complete silence while we chained three fags straight away. Iwan tried to interject with a question but was swiftly dismissed with a flap of Woody's hand. Smoking first, talking later. We had our priorities.

Once I'd sated my craving for nicotine I was able to turn my attention to the newcomer. He was staring at us with an expression of disbelief. 'Sorry,' I said. 'It's been a bit rough here lately. Let me show you around.'

We started the tour in the ops room, where I introduced Iwan to Harry and Phil. A loud bang suddenly reverberated through the room and I felt the adrenaline surge again. No explosion this time, just Woody, bringing his fist down hard on the map table. We looked at him and waited for an explanation.

'The RAF! I can't believe it. They've called Code Black.'

CHAPTER THIRTY-FOUR

August 2009

I sat opposite Christina in her small office on Harley Street and over the course of the next few months we talked about everything. I told her why I'd joined the Army, what had happened in Afghanistan and everything I'd done since. She just listened, prompting me with an occasional question when the words dried up. All the things that I'd been keeping bottled up, the worries I had about whether I'd done a good job, all the fear I still felt, everything came spilling out in a tidal wave of emotion. She didn't judge me or try to tell me what it was I ought to be thinking. She simply let me know that it was OK that I felt what I did.

Christina explained to me what PTSD was and why I was feeling this way. She told me how we all possess both an instinctive and a rational mind. The instinctive mind facilitates the primary activities required for survival, such as hunger that prompts us to search for food, or sexual desire, leading to procreation. Our emotions, fear and anger for example, are also governed by the instinctive mind, pushing us to fight our enemies or to flee. These feelings usually only last as long as they fulfil a need, so when our enemies no longer present a threat the anger or fear should dissipate.

The rational mind, on the other hand, is what allows us to analyse situations and override our instincts when appropriate. Hence we might be hungry but turn down a cream cake, or feel frightened but not be compelled to run. For example, when we watch a scary film the instinctive mind will generate fear but our rational mind can tell us that running away is not necessary. The same is true of war. In Afghanistan my instinctive mind told me to be afraid when the Taliban were shooting at me, but my rational mind had to push down the instinct to flee in order to allow me to carry on with my job. The problem is that my instinctive mind continued to produce fear, and my suppressing it meant I kept it with me. I was no longer able to process it and let it go. Essentially I had been highly stressed for two months in Nad Ali and somewhere along the road I had lost the ability to recover. The relentless feelings of anger and fear, coupled with the flashbacks I'd experienced since coming home, were signs that I was no longer able to deal with the safer, calmer environment I found outside Afghanistan.

Of course PTSD is much more complicated than Christina's explanation allowed, but the truth is that even the psychiatrists and neuroscientists who research the condition are yet to fully understand the effects that stress and trauma have on the brain. This gave me momentary pause – did I really want people messing around inside my head when they freely admitted that they had only the sketchiest idea of how it all worked? For now, however, I was just happy to be told that what was happening to me had a name and, more importantly, there were things that could be done to help.

My case, it seemed, was more complicated than most. The first difficulty was that my PTSD was not triggered by a single event. No one firefight had sent me over the edge, although things like the mine-strike in Gereshk or the Apache attack in Nad Ali had certainly contributed. Christina would have found it much easier to rewire the way I felt if the trigger for my condition had been more straightforward. Instead, it was the sheer length of time I had spent being frightened and under pressure that had done for me, and this was a considerably harder problem to unravel.

Christina went on to explain the second major complication in my history – I was a soldier. Military training is designed to make a person think in a particular way and while this is important to ensure one is able to fight effectively, it is not conducive to a healthy state of mind when the war is over. Throughout long exercises at Sandhurst I had been conditioned to push down my fear, so that when the bullets were raining down for real I would be able to get a grip and do what had to be done. We were encouraged not to feel fear. Publicly acknowledging its existence was taken as a sign of weakness.

On top of this, the Army heaps an extra layer of pressure by instilling a deep sense of honour and duty. 'You do not let down your men,' we were told at every opportunity. And quite right too – it's an officer's job to look after those under his or her command. But what happens when things go wrong, as they inevitably will in a war? Ever since Mason, Gee and the others had been taken away to hospital, not a day had passed when I hadn't questioned whether their injuries were my fault. Every decision I'd made in Afghanistan I'd gone over countless times, asking myself if I'd done the right thing. Christina was now helping me to be rational about these questions. There were times in our sessions when I thought I could do just that, but each week after our time was up it was a different story. I felt empty and drained. Acknowledging my problems to someone else brought them bubbling to the surface, releasing them from the depths of my consciousness where I had tried to keep them hidden. Again and again I went looking for answers at the bottom of a vodka bottle. For a while it helped, but every time I sobered up I found myself right back where I'd started.

Christina told me there was a kind of therapy available that could help me deal with some of my worst flashbacks. 'It's called EMDR,' she said. 'By stimulating your brain in a certain way, I can alter the neural pathways that are causing you to relive the most traumatic parts of your tour in Afghanistan.'

'Stimulating my brain?' I asked. 'Are we talking about electric shocks here?'

Christina laughed. 'Nothing so dramatic. I just have to touch you on the arm a few times while I talk you through the situation that you are trying to deal with and afterwards you won't be forced to relive it every time you think about it.'

It sounded like science fiction. I wasn't sure I wanted to be brainwashed. There was, however, one day that I would willingly wipe from

255

my mind. I relived being blown up almost constantly. All kinds of things could set it off – the view through the windscreen of a car, or the smell of bitumen being laid on a road. I would be transported back to the desert, scrabbling to get clear of the wreckage while Stocky screamed next to me. I wanted all that out of my head, but it had been part of me for so long now I feared that in letting go of it I'd be losing a part of my identity. And didn't I owe it to myself, and my men, to remember?

Christina was gentle yet persistent; EMDR would help. After a particularly hideous flashback I finally agreed to do it. First of all she made me think of a place where I felt particularly safe and happy. I picked the beach at Lyme Regis, where my parents had taken me on holiday when I was ten. The sun had shone all week and I ran around, climbing rocks, collecting fossils and swimming in the sea.

'Now,' said Christina, taking hold of my wrists. 'I want you to relax completely. I'm going to talk to you about the day you were blown up.'

I'd been over the story so many times with her now that she knew the chronology of events around the explosion as well as I did. I listened to her low, quiet voice as she told me the tale that I knew so well. As she talked, she began to tap rhythmically on my forearms with her fingertips. My heart began to beat faster as I visualised the scene in the desert. I began to sweat. Panic welled up inside, just as it always did when I had one of my flashbacks. I fought the urge to scream. And then, suddenly, I was calm. All the worry and fear dropped away. I could hear Christina talking about the vehicle somersaulting over but it was as though it was happening to someone else, far away. I knew that person was me but I was no longer living the story. It was just another memory.

Two days after the EMDR I walked past a gang of labourers repairing a road. The air was thick with the smell of hot bitumen. I kept on walking. It was only 100 metres down the road that I realised the smell hadn't triggered a flashback – for the first time since the explosion. Without knowing why, I began to cry. I felt enormous relief but at the same time it was like I was saying goodbye to a piece of who I was.

After a few more months of therapy I began to feel better. My thoughts still raced and I frequently found myself immersed in bouts of recollection but gradually these were becoming shorter and less intense. I started telling myself that the cure had worked and the future was bright – the same story I'd give to my friends and family. Christina was more cautious in her assessment. 'You might benefit from going away somewhere for a while,' she said. 'The Priory's very good. Here's a number you can call. Think about it.'

I took the proffered card reluctantly and stuffed it into my pocket. I won't need that, I thought.

CHAPTER THIRTY-FIVE

In the days that followed the declaration of Code Black, our situation became desperate. With the RAF refusing to land at our location we were entirely cut off. We had a love–hate relationship with them, especially since the Apache, but the helicopters had been our lifeblood, providing us with the supplies that were crucial to our survival. Now we had no source of food, water or ammunition. If something didn't change immediately we would be rendered completely ineffective, we'd be fish in a barrel for the Taliban. We were still surrounded, outnumbered and we lived in fear of another full-frontal assault.

The ANA had all but run out of food completely. They didn't eat the same ration packs that we relied upon but instead prepared their own meals of rice and beans and, once upon a time, the odd bit of goat or mutton. For the last two weeks, with the exception of the odd feast this diet had been reduced to small portions of plain rice. All the other ingredients had gone. Wadood showed me his storeroom, now completely empty. We tried to share our own limited rations with the Afghans but there were just too many of them. In addition they found it difficult to stomach the staples of our ration packs, such as corned beef hash or treacle pudding. I watched Afghans gagging as they tried to force down a mouthful.

We looked at our own storerooms once more and figured out how much longer we could hold out. The OMLT had food for at least another week and enough ammunition for perhaps three or four more sustained contacts. The Jocks had about the same. Our real problem was water. We were running dangerously low.

Up until now, we'd been resupplied by helicopter every three or four days. On each flight, at least half of the pallets were loaded with plastic bottles of drinking water. If we'd ever started to run out, we had a backup. Before today we hadn't used it. Now it would really come into its own.

At the back of the schoolhouse was a well, dug in by some American engineer when the school was built. A borehole had been sunk into the ground and then concreted over, with a plastic standpipe providing a conduit for the water. An electric pump drew the water up and once it was boiled or treated with purification tablets it was entirely safe to drink.

The Company Sergeant Major went to try the system. He pressed the switch on the pump and we heard the mechanism whir into action. A gurgling sound emanated from the well and the standpipe coughed out a short spurt of brown liquid. The machinery ground away for a few seconds. Then it fell silent. The Company Sergeant Major flicked the switch on and off several times but nothing happened. We prised the cover off the pump and found inside a rusted mess of cogs and gears. None of us was an engineer – this was a problem far beyond our technical know-how. I looked down at the small dirty puddle beneath the standpipe and was overcome by a wave of thirst.

The temperatures in Helmand meant that everyone had to take on enormous amounts of water to avoid crippling dehydration. If a man stayed still all day and kept out of the sun, he'd still need to drink around three litres to avoid suffering any ill effects. Patrolling in full kit put that figure up to at least seven. Each time we went out we emptied our bodies of fluids as the sweat ran like a river in spate. I'd lost about a stone and a half in weight over the past few weeks and my body armour hung loose about my diminished torso. Soldiers were walking around camp looking more like living skeletons than men – hollow-eyed and exhausted.

The ANA weren't reliant on resupply for their water and had already taken to drinking from the irrigation ditches, but one look at the murky sludge that we splashed through on patrol told us that this was a real last resort. The last thing we wanted was to bring the entire base down with dysentery. The Afghans had developed stronger stomachs than us.

We moved to a rationing system. Each soldier was allowed just two litres of water a day and all washing was banned. Morale plummeted. After fighting for hours in the sun there was nothing we wanted more than to throw water down our necks. Instead we were forced to confine ourselves to a few judicious swallows, just enough to stave off collapse. I was thirsty all the time, my body crying out for water. Coming in from patrol I'd slug back a bottle, gulping down my day's ration, a few glugs of hot, stale liquid. It was sweet relief, but for the rest of the day I'd sit, mouth parched, tongue stuck to the roof of my mouth, and imagine pints of crystal clear, ice-cold water. The sweat evaporated from my body, leaving behind a thin, salty crust. The physical strain that the water shortage imposed on the soldiers meant that we would have to limit the duration of patrols, shrinking the area we held to a small footprint extending only a few hundred metres beyond the patrol base.

'So we're giving the Taliban the run of the place?' Iwan asked. 'We're just kicking our heels, waiting for them to attack again?'

'Don't worry. We'll probably all keel over before they get a chance,' Woody said dryly, kicking away his empty water bottle.

None of us laughed. If we didn't get resupplied in 72 hours we were as good as dead.

Harry got on the net and explained our problem, his voice rising to a shout as he vented his frustration. Woody and I sat opposite him as we waited for the great minds at Brigade to formulate a solution. After a long pause while they considered our dilemma, the radio crackled and the plan was revealed. Airdrops. They still wouldn't risk landing but given the desperate nature of our situation they were willing to parachute supplies to us, flying over in planes and pushing boxes out of the back. Woody looked over at me, anger etched on his face. 'Air-drops never land where they're supposed to. We're screwed,' he said.

Harry remained calm. 'Don't worry about it,' he said. 'It's not like it used to be. The equipment they use to target the drop zones is much more sophisticated. I've been on exercises where stuff's been dropped into a box much smaller than our base.'

We took Harry at his word. We had to. We all knew there was a high chance that the air-drops would land outside of the schoolhouse. If they did, that meant a potentially deadly mission to go out and collect the provisions that were designed to keep us alive.

I hadn't spoken to my family since I'd arrived in Nad Ali, always surrendering my turn on the satellite phone to someone else who was more eager to reach out to their relatives. My parents must have been worried about me but I didn't know how to talk to them. They were so far removed from everything that had happened in Nad Ali. They wouldn't understand. But now I was scared that if I didn't talk to them I might never get the chance again. I gave in and made the call. My mother answered, her familiar gentle tones quite incongruous in this setting.

'Hi,' I said awkwardly.

There was a long pause at the other end. I didn't know if it was the delay over a long-distance line or whether I'd stunned her into silence.

'Hello? Mark? Is that you?'

'Hi Mum. Yes, it's me.'

'Oh, we've been so worried. Are you OK? Are you safe? What are you doing? Where are you?'

So many questions, none of which I could bring myself to answer fully.

'Still in Afghanistan. Everything's fine. What's new at home?'

'It's been so long since you called. I thought something had happened to you.' My mother's voice cracked. I wanted to console her, to make her believe that everything was OK, but I couldn't do it. My own voice was stiff and formal. I just wanted the conversation to be over and to get back to what passed for normal life now. This emotional crap was more than I could take.

'No, I'm OK. How's Dad?'

There was another pause and then, 'He's well. He's out at the shops at the moment but I know he'd love to speak to you if you can call back. Your brother visited yesterday with his girlfriend ...' And she was off, gossiping away like she always did, filling me in on all the latest familial goings on. I let her talk, not listening to a word, aching for the ten minutes to pass. I didn't have to wait that long. A crackle of gunfire nearby cut her monologue short.

'Got to run,' I said. 'Love you.'

I pushed the button to end the call and ran to the ops room. It wasn't serious, just a brief skirmish outside the gate as one of the Jock patrols made its way in. I should have called my mother back but couldn't muster the will. It would be the last time I spoke to her from Afghanistan.

The first air-drop was planned for that same evening. They told us that the supplies would be parachuted right onto the base. We wouldn't have to push out patrols to secure a perimeter like we had for the helicopters. Instead we'd just relax and wait for the supplies to come to us.

An hour before the plane was due over, the entire base was stood to, manning the sangars, alert to any enemy action that might interfere with the air-drop. Two platoons, DB's and Wali's, waited with their kit on, ready to deploy at a moment's notice to hunt for the supplies should the air-drop miss its target. As midnight approached, all the men were awake, staring up at the clear night sky waiting for deliverance.

A low rumbling heralded the coming of the C-130, flying low to make the drop as accurate as possible. It passed right over the schoolhouse. Iwan tapped me on the arm and pointed. 'There,' he said. High up in the sky I could see a dark silhouette plummeting downwards. It jerked sharply as its parachute opened and then came on, moving more slowly now. It was followed swiftly by a second, third and fourth shadow. The sound of the plane faded away and we watched the crates as they grew steadily larger. For one beautiful moment it seemed like they were falling true, straight towards us.

'Hang on a minute,' said Iwan. 'They're going off target.' I squinted upwards. He was right. The crates were drifting steadily away, off towards the east, beyond the DC. The pilot had failed to account for the wind that evening; we watched as our precious supplies wafted further and further away. We stayed silent, all eyes fixed on the crates, and collectively willed the wind to change.

It didn't. We would have to go out and track the supplies as they fell. Hopefully we could spot where they landed and get there before the Taliban did. Iwan, me and the new OMLT replacements went with Wali's platoon in the Toyotas. We'd never be able to hump all the supplies back on foot, so we were forced to expose ourselves to the risk of IEDs which were much harder to spot from a vehicle, DB's men went in front of us on foot to provide protection while we loaded up the supplies. Phil would support us from above, help guide us to the crates and look for the enemy.

We sped along the deserted tracks through the DC, desperate to reach the supplies before the Taliban found them first. Woody talked to me over the net. 'We're getting a lot of chatter about enemy activity,' he said. 'They've seen the drop and are moving now.'

Occasionally we managed to tap into the Taliban's communications systems. We had a piece of kit we called the Icom which monitored shortwave radio transmissions. Whenever they picked something up we'd shove them in front of an interpreter and try and work out what the enemy was up to. Of course the Taliban knew that we had this capability, and so they liked to play games with us, loudly broadcasting their intentions but then doing something completely different. Then sometimes there was the double bluff where they did exactly what they said they would, assuming that we'd interpret it as misinformation. Either way, it rarely handed us much advantage. Tonight it just made me nervous.

The first crate was quickly discovered, conveniently deposited at the side of the track. It had broken open on impact and was listing at an alarming angle into the irrigation ditch. Many of the water bottles in the crate had split open and their contents had drained into the dust. For once the Afghans hadn't been forgotten, and half the crate contained food. Unfortunately, with an alarming lack of foresight, the food had been packed in glass jars, the broken remnants of which were strewn all around. The food that we managed to salvage seemed to consist of a peculiar paste, more akin to baby food than anything a soldier might eat.

As our search continued, the Taliban radio chatter intensified and we peered into the darkness, sure that we'd be hit at any moment. We found the second crate on a patch of open ground, its contents mostly intact, and we loaded them quickly onto the trucks.

The third crate had landed in a field, some one hundred metres from the track, around the perimeter of which ran a wide irrigation ditch. Luckily a bridge was located nearby. Another relic of American aid, it was reinforced steel and easily sturdy enough to take the weight of our vehicles. We rumbled across and drove out into the field. Whatever crops were planted here did not grow tall and we were confident that we would have little trouble going off-road.

We made it across to the crate, which was intact, the impact absorbed by the soft, loamy soil. It was quickly packed onto the

Toyota and we were ready to move off. The driver pressed down on the accelerator but instead of moving seamlessly forward, the motor revved while the rear wheels span uselessly in the mud. We hadn't factored in the weight the supplies added to the truck. The driver pumped the accelerator, flinging mud out behind us. We sank deeper into the mire.

I ordered the men out and we fished around for implements with which to dig. One of the Afghans made to push his rifle into the mud but one of the OMLT men caught him just in time before he clogged the barrel. We had no shovels and ended up scrabbling in the mud with bare hands and broken pieces of wood from the pallet. We managed to improvise chocks from large rocks we found in the field and use the rest of the pallet to fashion duckboards.

While we'd been frantically digging in the mud, the others had continued the search for the final crate. Even with the dawn light flooding over the fields, they couldn't locate it.

DB was speaking to Phil on the net. His words were short. Almost desperate. I listened in intensely.

'Contact. Wait out.'

The Taliban had found our missing supplies and used the opportunity to ambush us when we were at our weakest.

'All call signs extract immediately.'

We pushed back to base under heavy fire. The sight of the schoolhouse gates had never looked so welcoming.

We never did find the fourth crate with our missing supplies. Perhaps they were concealed among the tall crops or maybe the Taliban had swooped in silently and taken them before they contacted us. It was a bitter blow. The missing crate had contained ammunition for the ANA. It was the same kind the Taliban used. If they'd managed to find it then the next time they attacked it would be our bullets flying towards us. With half our new supplies damaged and another quarter lost altogether we still faced severe shortages.

That day we didn't patrol again. Everyone was exhausted after the nocturnal misadventures. I don't suppose the soldiers really cared but I chafed at the inactivity and uselessness of our situation. We'd fought so hard to defend our position, to wrestle some advantage from the Taliban, and what were we doing now? Fuck all. Harry was similarly displeased and we took our feelings out on one another in a succession of ill-tempered exchanges.

The next night, they tried another air-drop with no more success than the first. Again the crates drifted wide and once more we traipsed after them for hours as vital supplies were lost once more.

Everyone looked broken. Men drifted listlessly around the base in filthy, torn uniforms. Some sported bloodstains on their clothes, poignant reminders of the battles we'd fought. No one could escape the fear that Taliban would take advantage of our weakened condition and mount an all-out attack on the base.

For one of the ANA soldiers the strain was too much to bear. An hour after we'd returned from the second air-drop patrol, just as dawn was breaking, he clambered up on to the schoolhouse roof where he began to yell at the top of his voice and spin around like a dervish, waving his hands over his head.

'What's he saying?' I asked Ash.

'He's asking the Taliban to come and kill him.'

Eventually the S2 managed to coax the man down and lead him away. He was subsequently confined to his dormitory. Sgt Taylor had a look at him but his was an illness of the mind and other than letting him rest there was little anyone in Nad Ali could do for him. The other ANA men treated him very gently and I was impressed with the compassion they showed. When I asked Wadood about him he said, 'It's war. This happens sometimes.'

I feared that I wasn't far off from the same thing happening to me. My nerves were stretched as taut as they could be and panicky premonitions of my own demise assailed me whenever my mind wasn't occupied. I didn't think that my fear showed outwardly but I could see in the wide, exhausted eyes of the other men that I wasn't the only one on the edge.

I needed to focus on a positive outcome or risk losing myself in a mire of hopelessness. The relentless treadmill of planning, patrolling and fighting was wearing me down fast. I still experienced a visceral thrill when in combat but now a gnawing fear had grown within me as I began to suspect that my luck was running out. When the austerity of rationing was piled on top of this, I slowly but surely began to crack. No one else could see this. We were all wrapped up in our own personal battle for survival and for all I knew, everyone's sanity might have been hanging by a thread. There was in any case no time for self-pity as the treadmill wouldn't stop until we all got the hell out of Nad Ali.

A week after Code Black had been declared I was in the ops room, preparing for the next air-drop when a message came over the radio.

'Code Black rescinded. Helicopter resupply to resume within 24 hours.'

That was it. No explanation given. I couldn't see what had changed – the HLS was as dangerous as ever – but I knew better than to question the decision. It should have been a moment of celebration but no one could muster the energy. No one even smiled. I passed on the message to the OMLT. The men just nodded. No cynical retort, just blank faces. It was good news, but we knew that even though helicopters would rejuvenate us, the Taliban still had us in a noose.

CHAPTER THIRTY-SIX

September 2009

Leaning over the side of the restaurant balcony, the ground below looked very far away. The Coq d'Argent, located in the heart of the City, had acquired an ugly reputation in recent years as a suicide spot where bankers go to hurl themselves from the roof terrace after a bad day on the markets. Gin and tonic in hand, I stared down at the traffic and wondered what passed through their minds during those last seconds as the pavement rushed towards them. Did they have second thoughts? Or did the whistling wind in their ears silence the screaming in their head?

I dismissed these gloomy thoughts and turned my attention back to my date, Annabelle. She was something big in finance. I was trying to listen while she explained some deal that she'd recently brokered but was struggling to concentrate. I forced myself to appear normal, nodding my head and making vague murmurs of interest at appropriate junctures. It seemed to work and Annabelle didn't appear to notice anything awry. My lack of engagement had nothing to do with what she had to say or how much I liked her. The problem was, as ever, Afghanistan. I still couldn't stop myself from dwelling on the events that had taken place in Nad Ali. Time after time I went over the same old ground, looking for resolution but finding none. Despite all Christina had done to help, I was still trapped in the same loop of remembrance. The endless repetition was at once agonising and boring, if that's possible, but I didn't want to break free. This was now my world and, painful as it was, it was familiar. The present was the unknown and I didn't know how to live there.

It was early autumn and a bright evening up on the rooftop. All around us people were enjoying themselves. I gulped down my drink, hopeful that the alcohol would work its usual magic and allow me to join everyone else in their merriment. I waited for the gin to hit my bloodstream, but before I could discern any noticeable effect the helicopter intervened.

It might have been a police helicopter, or perhaps it was filming for a news channel. Either way, the chopper buzzed incessantly as it circled above us. Round and round it went. It was flying low – any lower and we'd have felt the downdraft. I felt suddenly sick and the noise of the rotors thundered in my ears. With incredible clarity I knew that I was about to die.

The walls were shaking as the Apache poured lead from above. Blood flooded the floor and my own hands were stained crimson. I looked up and saw that all eyes were turned towards me.

'I don't know what to do!' I screamed. 'It's not my fault!'

The soldiers around me kept on staring. I screamed for the medic – he should have been here by now. A hand on my shoulder jerked me round; it was Gee. No. It was Annabelle. Why was she here? She hadn't come out on patrol today. My vision began to blur and Annabelle, Gee, Mason, everyone fell away. The noise of the helicopter became muffled, as though cotton wool had been stuffed inside my ears. Everything went dark.

I came to lying on a gurney staring up at the roof of an ambulance. A paramedic leant over me. My head was throbbing and my mouth felt stale and dry, as if I'd smoked too many cigarettes. I sat up and cast about wildly, searching for the Apache.

It was swiftly apparent that I wasn't in Afghanistan after all. As I realised this I felt a rush of embarrassment. Time to get out of here. I swung my legs over the side of the stretcher.

'Whoa there,' said the paramedic. 'Where are you going?'

'I'm fine,' I said. 'Don't know what I'm doing here.'

'You were collapsed on the pavement. Someone called an ambulance.'

'Where's Annabelle?'

'We called her. You were on your own so we dialled the last number on your mobile to try and reach someone who knew you. We spoke to Annabelle. She just said to take you to Wellington Barracks. Are you a soldier?'

'Where did she go? The last thing I remember is talking to her in a bar.'

The paramedic looked at me pityingly. 'You've had a lot to drink. Maybe you don't remember.'

He was right, I didn't remember – but I'd only had two drinks, hadn't I?

'The young lady on the phone said that you stopped talking to her and started "drinking like a maniac". She said that she left you after you started shouting abuse at her.'

I refused to believe what Annabelle had told him.

'Bollocks. So are you going to take me to Wellington Barracks?'

Despite my rudeness, the paramedic's kindly attitude continued unabated and I was driven directly to the barracks and dropped off at the guardroom. I'd suffered memory loss through drinking on many occasions but this felt different. I could remember nothing from the point when the helicopter started circling. Of the subsequent bender on which I'd embarked I had not the slightest recollection. Looking up at the night sky, it was clear that hours had passed and I couldn't dispute Annabelle's testimony.

The soldiers on guard offered to help me find my way back to the Mess. I told them to fuck off and weaved an unsteady course across the parade square. When I finally made it through the front door, the stairs up to my room presented a quite insurmountable obstacle and so I stumbled into a downstairs changing room where I found a discarded ceremonial greatcoat, which I pulled over myself, and passed out.

I awoke to find myself being roughly shaken by one of the other officers. 'You shit, Mark,' he said. 'You've slept in a puddle. My coat's soaking. I'm mounting guard in ten minutes.'

I looked blearily around, feeling the wetness soaking through my clothes. The puddle was warm. I chose not to divulge this information to the already angry man standing in front of me. 'Use someone else's,' I said.

'What about yours?'

'Sorry, no. I spilled wine on mine the other day and haven't got round to getting it cleaned.'

'You fucking twat! Seriously, you're a liability. You need to sort your shit out or people are going to stop putting up with you.'

The officer stormed out of the room in search of a serviceable coat. It was nothing that I hadn't heard before. I knew I was in the wrong. I knew I was losing control. I just wasn't sure that I cared. Dimly, it occurred to me that I had a choice. Either continue down this road into alcoholic oblivion or take the therapist's advice and seek more professional help. My watch showed that it was nine o'clock in the morning. I had nowhere in particular to be. Thrusting my hand into my pocket I felt a crumpled up piece of cardboard. I pulled it out. It was a business card that my therapist had given me at our last session a week ago. The Priory Hospital, it read. There was a telephone number. Upstairs in my room was an unopened bottle of vodka. I closed my eyes.

CHAPTER THIRTY-SEVEN

Helicopter supplies had resumed. We were able to hydrate again and now had enough ammunition for a real fight. Thoughts turned once more to offensive operations. Brigade felt that our reduced capacity for the duration of Code Black had allowed the Taliban too much freedom of movement. It was time to take back the initiative.

We began our fight back gradually, starting with a short patrol around the area to familiarise Iwan and the gunners with the environment. There were a few shots fired at us from the roof of a compound but as soon as we returned fire, they ran off.

Once back in the Patrol Base, Iwan, pumped by his experience on the ground, was keen to discuss the contact – his first. 'That was a bit hairy,' he said, excitement shining in his eyes. There was nothing I wanted to talk about less, and swiftly closed down the conversation. I was being unfair, but felt quite powerless to behave any other way. Iwan's attitude was exactly the same as mine had been when I'd arrived in Afghanistan but now I found his eagerness irritating and naïve. I wanted to sit him down and tell him how it was, but couldn't muster the energy. He'd find out in his own way soon enough. Anyway, there was work to be done. Tomorrow we were going back to the orchard.

During Code Black, the orchard had once more become infested with Taliban. They had taken up permanent residence there, turning it into a kind of FOB from which they could launch attacks on the schoolhouse. Col Wadood was keen that we evict them. Together we planned an operation. The scheme of manoeuvre was fairly straightforward – one platoon would provide fire support from the buildings that overlooked the orchard from the west, while a second would assault through the gate. The assaulting platoon would then push through the trees until the place was cleared.

As was our habit by now, I briefed the ANA platoon commanders and sergeants who then took charge of their own men. The OMLT guys I briefed separately using the photo map in the ops room. There wasn't much to it and I was done in around fifteen minutes.

When I ducked outside for a smoke, Iwan followed me. 'Is that it?' he asked.

'What do you mean?' I said.

'Those were your orders for the operation?'

'Yes. Is there a problem?'

'Bit brief, weren't they?'

I sighed. 'Look. We're not at Sandhurst now. It's not all about making complex models and going into every last detail about how sunny it's going to be. It's about getting the information across clearly and not wasting everyone's time, doing it all by the book as if your boss is watching and marking you on your presentational skills.'

'Even so . . .' Iwan was not to be persuaded.

'Look, do you understand what we're doing tomorrow?'

'Well yes, but . . .'

'No buts. That's it. If you get it, then so will the blokes. Don't try and do too much. If you spend all your time writing the perfect set of orders every time you walk out of the gate, you'll burn out in a fortnight.'

Even as I explained it to Iwan, I couldn't quite believe my own words. I knew it worked but this improvised approach that I'd adopted since I'd arrived in Nad Ali wasn't how we were taught to do it. Maybe Iwan had a point. Maybe if I'd done things differently, Mason, Ram and the rest of them would still be with me now. I shook myself. There was no time for contemplation of the road not taken. There was more fighting to be done.

The first part of the operation went smoothly enough. We split the OMLT between the two ANA platoons. I went with Wali's platoon into the fire support position, along with three of the newly arrived gunners. Iwan, eager to get stuck into the action, joined the assaulting troop, taking with him the rest of the OMLT. I hadn't argued with him and was now quite content to hang back and let him take the glory. My lust for war was running dry.

I crouched behind the wall of the compound and checked my watch, waiting for the appointed time to open fire. Phil's voice came over the radio. On his screen he could see armed men moving through the orchard, taking up positions near the perimeter wall. 'We'll have them,' he said.

Moments later, an Apache arrived on the scene. A few weeks ago this sight would have been a cause for joy, but now my muscles tensed and my stomach turned over.

This time the pilot correctly located his target and fired two Hellfire missiles into the trees. We saw orange flames leap momentarily above the orchard walls and two columns of black smoke rose up into the air. The gunners whooped but I watched silently and thanked God that the pilot three weeks ago had confined himself to using the chain gun. If he'd used Hellfire then my men would be lying in coffins, not hospital beds.

The Apache continued to hover menacingly while the assaulting platoon sprang forward. Their way into the orchard was via a narrow wooden bridge that led over the ditch to a small gate. It was a tight squeeze – only one man could enter at a time. This would have to be done fast or I feared the Taliban would pick off each man as they came through. That they didn't was testament to the damage the Apache had inflicted on their numbers.

The first man into the breach was 'PKM man'. He sprinted across the track and paused on the bridge to rake the gateway with a long burst from his weapon. Then he was across and through the gap. Another thunderous burst rang out before an arm darted back through the gate beckoning his comrades forward. 'That man is a lunatic,' chuckled Wali.

Most of the orchard's defenders must have been done for by the Hellfire missiles but sporadic bursts of fire suggested a few Taliban fighters were still holding out. I watched Iwan dart through the gate and was suddenly seized by a moment of jealousy. I wasn't so jaded that I couldn't still be moved by the thrill of combat once the bullets started to fly.

I couldn't see what was going on inside the orchard but Iwan kept me informed over the PRR. 'The enemy's fallen back,' he told me. 'I can see bodies at the edge of the trees. There are unarmed men moving in to pick them up.'

I relayed the information to Wali and told him to order his men in the orchard not to engage. Our rules of engagement dictated that we could only fire upon the enemy if they were armed. Wali couldn't understand the distinction. 'But they're Taliban,' he insisted. 'They're still Taliban whether they're carrying their rifles or not. These same men were trying to kill us just ten minutes ago.'

The man's point was not lost on me. I desperately wanted to let the Afghans off the leash, to finish the battle we'd begun. My better angels, or in this case Iwan, prevailed. 'We can't attack,' he said over the PRR. 'They're officially non-combatants.'

'It's a no go,' I told Wali. 'Let them go.'

He shook his head and muttered under his breath. He thought I was weak. Maybe I was.

At that moment the sound of gunfire erupted from the orchard. The unarmed men sent to recover the Taliban bodies had picked up the dead men's weapons and opened fire. Our scruples about non-combatants no longer applied and Iwan and

275

the ANA returned fire. They must have been crazy to take us on with the Apache still on station. A burst from the aircraft's cannon put an end to the counter-attack. This time there were no mistakes.

The battle was over and we returned to the schoolhouse. We reckoned that we must have killed at least a dozen of the enemy. We watched the recorded footage on Phil's screen of bodies being dragged away to the east of the orchard and loaded onto trucks. Phil flicked a switch and the picture flickered as he brought up the live feed. It was now dark outside but the picture remained clear, a green glow the only sign that dusk had fallen. 'Watch,' said Phil, pointing at the corner of the screen. As we looked on, figures emerged through the trees and scuttled towards the buildings. There must have been twenty or thirty men. The Taliban were taking back the same ground we'd just wrested from them.

'Hang on,' said Phil and picked up his radio handset. 'Hello Zero, this is Widow 52. Can I call in a strike on multiple Bravos near my location?'

'Can you identify them as hostile?' came the reply.

'They're taking back a position my ground call sign cleared two hours previously.'

'Can you see that they are carrying weapons?'

We all peered at the screen. 'No but they are definitely enemy fighters.'

'Sorry, Widow, we can't engage.'

Phil threw down the handset. 'For fuck's sake,' he said to the world in general.

What kind of war were we fighting here? We were ordered to kill the Taliban but when we had the chance we tied ourselves in moral knots. We risked our lives to take back their territory but without the men to hold it they just came back. What end could there be to a war like this?

CHAPTER THIRTY-EIGHT

January 2010

It was dark when I arrived at the Priory and the front door was locked. I should have been there hours before but I'd been frightened to make the six-mile journey from Wellington Barracks. My weekly therapy sessions with Christina were one thing but being admitted to an institution was an acknowledgement that I was truly insane. Screwing up my courage, I rang the bell. After what seemed an age, the door was answered by a uniformed security guard. I explained who I was and the man checked my details against a list. 'You're late,' he said.

'Yes, sorry about that. I'm mad, you see.'

The guard didn't laugh. 'Follow me,' he said.

He led me away down a maze of winding corridors. The place was huge, like some old country house hotel, albeit one with no guests. 'Lights out at eleven o'clock,' the guard told me after I commented on the quietness. We emerged into a brightly lit room where a uniformed man sat beside a desk. Behind him was a window with the word 'Dispensary' painted above the frosted glass in red letters. The two men nodded silent acknowledgements and we went on our way.

We finally arrived at my room. It was not what I was expecting. Christina had told me that I would be accommodated in luxury with a double bed, flat-screen television and a view out across the gardens. Instead I found myself in the most basic surroundings. There was a narrow single bunk, a small table and a chair bolted to the floor. In fact, everything was bolted down and the window couldn't be opened.

Overhead, the electric light that bathed the room in a sickly yellow glow was set into the ceiling, ensuring that I couldn't unscrew the bulb to do mischief to myself, or anyone else.

'Please open your suitcase,' said the guard.

I complied and the guard proceeded to rummage through it and remove anything that might conceivably be used as a weapon. Out came my razor, nail scissors and even my belt.

'I know I told you I was mad,' I said. 'But I'm not that insane.'

'Standard procedure,' he said.

Eventually I was left alone and I was surprised to hear the key turn in the lock on the other side of the door. I was in for the night. With nothing else to do, I climbed into bed and tried to will myself to sleep. Drifting off was made even harder due to half-hourly interruptions when a guard scraped back a viewing hatch in the door and peered in to make sure I was still alive.

The door was eventually unlocked at seven in the morning. I immediately dressed and made my way downstairs. A friendly nurse now manned the front desk. 'Go and get some breakfast in the restaurant,' she said. 'The doctor will be along soon and he'll be able to discuss the details of your treatment with you.'

There weren't many people in the restaurant when I arrived. I helped myself to a hearty portion of bacon and eggs, sat down at a table and tucked in. I'd only eaten a couple of forkfuls before a tall man wearing a black T-shirt and spectacles took a seat beside me. 'Hello,' he said, thrusting out a meaty hand to shake. 'You're new.'

'Er, yes,' I said. I didn't know what to expect from the other patients. I mean, they were all mental, weren't they? What if they turned violent? I glanced around, looking for a member of staff who could intervene if my companion decided to attack me with his cutlery.

'I'm Dan,' the man said. 'What are you in for?'

'I've got post-traumatic stress disorder.'

He nodded. 'Yeah, thought it would be something like that. You get a nose for these things after a while.'

'Oh, right.'

'Take that girl over there.' He pointed over at a painfully thin young woman hovering nervously around the edge of the buffet.

'That's easy,' I said. 'She's anorexic.'

'You'd think so, and she probably is, but that's not why she's here. The really serious anorexics are all kept together in a separate unit where they can monitor everything they eat and do. This one is your basic depressive. Blank stare, not interested in anything that's going on. Avoid them − depressives are really dull to talk to.'

Dan noticed my discomfort as he picked apart the lives of the other patients around us. 'Spend long enough in this place and you'll soon develop a pretty dark sense of humour. It's the only way to stay sane.'

'Is that what you are?' I asked. 'Sane, I mean.'

'God, no. I wouldn't be here otherwise, but I like to think that I'm one of the slightly less loopy ones. I've just had a bit of a nervous breakdown. It happens to me every so often and I come here to relax until I feel I can go back to work again.'

Dan went on to tell me that he worked for an investment bank in the City. I didn't understand what it was he did there but he clearly made a lot of money for his bosses as they were willing to hold his job open for him and cover all the costs of his stay in the Priory. Apparently this was the fourth time he'd wound up here. The ethics displayed by his employers seemed a little dubious − working a man until he collapsed and then helping him recover just in order to start the same destructive process once more. Dan seemed happy enough and was sufficiently convinced of my sanity to offer to show me around later on. In the meantime I finished my breakfast and went to find the doctor.

The doctor, a scholarly looking man, apologised for how I had been treated on my arrival. 'There seems to have been a bit of a mix-up,' he said. 'The man who admitted you thought that you had been sectioned and so automatically put you on suicide watch.'

He showed me to a new room, which was much more comfortable and afforded me the ability to open the window. My therapy, he explained, was to centre around continued meetings with Christina. Beyond that, all the group therapy sessions that were held at the Priory would be available to attend, should I so wish. The doctor recommended that I avail myself of as many as possible and presented me with a timetable. Sessions started at nine in the morning and went on until after dinner. I could, if I wanted, be in therapy for almost twelve hours a day but there was no obligation. In addition to the sessions I could use the gym, watch television or go for a walk. 'You've tried a few different types of therapy by now,' the doctor said. 'Your stay here will build on the good work that you've already begun. But most importantly we want you to relax and feel safe.' The main purpose of my stay here was to get away from the Army for a while. Hopefully this would help me to slow the thoughts that still raced through my brain.

Flicking through the timetable revealed a veritable smorgasbord of treatments, ranging from the rather ho-hum conventions of group discussions to the more esoteric aromatherapy, where we talked about how different smells made us feel. At first I was reluctant to open up in the presence of strangers, but as the days went by I grew in confidence and threw myself onto the therapy-go-round with gusto. My favourite was movement therapy, where a shrink asked us to adopt certain positions that were unfamiliar to us. For instance, I was accustomed to a defensive posture with my arms folded and legs crossed, so the therapist told me to stand up and put my hands by my side. I then had to discuss how this open stance made me feel. I found it intensely uncomfortable, but somehow it reminded me of the person I used to be. Others didn't react quite so well to being taken outside their comfort zones and the session frequently deteriorated into tantrums, arguments and, on one memorable occasion, a physical fight.

I was surprised to discover how some of the most effective therapies weren't focused on talking to a therapist. I've since learnt much more about trauma, how we process our emotions and how to release them. At the time all I knew was that so called 'alternative' therapies succeeded where constantly revisiting my time in Nad Ali over and over again had failed.

Smoking was popular in the Priory. It got you outdoors and was a fiercely social activity, offering the chance to get to know people outside the pressurised environment of the therapy sessions. It was over a morning cigarette that I met Michael. He was fiftyish, whippet-thin, with long white hair that straggled to his shoulders. All down his arms he sported tattoos while around his thick neck and wrists he wore heavy gold chains. He stood in stark contrast to the crowd of lawyers, bankers and accountants that made up most of the other patients here. I'd spotted him in one of the discussion workshops and remembered he was suffering from PTSD but had been cagey about the details of his past. Clearly he'd seen me too.

'You're the one who's in the Army, aren't you?' he asked in a thick Ulster accent.

'Yes. We were in the same session yesterday,' I replied.

Michael looked me up and down as though not quite sure what to make of me.

'I was in the army too,' he said.

'Yeah? What regiment? Royal Irish?'

Michael laughed. 'Not your army, mucker. I was in the Irish Republican Army.'

I was taken aback. I hadn't deployed to Northern Ireland but plenty of friends had, and they'd been in more than a few scraps with the IRA. It was a little bit like coming face to face with someone who'd admitted membership of the Taliban.

'Was in, or still are in?' I asked.

'Well you never really leave but you could say that my fighting days are behind me.' He leaned in close and I felt his breath on my cheek as he spoke. 'But I'll tell you now that if I'd met you a few years ago across the water then we wouldn't be having a conversation. And there's a good chance that you'd be lying down dead.'

Michael pulled his face back from mine and took another drag on his cigarette.

'That's good to know. Thanks for clearing that up. On the other hand, no one's managed to finish me off yet so maybe it would be you who'd have ended up dead.'

He held my gaze for a few seconds more before his face creased into a

281

smile. Clapping me on the back, he said, 'You might be right there. Let's call it quits, eh, and we can get back to talking about our feelings and how our mas didn't hug us enough when we were wee'uns.'

From then on, Michael and I were all right. He never became a friend but we did talk a little about the violence we'd seen. It was always slightly uncomfortable because I was aware that every time he referred to a gun battle or an explosion, it was British soldiers he had been fighting. Nevertheless, it felt like he understood something of what I'd been through. It also gave me pause for thought. If I was so messed up by the bloodshed I'd seen, what must it be like for the men fighting for the Taliban?

Over time I met more patients. It wasn't always easy to get to know people. After spending an hour-long workshop discussing the most intimate details of each other's lives it was hard to shift gear into a casual lunchtime conversation. People were in the Priory for all kinds of reasons. There was Monique, an Oxford-educated lawyer from France who had suffered a nervous breakdown; Kate, PA to a famous rock star – she was bipolar; there was even another soldier suffering from PTSD – he was US Army – sent here from his base in Germany after he had tried to hang himself. Everyone had a story to tell; it was comforting to be around so many other people who were suffering in a similar way to me. Just being around all the others put my own problems into perspective.

After I'd been there a week I received a visit from my parents. They brought with them a large chocolate cake topped with candles. I'd been so wrapped up in my therapy that my birthday had quite slipped my mind. We sat in my room, eating cake and chatting. It seemed easy and relaxed – the way our family used to be before I went to war. I was lucky to have them; my younger brother too. Throughout everything – my drinking, mood swings and hatred of the entire world – they'd been there for me at the end of the phone or with a place to stay whenever I wanted it. When it was finally time for my parents to leave I felt sad, but reassured that I had people I could trust beyond the walls of the Priory.

As the days slipped past, I gradually started to feel better. The change was imperceptible at first but by the beginning of the third week I *realised that whole hours were going by when I didn't think about Afghanistan. Just being away from the Army and talking to people whose lives didn't revolve around the war was helping me to let go. Even the urge to drink wasn't as strong. Alcohol wasn't allowed in the Priory but that didn't stop me and some of my new friends from slipping out to the pub for a pint, under the pretext of 'going for a long walk'. The amazing thing for me was that 'a pint' meant just that. I was able to enjoy a drink without needing to keep going until I passed out. I can't pretend that I was cured. I still lost hours stuck in Nad Ali, but the intensity seemed to be fading. For the first time since I came home, I started to look forwards.*

I realised there was no future for me in the Army. My resentment was beginning to fade. Christina helped me to realise that my anger was misdirected. I understood that the Army wasn't to blame for what had happened to me. I had volunteered, begged even, to go to war. There was no one responsible but myself. But I knew that I never wanted to go back to war and that meant I would have to leave, becoming a civilian once more. This decision at once liberated me and filled me with dread. For the past six years the Army had been my whole existence. It had put a roof over my head and fed me; it had paid my salary and told me where to go and what to do. Every part of my life had been prescribed. The thought of making my own way in the world was terrifying. There were boundless possibilities but I had no idea what I wanted to do or what I was qualified for. But I knew I had the support of my family and friends like Steph who had stuck by me. They remembered me before I went to Afghanistan. I wanted to remember that person too.

CHAPTER THIRTY-NINE

At the start of my seventh week in Nad Ali, we began to hear rumours from the ANA that senior Afghan commanders in Kabul had begun to take an interest in our situation and were planning a major operation to clear the Taliban from the area and lift the siege. Brigade couldn't confirm this but Wadood was buying it. In the past he'd been inscrutable in the face of rumour but now he agreed that something big was in the offing.

The first concrete information we had from Brigade was a radio message informing us that a platoon of Royal Marines were to be flown in as an advance party prior to the arrival of the relieving force. We made the usual arrangements, securing the HLS out on the football pitch, and waited for the helicopters to come. I stayed back in the ops room while Wali's boys were out on the ground with Iwan.

It felt strange to be sitting inside while the others were on patrol. There was a hush about the place that was quite unnerving. Phil sat in his usual corner spot, lost in a cloud of tobacco smoke as he scrutinised his screens. We didn't speak much. My supply of idle chatter had run dry weeks before. There wasn't much to say to the men on the ground either. After a flurry of radio chatter when the patrol went out and another as the men took up their defensive positions, it had all gone quiet. I didn't like it. When I was out on the ground it might have been my life that was on the line but at least I had some measure of control over what happened. Now if the enemy attacked I could only sit here uselessly and listen, while others shot back. Now I knew how Woody and Harry must have felt. I'd get fragmented bursts of the action from which to try and piece together a picture of the battle.

Ten minutes before the helicopters were due, the brigade net sparked into life, informing us that the choppers were airborne. I passed the information to Iwan and our vigil continued.

Another eight minutes went by and then I heard the noise of the two Chinooks. 'Can you see them?' I asked Iwan.

'No,' he said, 'but I can hear them and they don't sound like they're above us.'

Probably just being cautious, I thought. It was a fresh squadron, new in theatre, and the pilots weren't yet accustomed to this trip. The clatter of the choppers was faintly audible and then suddenly it wasn't. Had they left? I asked Brigade to advise. There was a pause. Then, 'The helicopters have landed at your HLS and are now en route back to our location.'

'Are the Marines they were carrying still with them?'

'No, they are now on the ground at the HLS.'

I checked in with Iwan but he reported no sign of either the helicopters or the Marines. Fuck. They'd dropped them in the wrong place. I asked Brigade to confirm the co-ordinates of the HLS. The officer at the other end reeled off an eight-figure grid reference and I checked it against the map on the table in front of me.

'Idiots! They've dropped them on the other side of the DC. Their co-ordinates were out by a half a grid square.'

It was unbelievable, the sheer incompetence that had led to this balls-up. I didn't know who was responsible but their error would now put dozens of men's lives at risk as they patrolled across the DC to lead the Marines back to safety – unless I did something about it myself.

Looking back now, I couldn't tell you what made me do what I did next. I'd been under too great a strain for too long, I guess.

In a kind of daze I walked out of the ops room and made my way across the courtyard. One of the ANA Toyotas was parked up next to the front gate, its driver leaning on the bonnet, smoking a cigarette. I knew the guy by sight. We had patrolled together many times. 'All right, let's go,' I said, clapping him on the shoulder before jumping up into the cab. The man looked at me as though I'd lost my mind, which I suppose I had. Then he shrugged, flicked his fag butt into the dust and walked round to the driver's side.

The engine roared into life and we were off, just the two of us, rolling out of the gate and into the night before anyone knew we were gone. I knew where we were going. It was only 500 metres through the deserted streets to where the Marines had been deposited. The window was open and a refreshing breeze blew in as we sped along our way. Somewhere out there in the darkness lurked the Taliban. It was OK though – I had a pistol and body armour was for cissies. For all I knew the road might be littered with IEDs. I didn't care. Whether I lived or died seemed rather beside the point; I just wanted to find this patrol, bring them in and go to bed.

We reached the eastern edge of the DC and I told the driver to pull over by the side of the road. The Marines should be around here somewhere. I stared out of the window into the blackness. Where were they?

A sudden tapping on the window of the cab made me jump. I turned my head and peered out and saw a face looming out of the darkness. As I squinted it resolved itself into a familiar set of features. Fuck me. It was CSgt Mason. He was supposed to be in hospital in Birmingham. He was illuminated by the glow of his trademark cigarette. He glowered at me with eyes full of reproach and I just knew I was in for a bollocking. 'What the fuck are you doing, sir? You're going to get this boy killed,' he said, jerking a thumb at the driver. 'Do what you like with your life but don't fuck around with everyone else.'

I blinked and looked away. The old bastard was right of course, as he had been about so many things. I became suddenly and keenly aware of my situation and how potentially dangerous it was. When I turned back, Mason's face had altered. I opened the door and saw a man dressed in combats with a corporal's stripes on the front of his uniform. 'Do you know where the patrol base is?' the man asked. I'd found the Marines. The rest of them were fanned out in defensive positions, alert and ready to deal with any potential enemy attack. Heavily armed and stern faced, they were the complete antithesis of my own ragged appearance. I told them to dump their heaviest kit in the back of the Toyota and follow me as I drove slowly back to the schoolhouse.

After we got in, I waited for the inevitable consequences. I had no justification for what I'd done. It had been the height of stupidity and I could have risked many lives if things had gone wrong. This was the sort of rule-breaking that could end a career.

But the repercussions never came. Harry barely grunted an acknowledgement of my presence when I saw him in the ops room the next morning. It seemed that my midnight ride through town had gone entirely unnoticed. It was a measure of just how topsy-turvy Nad Ali had become that I could pull a stunt like this without so much as an eyebrow being raised.

The Marines only stayed for a day. They'd come in to get a briefing from Harry before he took his company out of theatre. They informed him that Brigade would be taking him and his men out by helicopter two days later. I, on the other hand, had no idea when it would be my turn to leave. The prospect of being left here without the Jocks was nerve-wracking. We still didn't know when the relief would finally arrive so there was still plenty of time to get myself killed. For all my disagreements with Harry, I knew his soldiers had had my back.

Before Harry left, he insisted on overseeing one last push into enemy territory. The whole area was due to be cleared any day now. We'd heard from Brigade that a whole kandak was flying in from Kabul, supported by a fresh British company. They'd be better armed and better prepared for the job than we were. But Harry was resolute – we should keep up the pressure on the Taliban right till the end. I think he was motivated by his hatred of the enemy – he'd seen almost half his men wounded and evacuated home. Whatever his reason, it offered me one more chance to die.

We headed out again. For the first time since that initial patrol with Wadood, there were civilians in the fields. Not just one or two; they were everywhere. The harvest had finally begun. It was already a fortnight overdue and this was the last chance they had before the crop spoiled. It seemed the fear of financial ruin and starvation had finally outweighed the risk of getting caught in the crossfire between us and the Taliban. In fact, as Ash explained to me, they'd been given an additional impetus from a radio broadcast the previous evening in which General Mahayadin had announced the imminent clearance of Nad Ali. The ANA had decided to take matters into their own hands. 'Leave the area before then,' the General had warned. 'Anyone that's left will be considered an enemy combatant and will be killed.' I loved Afghan diplomacy, but more than that I loved the confirmation that our relief really was on its way.

Having the locals back in the area didn't make it any easier to patrol. Everywhere I looked there were men working the fields. Or were they? I had by now developed automatic and violent reactions to any man who wasn't wearing either a British or an ANA uniform. Any one of these farmers could be Taliban and several probably were. At any time they might turn on us and open fire. We stopped and questioned several men but each of them insisted that they were concerned only with the harvest.

Out of the corner of my eye, I saw two men running towards us. They seemed to be unarmed but their behaviour was peculiar in the extreme. Side by side they ran, charging down the track, heading straight for our point men. At once, every soldier in the patrol brought their weapon to bear. 'Stop!' shouted the front two ANA men. By now, the runners were just 30 or 40 metres distant. They pulled up short, huffing and puffing and staring at us in consternation. 'What?' their sweating faces seemed to ask. Hands on hips, they were pictures of righteous indignation. Wali ordered them to get down in the dirt, arms and legs splayed while he went forward to question them.

There was no explanation for the bizarre behaviour. Just a couple of idiots who didn't realise how close to death they had come. We left them lying in the road, with instructions not to get up until the patrol had gone past. I'm sure that a couple of the ANA soldiers administered an educational nudge with their boots as they filed past.

We moved on and occupied a nearby compound. From the roof we had a good view of the surrounding area. It was the same in every direction – farmers furiously at work. It was like a scene frozen in time. Dressed in traditional garb, the men hacked at the crops with scythes and sickles. Only the trucks that bore the harvest away signified that any time had passed since the eighteenth century.

Harry was on the net again. 'Push forward,' he was saying. 'We're hearing chatter over the Icom. Possible enemy movement 400 metres to the south of your position.'

I looked at Wali. 'What do you reckon?'

He grimaced. 'It's a busy day out here. Lots of people. Who knows what's going on?'

I turned back to the bustling fields. So many people. It would be a bad day for them if we started a fight and I'd done more than enough shooting over the past two months.

'Come on, Wali,' I said. 'Let's go back.'

That afternoon Harry left along with his company. In the two months they had been there they had endured countless attacks, killed hundreds of Taliban and had over half their number casevaced. Until the relieving troops arrived, the OMLT would be the only British presence in Nad Ali. It was another odd farewell. I know that he cared deeply for his men and that he'd been trying to do the best job he could. That said, Harry had often given me a hard time in Nad Ali and I couldn't forgive him for his apparent insinuations about my courage and leadership. Despite this, his departure fuelled my own sense of abandonment. When would it be my turn to climb on a helicopter? I still wanted to ask Harry straight out how he thought I'd done; put the question to him directly. Make him look me in the eye and tell me what he thought. Other than Wadood he was the only man senior to me in rank who might pass judgment on my performance. I couldn't bring myself to do it. There was already an inherent awkwardness to our goodbye, but more than that I was afraid of what his answer might be.

I shook Harry's hand and wished him a speedy journey home. He nodded curtly and went on his way. I never spoke to him again.

The relief of Nad Ali began two days later. Three kandaks lined up beside two British companies from 1 Rifles along the eastern edge of Luy Bagh – in all over 1,000 men. We, the garrison, were ordered to remain in our patrol base for the duration of the clearance operation. They didn't want to risk us fighting from east to west while the new troops moved in the opposite direction. The risk of friendly fire was too great. I'd experienced as much of that as I could wish for and accepted the order to do nothing with alacrity.

My enthusiasm for this passive role was short-lived. Although I knew that the end was near, the walls of our compound seemed to press in more than ever. I watched on Phil's screens as the troops formed up on the far side of Luy Bagh. They were stretched north to south along the track that ran along the edge of the town – dozens of vehicles and hundreds of men armed to the teeth, all itching for a scrap. I knew what fighting around here was like and the price at which it came. Guilt enveloped me. It felt as though it was my fault they were fighting here.

Iwan and the new OMLT had their own reaction to the impending relief. To them it meant the coming of superiors with sharp eyes and caustic judgments on the state of this outpost. The men were set to work reorganising stores and cleaning equipment. Iwan busied himself preparing briefings for the newcomers, polishing his delivery, every inch the professional young officer. I sat on the veranda or in the ops room smoking, wishing Woody was still here. It was clear that Iwan thought me slovenly but I didn't give a fuck. It wasn't his fault. He was a good bloke and under different circumstances we might have been friends but for now his raw keenness just made me angry. Watching him pore over the maps, making notes and rehearsing the words of his presentation I was overwhelmed by a desire to punch him. I pictured his nose exploding with a satisfying crunch as my fist hit home. Involuntarily my hand curled into a tight ball, the nails digging into my palm.

'What?' he said, looking up at me. Suddenly I felt Mason's disembodied gaze upon me. I thrust my right hand deeply into my pocket.

'Nothing,' I said and walked away.

Col Wadood was the only man left in Nad Ali whose opinion mattered to me, but more and more he kept to himself, holed up in his office, co-ordinating with his ANA comrades on the radio. As the end of siege drew nearer, I could only think of returning home. Nad Ali would be my whole war, but for the Colonel it was merely another step on a much longer journey.

The clearance operation began and it quickly became apparent that the Taliban weren't going to cede the district without a fight. As the relieving troops pushed up to the edge of Luy Bagh they came under heavy fire. It would have been so easy to bring in the fast jets with their JDAMs but the rules of engagement were now stricter than ever – no unnecessary damage to Afghan property. I followed the action obsessively both on the radio and on the screen. I didn't feel jealous of the men out there but experienced a pang of regret that I couldn't do more to help. I'd spent the past two months walking the ground now being contested so fiercely. I felt irrationally proprietorial. This was my corner of the war. I wanted to show them how it ought to be fought. The waiting and the smoking went on.

By the end of the first day, the troops had gained just a few hundred metres and were now poised right on the edge of the town. They weren't bogged down but progress was achingly slow.

The near deadlock was broken not by the ANA or the British but by the ANP. A small police contingent had joined the fight and, lacking the patient discipline of their military colleagues, piled straight into Luy Bagh through a hail of gunfire. The British had little choice but to follow and together they pushed the enemy from their strongholds across the northern edge of the town in a bravura frontal assault that bordered on the suicidal.

By lunchtime on the third day of the operation, the commanders of the relieving force stood on the crossroads at the centre of Luy Bagh. The town was theirs. Col Wadood emerged from his office. 'Mark!' he called out to me from across the courtyard. 'We've sat around long enough. Now we go to Luy Bagh. Get your men. We're driving out in twenty minutes.'

The prospect of action was a welcome relief. I knew Wadood would have been chafing at the inactivity as well. He saw another commander standing in the centre of Luy Bagh as an affront to his own authority and prowess as a warrior. He refused to cower behind the walls of the base any longer. His men had fought hard to hold on here and he refused to cede the glory to these Johnny-come-latelies. The victory was rightly his.

I rounded up the OMLT and ordered them into the WMIKs that had sat unused in the schoolyard for two months. Iwan was more cautious. 'They haven't cleared the roads yet,' he said. 'We can't take vehicles down there until they've been cleared for IEDs.'

'The Colonel's going,' I said. 'Where the ANA goes, we go. It's our job.'

Reluctantly he acquiesced and picked up his kit. Ten minutes later we were driving out, bringing up the rear of Wadood's convoy. But Iwan didn't let up. He was two vehicles further back and continued to voice his concerns over the PRR. 'This is stupid,' he said. 'They don't need us for this. We're risking everything for Wadood's pride.'

'They take risks for us,' I said. 'And we do the same for them. That's how this works. I owe it to the Colonel.'

It was no longer just between me and Iwan. The rest of the OMLT was listening in on the same channel and as our disagreement escalated, I could feel the nervousness growing amongst the men. We could see the orchard, a couple of hundred metres away, straight down the road. I thought back to the IEDs that Beattie had found all those weeks before. As the relieving force pushed through Luy Bagh, why wouldn't the Taliban have mined the route to the DC? Iwan was right. This was lunacy. I did owe it to Wadood; he and his men had fought hard with me. But that was my debt. Iwan and the gunners owed Wadood nothing and their lives weren't for me to play with.

I called a halt and watched as the ANA vehicles drove away towards Luy Bagh. 'Fuck!' I shouted and slammed a fist into the dashboard of the WMIK. My driver stared at me in consternation. 'What the hell are you looking at?' I yelled.

I sat there for several long minutes, while Iwan wittered in my ear. 'Turn around,' I said. We drove back in silence.

After a few hours, Wadood returned. I met him as he came back into the base and explained why I'd turned around. He nodded. 'I understand,' he said. But there was something in his eyes, a glimmer of contempt, and I was sure that I'd lost his trust once more. I hung my head.

The next day the Rifles company mineswept the road up towards us. When they reached the edge of the DC we set out on foot to meet them. Along the way, we were contacted. It was just a few short bursts, too quick for us to identify the firing point but enough to send us scuttling into the ditch. We soon picked ourselves up and resumed our patrol.

I saw the British riflemen coming slowly up the track and pushing through the fields on either side. They were almost strolling it seemed to me, the kind of confident swagger of men who'd just won their first victory and were yet to experience how bloody war really gets. There in the middle of them, lost in conversation with an ANA sergeant, was their commander, a captain.

I barged straight in. 'What the fuck are you doing? There's Taliban all round here and your men are wandering around without a care in the world. We've just been shot up 200 metres down the road!'

The captain stood there and blinked at me in utter amazement. I must have cut a peculiar figure, sporting a full beard, tattered rags for a uniform and staring with wild, furious eyes.

'Who are you?' the captain asked.

'I'm the guy who's trying to save your life.'

He shook his head. 'Fuck off,' he replied.

Once again, violent thoughts began to pile through my mind. I felt the urge to switch my rifle to automatic and start firing bullets into his head until the magazine was empty. I realised that I was shaking, my finger tight on the trigger of my weapon.

Iwan appeared on my shoulder. 'Come on,' he said. 'There's nothing to do here. Let's go back to the schoolhouse and wait.'

I don't know what Iwan said to the Rifles officers about me but I was largely left alone. I introduced the major commanding the company to Wadood when he arrived but left all the briefings to Iwan. He was in charge of the OMLT now. Someone told me that I would be able to leave tomorrow. Now the road was secured, I'd be driving back to Lash on a convoy. This was the news for which I'd been waiting for weeks but now the moment had come, I felt little emotion.

That evening, I accepted Wadood's invitation to a farewell dinner. It was just me, him, Ash and the S2, all sat around the table in his office, as it had been most evenings since the Apache. Now that the road was open once more, the kandak was no longer reliant on British helicopters for its supplies. As soon as Luy Bagh had been cleared Wadood had dispatched a convoy to Lash, just a couple of hours' drive away. They'd come back that same day and now, for the first time in a long time, we had meat for dinner.

The conversation was light. We didn't speak about Afghanistan, the war or our time in Nad Ali. Instead we talked about home, our families and what awaited us when we left this place. The S2 told us about buzkashi matches he hoped to play. Wadood talked of his sons and how he hoped that they would follow him into the army one day.

When it came time for me to go, I told Wadood how much I had felt that I'd learned from him and how sorry I was to leave him behind. He shrugged. 'There'll be other officers,' he said. I couldn't help but feel hurt. To the Colonel that's all I was, just another Brit, here today and gone tomorrow. Only the Afghans endured in this war. Then he reached into his desk draw and pulled out a scarf. It was black silk, with an elaborate gold thread woven in a swirling pattern. 'This is for you,' he said. 'Something to remember Afghanistan. You can give it to your bride when you get married.'

'If you get married,' said the S2, chuckling. 'It doesn't count if you try and marry a man.'

I laughed and we all shook hands. Then I turned and went out of the office, walking away and out of their war.

The next day I jumped aboard a WMIK and drove out of Patrol Base Argyll for the last time. I was a passenger on this trip.

Some lieutenant from the Rifles was in command. I just sat in the back, my bergen between my legs and watched Nad Ali flash by. We took the familiar track down past the orchard, through Luy Bagh and headed west towards Lash. Along the way we passed the scenes of many of my firefights. There was the spot we'd found the IEDs; my first real encounter with the enemy. I felt nothing. Off in the distance was the shack where I'd stood, shaking, when the Apache had unloaded. Still nothing. It was like touring around a First World War battlefield. So hard to imagine the chaos that had once reigned here.

I was going home.

I was in Lash just a few hours before a helicopter came to whisk me off to Camp Bastion but this was quite time enough to get in trouble. I stuck my head into the ops room, on the off chance that someone there needed to pick my brains on Nad Ali. I approached the commando major who was running the show. He was a big man, immaculately turned out and exuding a cool efficiency. His gaze swept over me, taking in my filthy beard and my ripped, travel-stained clothes. The curl of his lip told me that he didn't like what he saw. 'What the fuck do you look like?' he said. 'What are you doing, waltzing into my ops room like this?'

'I thought you might want to speak to me about Nad Ali. I was there from the start and fancied I might have some useful information for you.'

'Get a shave,' he said. 'Start looking like a British officer and I might start treating you like one.'

'Oh. Sorry.' I walked straight back out again. Cunt. I felt like a visitor from a different planet. What did beards and dirt have to do with anything? Did no one realise there was a war on? I went to find some obscure corner in which to hide until it was time to leave.

There was another short stop in Bastion where I dropped off my rifle before being ushered aboard a C-130 back to Kandahar

– the last stop on the way out of Afghanistan. No one from my Brigade was left now and the new lot weren't interested in me or what I'd been doing. I was just a minor administrative hassle. Get him out of here as fast as possible was the response everywhere. He's not part of our war. Suits me, I thought.

Kandahar air base was huge. I'd come through here on my way in but now the sheer enormity of the place seemed incongruous after the tight confines of the schoolhouse. Americans were everywhere.

The scale of the operation was impressive. Dozens of huge transport planes lumbered across the tarmac in a ponderous ballet while hordes of men in helmets and jumpsuits unloaded box upon box of supplies and equipment. Beyond the high chain-link fence that marked the edge of the airfield rows of prefabricated huts extended into the distance; soldiers bustled between them in a sort of Brownian motion of military activity.

Despite the constant hubbub there was little sign that a war was raging here. Soldiers wore their uniforms with carefully pressed creases and threw up crisp salutes. Joggers puffed their way past me in army-issue PT kit with luminous waist-belts to warn traffic of their presence, while the cries of drill sergeants rent the air. Off to my right a row of signs announced Pizza Hut, Subway and Burger King, all open for business.

What did all these people do? It was like being on a base in the United States. Of Afghans there was no sign.

I spent two days in Kandahar, waiting for my flight. I wandered around, did a little shopping – rugs, DVDs, other random souvenirs – but mostly I tried to sleep. It was a pointless endeavour; my body might have left Nad Ali but my mind was still there, waiting for the Taliban's next move. I smoked a lot.

Eventually it was time to leave and I climbed aboard the big, silver passenger plane for my final journey home. In the seat next to me was an American officer, a full colonel. He had a bored, glassy-eyed way about him and he spent the first few hours of the flight plugged into an iPod. Somewhere over the Mediterranean, he engaged me in conversation for the first time. 'Where've you been, son?' he asked. I told him a little about Nad Ali and in turn he spoke about his time at ISAF HQ in Kabul, planning strategy across Afghanistan. Here was a man who had oversight across the entire war, not just the small corner in which I'd fought.

'So what do you think is going to happen?' I asked.

He looked straight into my eyes. 'Son,' he said. 'There's only one thing to do with that country.' He paused and I waited for the answer, the rationale I'd been searching for since that first dinner with Wadood in Nad Ali. 'Turn it all to fucking glass,' he said.

I waited for the telltale smile, the 'no, but seriously' that would precede his real answer. It never came. He turned away and went to sleep.

As we began our final approach to the airbase at Brize Norton, I stared out of the window. The first bit of green emerging through grey clouds is something I always look forward to. It's a shade peculiar to the English countryside that you don't get elsewhere. I think it's imprinted on the psyche of every Englishman. It means coming home.

Today it was different. I watched the familiar patchwork of fields and hedges slip beneath us, growing ever closer, but the tightening of breath, the swelling in my chest was absent. Over the past six months coming home had been a fixation, the subject of my dreams, awake and asleep. Now I was almost there, I didn't know what to feel. All the emotions of the past few months bubbled up inside me and I wanted to shout, scream and laugh all at once. Instead, I checked my sleeves were rolled to regulation length and moved my seat into the upright position.

The plane bumped on the tarmac and we lurched slightly as

the tyres found their purchase. I gathered my gear and followed the column of soldiers disembarking and making their way through the baggage reclaim area.

Minutes later, I was standing outside in the grey Oxfordshire drizzle, smoking a quick cigarette while I waited for my parents to arrive. I wanted a drink.

CHAPTER FORTY

April 2010

I'd been drinking solidly for three days. There was, it seemed, no particular reason to stop. When I'd left the Priory I'd felt like I was through the worst of the PTSD. I'd resigned from the Army straight away and for a few weeks it had seemed as though I was making progress, moving towards a better future. But then reality reasserted itself. The expeditions I was running were cancelled and I suddenly had no work to do. My days became empty. I was officially still an officer, with the salary and a room in barracks, but I had no duties. In two weeks I'd be a civilian again, with no job, no income and nowhere to live. Some mornings I got up and went running but mostly I just hung around the Mess and worried about the future.

Now I was alone at a station somewhere near the outskirts of Bristol. There had been a party but that was a long time ago. I was still in my dinner jacket. Looking down I saw that the trouser legs were smeared with a dry crust of vomit. It was dark and I shivered as sobriety began to bite. This was bad. I had started drinking to fog my brain and exorcise the old, familiar ghosts that had begun to re-emerge. As the alcohol leaked from my bloodstream, so the mist parted and the dead men rose up once more.

I looked at my watch – 3 a.m. There was nowhere to get any more booze at this time and the next train didn't leave for another four and a half hours. A sensible man would have gone and found a hotel in which to crash until dawn. I sat down on the platform, my back to the wall and hugged my knees against the cold.

The images of Nad Ali began to turn over in my mind. I was beginning the same patrol all over again. Planning the route, giving the orders and then we were off out of the gate. The radio hissed in my ear, and I listened to the same conversations over the net. I'd passed this way so many times now that it had become almost comforting in its familiarity. Except I knew where this path ended up. Somewhere in the sky above us was the Apache.

Every time I've set out on that journey again I've hoped that it would take me somewhere else and that I'd be able to think my way into a different reality. This time it'll be different, I'll make another call and take the blokes through some different field. But no matter how hard I've tried to change the ending, the film inside my head has spooled on regardless.

I thought about everything that Christina had told me and summoned the strength to wrench myself back to the present. Screwing my eyes shut, I forced myself to focus. When I opened them again I was back on the platform. The cold platform. The dark platform. Where I'm all alone. It suddenly occurred to me that the uncertain present was no better than the war had been. Even if I could stop the memories that plagued me, my life would still add up to nothing. I had no future.

Out of the darkness I heard a rumbling. My mind transformed the sounds to that of a helicopter and my eyes darted upwards. There were only clouds overhead and I realised that I was hearing a train coming down the track.

Before I had time to process what I was doing, I stood up. I was walking forward across the platform. My head was still so full of Afghanistan that I was only half conscious, half aware of what it was I was contemplating. I just knew I needed the noise in my head to stop.

I was near the edge now. 'Keep behind the line,' it said in yellow painted letters beneath my feet. That wasn't meant for me. That was for those other fuckers, the ones who still slept at night. I took another step forward and my toes hung out over the edge. The rumbling was getting louder now. This train was fast and it wasn't stopping here.

I could make out the lights as the engine rounded the final bend

– *two white circles that got bigger and bigger. My hands curled into tight balls and the nails dug painfully into my palms. I sucked in a huge lungful of air. The lights were massive now and the rattle of the wheels screamed in my ears. Nearly there now. Get ready.*

I staggered backwards and fell hard on the floor as the train blurred past just inches away. 'Fuck! Fuck! Fuck!' I screamed. Kneeling on the ground, I pounded my fist against the tarmac until my knuckles were bleeding freely.

Why couldn't I do it? I wanted to do it, didn't I? Why wouldn't I? My life was shit. But a small voice in the back of my mind answered tentatively, 'But it might get better.' It might. And that was enough.

In the distance I heard another train making its approach. The last remnant of common sense I had told me to get out of there. I might be scared of dying but what if I remembered how to be brave? I turned and ran. The door to the waiting room was open and I fell inside. A vending machine stood beside the door. I crouched beside it and pushed my shoulder hard against it, heaving until the thing began to budge. Inch by inch I shifted it sideways until it came to rest flush against the door. My way onto the platform was blocked.

I sat down on one of the hard plastic chairs and watched through the window as the train flashed by. In here I was safe. I thought about all the things that made life worth living – my friends, family, the other guys who'd made it through Nad Ali with me. Just knowing that those people were out there, getting on with their lives, whether I saw them again or not, made me feel comforted. In Afghanistan I'd gone through hell and made it back; I could do the same again now. I sat in the dark, alone but alive, and waited for the sun to come up.

EPILOGUE

It's now four years since I left the Army and six since I returned from Afghanistan. I think about it often. I wonder what happened to Wadood. What part he has gone on to play. I remember the headscarf he gave me, the meals we shared, how he defiantly walked through Luy Bagh daring the Taliban to take him on. I imagine him holding court in the headmaster's office, laughing off their every attempt to kill him and take his country.

The reality is that in the immediate aftermath of the operation that lifted the siege of Nad Ali the Taliban melted away, scared off or killed during the relief. With the threat now apparently gone, our focus and main force moved elsewhere. The OMLT remained to hold the ground and mentor the ANA, but gradually the Taliban crept back towards the DC. Within months they had built up their forces to the same level they'd been at the height of the siege.

In summer 2009, Operation Panther's Claw was launched to win back territory across Helmand, including Nad Ali. Some 4,500 British, American and Afghan troops were involved. Over twenty soldiers died and many more were injured. They succeeded in capturing their objectives and the British Government declared the operation a success. It was the same old story though. Without sufficient troops to hold the ground, the Taliban came back once more.

So what success has the British Army achieved in Afghanistan? For what did all those soldiers fight and die? Well there's the turbine, I suppose – they did get it all the way to the dam after all. As I write this in the spring of 2014, a few months before the British Army leaves Helmand for good, the turbine is still sitting there – never installed, never producing a single watt of power – slowly rusting in the sun.

Afghanistan is still wracked by war, but three thousand miles away in London I have found a measure of peace. I have slowly rebuilt myself and my life. I have learnt to accept help. I've learnt not to blame other people. Slowly, I have begun to talk openly about my experiences. Yoga, meditation and therapy have all played their part in my recovery. I still have memories, but now I can manage them. They are a part of the story of my life rather than the whole of it.

A few weeks ago I was walking in the New Forest near to where my parents live. It was a beautiful spring day and my mother and father were by my side. Suddenly, off in the distance, I heard the sharp report of a car backfiring. I stiffened and just for an instant I thought of Nad Ali. But then I looked around at the trees and the stream running beside the path and remembered where I was. The tension ran away just as quickly as it had come. I glanced over at my father and saw that he was smiling..

ACKNOWLEDGEMENTS

In writing this book I was gifted the opportunity to tell the story of the brave men I fought with in Nad Ali and to give an insight into what so many soldiers and their loved ones have been through, both at war and when they return home. It is solely my memory of those events, memories that nearly killed me, but today serve as reminder to me of how lucky I am and how many great people I have the honour of calling family and friends.

I would first like to say thank you to the people who have worked tirelessly with Andrew and myself over the past 18 months to make this book possible:

To Hodder and our publisher Mark Booth for taking a chance on two new writers, letting us tell this story, and understanding what we were trying to achieve.

To Fiona Rose for her exceptional administration, Tara Gladden for her edit, the marketing team and Rachel Dudley for her patience.

To Ken, whose camera I called upon yet again and Col Lockheart for his words of wisdom from within the MOD.

To Gwyn Evans, Tristan Evans, Charlie Foinette, Jonathan Cooper, Ros Tendler and Saethryd Brandreth who read the book in its many stages and helped shape the final manuscript.

To Andy McNab, Bernard Cornwell, Patrick Hennessey and Damien Lewis who all took time out from their busy lives to read Code Black and let you know what they thought of it; and to Annabel Merullo and Laura Williams who helped with this.

To the writing and insight of Winston Churchill (from My Early Life by Winston S. Churchill) reproduced with permission of Curtis Brown, London on behalf of the Estate of Sir Winston Churchill. Copyright © Estate of Sir Winston Churchill.

The book is only part of this story and there are many others without whom it would not have existed.

My sincere thanks to all those I am proud to have served with: the soldiers and officers of the Coldstream Guards, 13 Platoon (Sandhurst), Catterick, C Battery 3 RHA, 1 Royal Irish, 1 Rifles, B Company 5 Scots and the of course the ANA. To Jeremy Bagshaw, Col Cowan, Dr Smith, Col Toby and Karen who supported me in my difficult time at Horse Guards. And Charlie Foinette, Jamie Russell and Dr Khan who pointed me in the right direction when I was falling apart at battalion.

To those who worked so hard to cure me of my PTSD: Andy Cottom, Cristina Garcia-Llavona, Dr Wilkins, Capain Tony Penny, and Sophia Davis. And the guys from the Priory (I hope you're all doing well) who I can't name, but made my time there so enjoyable, eventful and memorable.

To my friends who stood by me – there are simply too many to mention by name – but I hope you know who you are and how much your friendship and support has been appreciated. A very special thanks goes to Steph and John Matthews, and Piers and Sarah Musgrove Sanders whose floors were my home. Fonz, Lou and Jon Drori who have all been so kind as long as I have known them. Ellie Fox and the Hannahs who were always there at the right time. To Helen Fairclough – I'm still waiting for you to knit me something; Jim Horton, for the most timely coffee of my life; and to Mark Elliot for being in the right place at the right time. Not forgetting the Blue Cow team and investors who might not know how important they were in helping me get to where I am now, and the 'crew' of the Sea Ferrari – what an experience that was!

A special thanks goes to Gyles and Michèle Brandreth who

guided me through the publication process and provided the very best of support and advice to me unreservedly.

To Andrew Sharples who I trained with at Sandhurst and have been friends with for over 10 years – I'm looking forward to the next chapter.

Col Richard Clements, Stocky, Greyman, the OMLT and ANA from Gereshk.

The guys from Nad Ali: Woody, DB, Wadood, the S2, Chantel, the Company Sergeant
Major, Nick Bridle, Iwan Williams, the Jocks, the ANA, the OMLT. All of you I don't mention by name. To Ash and his fellow interpreters who day after day put their lives on the line to help us. And to Phil, who will sadly never get to read about how he kept us safe.

To Colour Mason, Magoo, Beattie, Gee, Stan, Ram, Griff and Charlie. I will never forget those days we spent together. And Harry – we had our differences but you kept us safe and I can't thank you enough for the tough decisions you were brave enough to make.

To my family, my brother and Tiff, my mum, my dad and my grandparents who helped me more than they know and whose love I will forever be grateful for – I am very lucky to have you. Your support has been incredible and my love for you is forever unconditional.

And last but by no means least to Rory (he's 8) for putting up with my madness and welcoming me into his life and home. And his mother Saethryd, a fantastic writer and editor in her own right, and the most amazing partner and friend I could have ever found. This book and my life would not have been the same without you.